Royalty Rates
for Licensing
Intellectual Property

Royalty Rates for Licensing Intellectual Property

Russell L. Parr

John Wiley & Sons, Inc.

This book is printed on acid-free paper. ∞

Copyright © 2007 by John Wiley & Sons, Inc. All rights reserved.

Published by John Wiley & Sons, Inc., Hoboken, New Jersey.

Published simultaneously in Canada.

Wiley Bicentennial Logo: Richard J. Pacifico

No part of this publication may be reproduced, stored in a retrieval system, or transmitted in any form, or by any means, electronic, mechanical, photocopying, recording, scanning, or otherwise, except as permitted under Section 107 or 108 of the 1976 United States Copyright Act, without either the prior written permission of the Publisher, or authorization through payment of the appropriate per-copy fee to the Copyright Clearance Center, Inc., 222 Rosewood Drive, Danvers, MA 01923, 978-750-8400, fax 978-646-8600, or on the web at www.copyright.com. Requests to the Publisher for permission should be addressed to the Permissions Department, John Wiley & Sons, Inc., 111 River Street, Hoboken, NJ 07030, 201-748-6011, fax 201-748-6008, or online at http://www.wiley.com/go/permissions.

Limit of Liability/Disclaimer of Warranty: While the publisher and author have used their best efforts in preparing this book, they make no representations or warranties with respect to the accuracy or completeness of the contents of this book, and specifically disclaim any implied warranties of merchantability or fitness for a particular purpose. No warranty may be created or extended by sales representatives or written sales materials. The advice and strategies contained herein may not be suitable for your situation. You should consult with a professional where appropriate. Neither the publisher nor author shall be liable for any loss of profit, or any other commercial damages, including, but not limited to, special, incidental, consequential, or other damages.

For general information on our other products and services, or for technical support, please contact our Customer Care Department, within the United States at 800-762-2974, outside the United States at 317-572-3993, or fax at 317-572-4002.

Wiley also publishes its books in a variety of electronic formats. Some content that appears in print may not be available in electronic books.

For more information about Wiley products, visit our Web site at http://www.wiley.com.

Library of Congress Cataloging-in-Publication Data:

ISBN: 978-0470-06928-8

Printed in the United States of America

10 9 8 7 6 5 4 3 2 1

Amy Lynne Shanahan saved me during the summer of 2006.
This book is dedicated to her, with gratitude and love.
Thank you Amy

Contents

About the Author xiii
Acknowledgments xv
Preface xix

CHAPTER 1 **Intellectual Property and Corporate Value** **1**
    Patents 3
        Patent Trends 4
        Who Owns the Most Patents? 4
        Technology Classifications 6
        History of U.S. Patent Applications 6
    Trademarks 8
    Copyrights 10
    Trade Secrets 13
        Evaluating Trade Secrets 14

CHAPTER 2 **Licensing Intellectual Property** **17**
    Forces Behind Licensing 19
    Licensing Motivation 22
    Reasons Companies Engage in Licensing 25

CHAPTER 3 **Use of the Twenty-Five Percent Rule in Valuing IP** **31**
    Introduction 31
    History of the Rule 32
    Explanation of the Rule 33
    Illustration of the Rule 36
    Application of the Rule 39
    Justification for the Rule 41
    Criticisms of the Rule 42
    Empirical Test of the Rule 44
    Royalty Rates 45
    Industry Profits 46

	Licensee Profits	46
	Royalty Rates and Licensee Profits	48
	Successful Licensee Profits	50
	Royalty Rates and Successful Licensee Profits	50
	Conclusions	51
CHAPTER 4	**Royalty Rate Guidelines**	**53**
	Royalty Rates for Technology, Third Edition	55
	Royalty Rates for Trademarks and Copyrights, Third Edition	57
	Royalty Rates for Pharmaceuticals and Biotechnology, Sixth Edition	58
CHAPTER 5	**Comparable Licenses**	**61**
	Internal Licenses Are Often Self-Serving	62
	Relevant Time Period	62
	Financial Condition of Both Licensing Parties	63
	Relevant Industry Transactions	63
	International Transactions	64
	Non-Monetary Compensation	64
	Exclusivity	64
	Package Licenses	65
	Comparative Analysis Summarized	65
CHAPTER 6	**Technology Royalty Statistics**	**67**
	Automotive	67
	Battery Terminals	68
	Transaxles	68
	Manufacturing Technology	69
	Self-Dimmable Rearview Mirrors	70
	Chemicals	70
	Flame-Retardant Products	71
	Fuel Reactor Technology	71
	Fuel Technology	72
	Communications Equipment and Services	72
	Third-Generation Wireless Technology	73
	Video Patent Pool	74
	Code Division Multiple Access Technology	75
	Wideband Code Division Multiple Access Technology	76
	Computer Hardware	76
	Macintosh Enhancement	77
	Computer Architecture	77
	PS/2 Computers	77
	Modem Standards	78
	Modems	79

Computer Software	80
Apple Operating System	80
Decision and Data Mining	81
Windows OS Code	82
Construction	82
Paving	83
Polyvinyl Chloride Pipe Products	83
Electronics	84
DVD/Video Players	84
Detection Monitoring	85
Flat Panel Display Technology	85
Remote Metering	86
Food and Beverage	86
Mineral Water	86
Packaging	87
Eggs	87
Medical Equipment	88
Breast Cancer Detection	88
Cancer Screening	89
Catheter	89
Digital Scanner	90
Laser Finger-Perforator Technology	90
Laser Hair-Removal	91
Pharmaceuticals and Biotechnology	92
Semiconductors	97
High-Bandwidth Chip Connection Technology	98
Lightning Resistance	99
Manufacturing	99
Pentium II Processor	100
Power Conversion	101
Thin Film Ferroelectric Technology	101
SIMMs	102
Waste Management	102
Recycling of Asphalt Roofing Debris	103
Used Oil Recovery	103
Tire Recycling	104

CHAPTER 7   Trademark and Copyright Royalty Statistics   107

Apparel	107
Everlast™	108
Lotto™	108
Disney	108
Ralph Lauren and Polo	108
Artwork	109
Textile Patterns	110
Andretti™	111

	Big League Chew®	111
	Dannon/Yocream™	111
	Condiment Names	112
	Personal Care	112
	Hawaiian Tropic®	113
	Tapazole®	114
	Vidal Sassoon	114
	Publishing	114
	Restaurants	116
	Ruth's Chris Steakhouse	117
	Capital Grille Steakhouse	117
	Benihana Japanese Restaurants	118
CHAPTER 8	**Profit Differentials and Royalty Rates**	**119**
	Business Enterprise Framework	119
	Beyond Commodity Earnings	122
	Driving Forces Behind Royalty Rates	124
	Infringement Damages Analysis	125
	The Analytical Approach	125
	Hypothetical Example	126
	General Profit Margins	128
	Generic Pricing	128
CHAPTER 9	**Investment Rates of Return and Royalty Rates**	**133**
	Basic Principles	133
	Investment Rate of Return Royalty Rates	134
	Royalty Rates	135
	Appropriate Return on Monetary Assets	136
	Appropriate Return on Tangible Assets	137
	Appropriate Return on Intangible Assets and Intellectual Property	139
	Royalty Rate for the Specific Patented Invention	140
	Benefits of Investment Rate of Return Analysis	140
CHAPTER 10	**Discounted Cash Flow Analysis and Royalty Rates**	**143**
	Generic and Mature Commodity Corporate Value	146
	New Pharmaprod Corporation Royalty Rate	149
	Risk-Adjusted Net Present Value	149
	Success Rates	153
	Success Rate Adjusted DCF Example	155
	Valuation Using the Relief-from-Royalty Method	156
	Inputs for the Relief-from-Royalty Method	157
	Remaining Life of the Patent Protection	157
	Forecast Revenue	158
	Royalty Rate	158
	Tax Rate	159

	Discount Rate	159
	Present Value Calculation	160
CHAPTER 11	**Court-Awarded Royalty Rates**	**163**
	Top Ten	163
	Frequency of Rates Awarded	165
	Industry Categorizations	166
	Considerations Cited by the Courts in Determining a Reasonable Royalty	167
	Existing Licenses	167
	Importance of Expert Testimony	169
	Use of Projections	170
	Entire Market Value Rule	170
	Federal Circuit Decisions on Royalty Rates	171
	Conclusion	173
CHAPTER 12	**Litigation Rates Are Higher**	**175**
	Comparison of Litigated and Non-Litigated Licenses	175
CHAPTER 13	**Royalty Rate Services**	**181**
	RoyaltySource®™	181
	RoyaltyStat®	182
	Intellectual Property Research Associates (IPRA)	183
	Securities and Exchange Commission EDGAR Archives	184
CHAPTER 14	**Monitoring License Agreements and Financial Compliance**	**187**
	Introduction	187
	Breaking Through Old Perceptions	189
	What Is a Royalty Audit?	190
	Red Flags	190
	Auditor Selection	191
	How Is the Royalty Audit Done?	192
	Desk Audits	193
	Drafting a License Agreement to Lower the Likelihood of Mistakes	193
	Common Errors	194
	Communications Between Licensor and Licensee	195
	Conclusion: Benefits of a Sound Monitoring Program	195

Notes   **197**
Index   **205**

About the Author

Russell L. Parr, CFA, ASA is president of IPRA, Inc. (Intellectual Property Research Associates). He is a consultant, author, publisher, and lecturer focused on the valuation, pricing, and strategic management of intellectual property. For over twenty-five years, he has advised his clients about the value and pricing of patents, trademarks, copyrights, and trade secrets. His books are published in Japanese, Korean, Italian, Chinese, and Russian. Mr. Parr's opinions are used to accomplish licensing transactions, mergers and acquisitions, transfer pricing, infringement damages litigation support, and joint venture equity splits. His clients include multinational corporations, universities, and private inventors.

Past assignments have included the valuation of the Dr. Seuss copyrights and the patent portfolio of AT&T. Mr. Parr has also conducted valuations and royalty rate studies, for technology and trademarks related to pharmaceuticals, semiconductor processes and products, agricultural formulations, automotive, biotechnology, photography, chemical formulations, communications, computer software and hardware, drug delivery systems, flowers, incinerator feed systems, lasers, medical instruments, and motivational book copyrights.

In addition to consulting, Mr. Parr publishes three royalty rate resource books sold all over the world. These books are *Royalty Rates for Pharmaceuticals and Biotechnology, Sixth Edition; Royalty Rates for Trademarks and Copyrights, Third Edition;* and *Royalty Rates for Technology, Third Edition*. These books are dedicated to reporting detailed information about the financial aspects of intellectual property transactions, including licensing and joint ventures.

Mr. Parr is a graduate of Rutgers University, having received a Bachelor's in Electrical Engineering and a Masters in Business Administration. He has also been awarded the professional designations of Chartered Financial Analyst, from the CFA Institute, and Accredited Senior Appraiser, from the American Society of Appraisers. He is a member of the Licensing Executives Society and is on the advisory board of three professional publications, *Licensing Economics Review, IP Litigator,* and *The Licensing Journal.*

As an author and co-author, Mr. Parr has created seven books published by John Wiley and Sons, about the valuation, management, and pricing of intellectual property, including *Intellectual Property: Valuation, Exploitation and Infringement Damages.* In addition he has written twenty-six articles for professional publications such as *Les Nouvelles* and *The Journal of Proprietary Rights.* He has made forty-three seminar presentations for organizations including the Licensing Executives Society, the American Intellectual Property Law Association and the World Intellectual Property Organization. He has testified at deposition or trial fifty-five times regarding intellectual property infringement. More information about Mr. Parr, his firm, and its publications can be found at www.ipresearch.com.

Acknowledgments

The following accomplished professionals have kindly contributed insightful chapters to this book.

DEBORA R. STEWART, CPA

Debora Rose Stewart is a managing director with Invotex Group's Intellectual Property (IP) Management and Finance practice, and leads the firm's IP Advisory Services, which include licensing and license compliance, technology evaluation, asset management and enforcement of IP rights. She has more than twenty years experience working with corporations, universities, and their counsel on IP matters. Ms. Stewart's experience includes IP compliance, valuations and licensing consulting, and reasonable royalty and lost profit damage calculations in patent, trademark, and copyright infringement. In addition she developed the proprietary Royalty Reporting Process™, to help clients manage royalty reporting and revenue, and the Audit Indicator™, a selection tool to identify licenses that should be audited. Ms. Stewart has worked with clients in a wide range of industries, from computer graphics and biotechnology to consumer goods. She has also authored several articles, and has given presentations and expert testimony on related topics. Ms. Stewart has been a member of the faculty of the Licensing Executive Society's Professional Development series. She is a member of the American Institute of Certified Public Accountants (AICPA), Association of University Technology Managers (AUTM), International Licensing Industry Merchandisers' Association (LIMA), Maryland Association of Certified Public Accountants

(MACPA), and the Licensing Executives Society (LES). Ms. Stewart holds a BBA in industrial management from Kent State University, and an MBA in finance and marketing from Case Western Reserve University.

JUDY A. BYRD, CPA, CIRA

Judy Ann Byrd is a director with Invotex Group's IP Management and Finance practice. She has more than fifteen years experience, providing a variety of accounting and consulting services including litigation, valuation, and royalty compliance services related to IP. Ms. Byrd's IP experience includes litigation related damage valuations and royalty audits for IP licensors. She also has more than seven years experience providing tax, accounting, and auditing services (including royalty audits) to clients in manufacturing, construction, property management, and other industries. She began her career as an accountant and auditor, specializing in business start-ups and small to medium sized business development. Ms. Byrd has co-authored several articles and frequently speaks on IP topics. She is a member of the AICPA, AUTM, MACPA, and LES. She has a BA from the University of Pittsburgh, and an MBA from the University of Baltimore. Ms. Byrd is a CPA in Maryland and Pennsylvania, and is a Certified Insolvency and Restructuring Advisor.

MICHELE M. RILEY, CPA, CFE

Michele Riley is a director with Invotex Group's Intellectual Property Management and Finance practice. She is responsible for providing a variety of consulting services, including bankruptcy and troubled company services, litigation services, business consulting, and business valuations. Ms. Riley's litigation services experience has included damage valuations in the areas of breach of contract, unfair competition, and IP. She has prepared damage analyses relating to patent, trademark and copyright infringement, and unfair competition and breach of contract claims for clients in computer hardware/software, retail merchandising, durable goods manufacturing, telecommunications, waste management, pharmaceutical, and business process automation industries. Ms. Riley has testified regarding damages in both IP and commercial cases. In addition, she has performed royalty audits of technology licenses for clients in numerous industries, and has assisted clients with the financial aspects of license negotiations, for both copyright and technology licenses. Ms. Riley's experience in bankruptcy and troubled company services has covered such industries as construction, manufacturing, hospital administration, and private medical practice. Her management and administration of these engagements have entailed developing financial models, preparing cash flow projections under varying scenarios, and analyzing business segments and operations.

ROBERT GOLDSCHEIDER

Robert Goldscheider is a specialist and recognized authority on the many commercial and legal aspects of the technology transfer process, both in the United States and worldwide. He has done pioneering work in the field of technology management, specifically corporate organization of research and development, to include marketing and acquisition of patented and unpatented inventions. As chairman and founder of the International Licensing Network, a technology management consultants firm, Mr. Goldscheider is a frequent lecturer on problems involving the transfer and commercialization of technology, addressing such topics as the creation of international joint ventures and strategic alliances, the Internet, and offering strategic advice on negotiations involving IP assets. Mr. Goldscheider graduated magna cum laude in 1951, with a BS from Columbia University and distinction in economics. He received his JD from Harvard Law School in 1954 and was a 1955 Fulbright scholar. His books and articles are widely read, and are foundations for the discipline of technology licensing. He has taught more people about this subject than anyone alive, having lectured on every continent of the world.

JOHN JAROSZ

John Jarosz specializes in applied microeconomics and industrial organization. He has given economic testimony, performed research, and provided strategy consultation in matters involving IP, commercial damages, licensing, and antitrust. Mr. Jarosz has significant expertise evaluating and testifying on damages in patent, copyright, trademark, trade secret, and unfair competition cases. He has also done substantial work in breach of contract and general tort litigation. Mr. Jarosz has assisted clients across a variety of industries, including semiconductors, telecommunications, computer hardware and software, medical devices, consumer products, biotechnology, and pharmaceuticals. He is a member of the American Law and Economics Association and LES. He has been a columnist and advisory board member for *The IP Litigator,* and is a frequent writer and lecturer on IP and damages issues. Mr. Jarosz holds a BA in economics and organizational communication from Creighton University, a JD from the University of Wisconsin, and is a Ph.D. candidate in economics at Washington University in St. Louis.

CARLA MULHERN

Carla Mulhern specializes in the application of economic principles to issues arising in complex business litigation. She has served as an expert witness on damages in commercial litigation matters, including IP and breach of contract cases. Her IP damages experience spans cases involving allegations of patent, copyright, and trademark infringement, as well as misappropriation of trade secrets. She has assisted clients in a variety of industries, including pharmaceuticals, medical devices, automotive, entertainment, consumer products, computer hardware and software, and semiconductors. In non-litigation matters, Ms. Mulhern has assisted clients in the valuation of IP and other business assets, in the context of strategic alliances and joint ventures. She is a member of the American Economic Association and LES, and is a frequent writer and speaker on issues related to intellectual property valuation and damages assessment. Ms. Mulhern holds an MSc in economics from the London School of Economics and Political Science, and a BS in mathematics from Bucknell University.

Preface

This book is all about royalty rate information. Over the years, I have collected articles, statistics, royalty rate data, and other key information about royalty rates. I have also collected, and tried to enhance, different financial models for deriving royalty rates. Rather than have this data scattered about my office, I created a central repository, which has served as the basis of this new book.

Intellectual property (IP) is the central resource for creating wealth in almost all industries. The foundation of commercial power has shifted from capital resources to IP. In fact, the definition of capital resources is shifting. No longer does the term "capital resources" bring to mind balance sheets of cash, or pictures of sprawling manufacturing plants. The definition of capital includes such IP as technological know-how, patents, copyrights, and trade secrets. Corporations once dominated industries by acquiring, and managing, extensive holdings of natural resources and manufacturing facilities. Barriers to entry were high because enormous amounts of fixed-asset investments were required, to attempt displacing well-entrenched players. Today companies that once dominated industries are finding themselves fighting for survival. Start-up companies are creating new products and services based not on extensive resource holdings or cash hordes, but on IP resources.

In this book I talk about the enormous contribution IP adds to corporate value. This is followed by a discussion about patent growth and licensing revenue. The remainder of the book presents royalty rate statistics, averages, and graphs. This is coordinated with information about the factors driving licenses and royalty rates. Real deal data is provided, along with models for deriving royalty rates from financial information.

I am also fortunate to be able to include three chapters from very knowledgeable friends. Chapter three, "Use of the Twenty-Five Percent Rule in Valuing IP" by Robert Goldscheider, John Jarosz, and Carla Mulhern, is the definitive article about the popular Profit Split Rule for estimating an appropriate royalty rate. The rule is clearly stated, and then tested against profit margin and royalty rate data.

Chapter eleven, "Court-Awarded Royalty Rates," by Michele M. Riley, CPA, CFE, provides information and data about royalty rates awarded in patent infringement court cases. The chapter provides balance and context for the other chapters about court-awarded royalty rates.

Chapter twelve, "Royalty Audits," by Debora R. Stewart, CPA, discusses the underpayment of royalties occurring through honest error and otherwise. The point of her article is to make it clear that, after all the effort put into negotiating a royalty rate, more effort is still needed to make sure proper payments are eventually collected.

Russell L. Parr
Townsend Inlet, New Jersey

CHAPTER 1

Intellectual Property and Corporate Value

In the last thirty years, intellectual property (IP) and intangible assets have become the dominant assets of major corporations. These assets are at the heart of competitive advantage. They are the foundation of new product categories and sometimes entirely new industries. They differentiate products, provide unique utility, and even permeate products and services with cachet. Often, they allow the manufacturer to obtain a premium price for an otherwise ordinary item. Other times, they provide the user with substantial cost savings.

Ocean Tomo is an integrated, intellectual capital merchant bank.[1] It conducted an analysis of the largest companies in the United States and found that patents, trademarks, copyrights, and other intangible assets have exploded as a percentage of the S&P 500's market value, from seventeen percent in 1975 to eighty percent in 2005 (see Exhibit 1.1). No longer do markets value companies based on balance sheet cash and fixed assets. Today, stock prices reflect the importance and value of all intangible assets, including patents, trademarks, copyrights, and trade secrets.

This is supported by a recent *Les Nouvelles* article, where the value of IP and intangible assets, as a percentage of corporate market value, is reported

2 CHAPTER 1 INTELLECTUAL PROPERTY AND CORPORATE VALUE

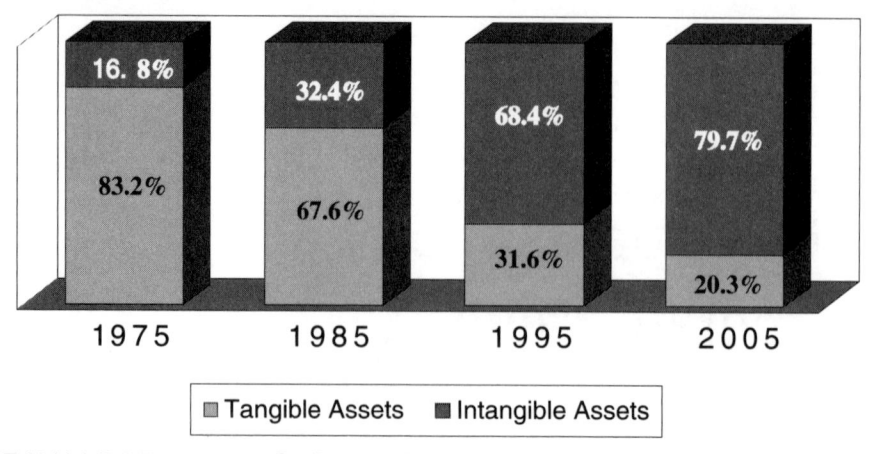

	1975	1985	1995	2005
Intangible Assets	16.8%	32.4%	68.4%	79.7%
Tangible Assets	83.2%	67.6%	31.6%	20.3%

EXHIBIT 1.1 **S&P 500 Components**

as the exact same value shown by Standard and Poor's index.[2] The article shows that the dominance of intangibles is not solely associated with high technology companies, but rather holds true for a diverse selection of industries. For many industries, the dominance of IP is easy to understand. Healthcare, telecommunications, and consumer discretionary products would be expected to possess high amounts of technology or trademarks. Some industries, like utilities, would not be expected to have such intangible asset dominance, yet it turns out that all industries currently rely on a significant amount of IP and intangible assets (see Exhibit 1.2).[3]

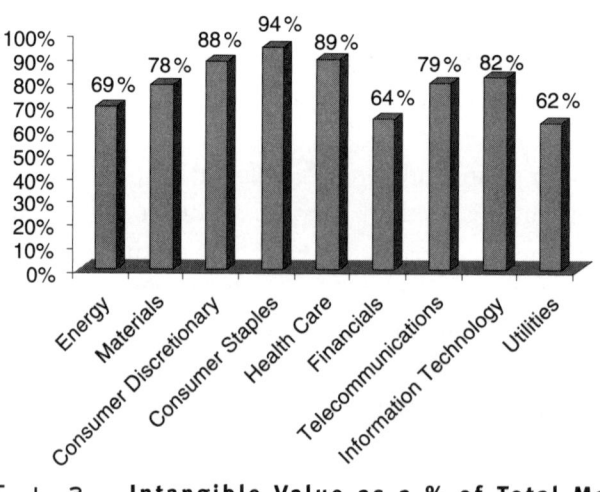

Industry	%
Energy	69%
Materials	78%
Consumer Discretionary	88%
Consumer Staples	94%
Health Care	89%
Financials	64%
Telecommunications	79%
Information Technology	82%
Utilities	62%

EXHIBIT 1.2 **Intangible Value as a % of Total Market Value for 2005**

Thirty years ago, the vast majority of a company's value was its monetary and tangible assets. These are the cash, inventories, accounts receivable, manufacturing facilities, warehouses, transportation systems, and office facilities of a company. Currently, these assets are almost an afterthought, replaced in importance by patented technology, trademarks, copyrights, and other intangible assets.

PATENTS

A patent for an invention is the grant of a property right to the inventor, issued by the United States Patent and Trademark Office (USPTO). Generally, the term of a new patent is twenty years from the date the application for the patent was filed in the United States or, in special cases, from the date an earlier related application was filed, subject to the payment of maintenance fees. U.S. patent grants are effective only within the United States, U.S. territories, and U.S. possessions. Under certain circumstances, patent term extensions or adjustments may be available.

The right conferred by the patent grant is, in the language of the statute and of the grant itself, "the right to exclude others from making, using, offering for sale, or selling" the invention in the United States, or "importing" the invention into the United States. What is granted is not the right to make, use, offer for sale, sell, or import, but the right to exclude others. Once a patent is issued, the patentee must enforce the patent without the aid of the USPTO.

There are three types of patents:

1. *Utility patents* may be granted to anyone who invents or discovers any new and useful process, machine, article of manufacture, composition of matter, or any new and useful improvement thereof.
2. *Design patents* may be granted to anyone who invents a new, original, and ornamental design for an article of manufacture.
3. *Plant patents* may be granted to anyone who invents or discovers, and asexually reproduces, any distinct and new variety of plant.

As more products incorporate many diverse technologies, there will continue to be more opportunities to enjoy the economic benefits of licensing. There will also be more need for licensing, so that the companies pursuing commercialization of technology will be able to enjoy freedom to operate, without the threat of infringement litigation. Consider, as an example, the ubiquitous personal digital assistant (PDA). The diverse proprietary technologies incorporated into PDAs includes inventions associated with

- Liquid crystal displays
- Operating software
- Applications software
- Keyboard and other input devices
- Wireless communications, such as Bluetooth®
- Modems
- Microprocessors
- Digital photography

Few companies possess all of the diverse technologies incorporated into today's products, so licensing technology is becoming fundamental to product creation.

Patent Trends

In 1974, the number of utility patents granted was 76,278. By 2004, the number of patents granted more than doubled, to 164,293. Corporations were granted the vast majority of patents in 2004; foreign and domestic corporations received eighty-eight percent of the total number of patents granted. Interestingly, forty-four percent of patents are owned by U.S. corporations and forty-four percent are owned by foreign companies. Foreign and U.S. individuals combined received ten percent of all patents, with the remainder going to U.S. and foreign governments. The 2004 distribution of patent ownership has remained largely unchanged for the past ten years (see Exhibit 1.3).

Who Owns the Most Patents?

Most patents are owned by U.S. and Japanese companies. The top ten foreign owners of U.S. patents are Japan, Germany, the United Kingdom, France, Canada, Switzerland, Taiwan, Italy, Sweden, and South Korea.

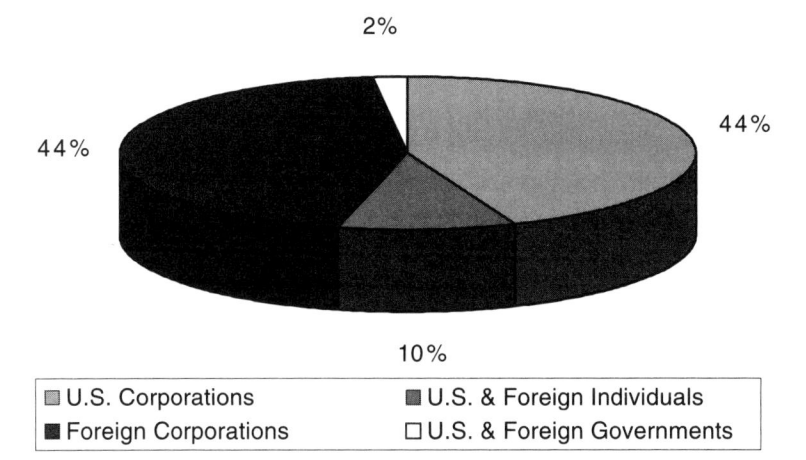

Source: United States Patent & Trademark Office.

EXHIBIT 1.3 2004 Patent Owner Distribution.

Listed below are the top twenty corporate patent owners. The number of patents they own counts all patents granted to these companies between January 1, 1969 and December 31, 2004.

Company	Number of Patents
IBM	42,591
General Electric	31,293
Canon Kabushiki Kaisha	28,202
Hitachi	26,369
Toshiba	22,888
NEC	17,626
Eastman Kodak	19,780
Matsushita Electric Industrial	19,611
Mitsubishi Denki Kabushiki Kaisha	18,985
Sony	17,604
Motorola	17,541
Siemens AG	17,095
US Philips	16,229
AT&T	16,130

Company	Number of Patents
E. I. DuPont De Nemours	15,385
Fujitsu	15,176
Fuji Photo Film	15,044
Xerox	14,743
Bayer AG	13,930
US Navy	13,408

Source: U.S. Patent and Trademark Office

Technology Classifications

Between January 1977 and December 2004, over 3.1 million patents were granted. At this writing, the total number of patents granted for all time was nearing 7 million.

The USPTO classifies patents by technology category. Technology classifications for which patenting is most active are shown in Exhibit 1.4.

Drug inventions clearly dominate. This is not surprising. Huge investments are required to invent and perfect medical therapies. Even larger amounts of profit are available from these successful inventions. Consequently, patent protection is of critical importance.

Further review of the most active technology classifications clearly reflects the state of our experience with commercial and consumer products. As an example, computer and digital products are part of every aspect of our lives. Not surprisingly, semiconductors and active solid-state devices are technology classifications that appear in the top five of the most active list.

Exhibit 1.4 counts all patent documents, including utility, design, plant, and reissue patents, as well as statutory invention registrations and defensive publications.

History of U.S. Patent Applications

Are patent applications an indicator of business confidence? The next graph shows the number of patent applications, by year, since 1850. By focusing on valleys in the graph, we can generally show that during times of turmoil patent applications drop. Listed below are some of the most shattering events in modern history. In all cases they correspond to substantial reduction in

EXHIBIT 1.4 U.S. PATENT TECHNOLOGY CLASSIFICATION

	Total
Drug, Bio-Affecting	108,492
Stock Material or Miscellaneous	52,004
Semiconductor Device Manufacturing	45,752
Chemistry: Molecular and Microbiology	44,041
Active Solid-State Devices	38,152
Measuring and Testing	35,325
Radiation Imagery Chemistry	31,923
Internal-Combustion Engines	31,712
Radiant Energy	27,964
Electrical Connectors	27,898
Furnishings	26,447
Metal Working	26,135
Liquid Purification or Separation	26,059
Optical: Systems and Elements	26,010
Surgery	25,217
Electricity: Measuring and Testing	24,596
Electricity: Electrical Systems	23,603
Surgery	23,157
Communications: Electrical	22,782
Static Information Storage and Retrieval	22,676
Land Vehicles	22,521
Multiplex Communications	22,360
Plastic and Nonmetallic Article Shaping or Treating: Processes	21,718
Adhesive Bonding and Misc. Chemical Manufacture	21,610
Recording, Communication, or Information Retrieval Equip.	21,557
Synthetic Resins or Natural Rubbers	21,238
Television	21,140
Computer Graphics Processing and Selective Visual Display	20,498
Electric Heating	20,250

Source: United States Patent & Trademark Office.

the number of patent applications. It appears that patent applications are an indicator of confidence in the future (see Exhibit 1.5).

1860's—Civil War

1893—Depression

1898—War with Spain

1915—World War I

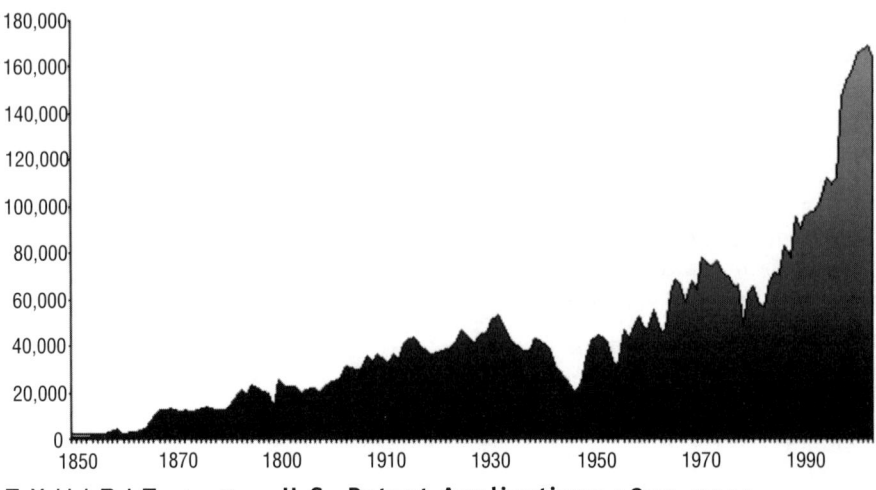

EXHIBIT 1.5 U.S. Patent Applications 1850–2004

1920—Prohibition

1930's—Great Depression

1940's—World War II

1950—Korean War

1968—Vietnam War at its Height

1970's—Oil Embargo

1990—Gulf War

TRADEMARKS

A trademark is a word, name, symbol, or device used in trade with goods, to indicate the source of the goods, and to distinguish them from the goods of others. A servicemark is the same as a trademark, except that it identifies and distinguishes the source of a service rather than a product. The terms "trademark" and "mark" are commonly used to refer to both trademarks and servicemarks.

Trademark rights may be used to prevent others from using a confusingly similar mark, but not to prevent others from making the same goods, or from selling the same goods or services, under a clearly different mark. Trademarks used in interstate or foreign commerce may be registered with the USPTO.

Between 2001 and 2005, over one million trademark applications were filed, at the general rate of over 200,000 annually.

Trademark Applications 2001–2005

Year	Applications
2001	232,939
2002	207,287
2003	218,596
2004	244,848
2005	265,506
Total	**1,169,176**

Source: U.S. Patent and Trademark Office.

In 2005, U.S. companies filed for 262,506 trademarks. States comprising the top ten number of filings are listed below. These ten states accounted for over sixty percent of the applications.

Trademarks Applications for 2005 Top Ten State Filers

State	Applications
California	56,167
New York	28,164
Florida	17,285
Texas	13,609
Illinois	11,782
New Jersey	10,227
Ohio	7,510
Massachusetts	7,491
Pennsylvania	7,376
Georgia	6,700
Total	**166,311**

Source: U.S. Patent and Trademark Office.

Also in 2005, nearly sixty-one thousand trademark applications (twenty-three percent of the total) were filed by business entities of over one hundred sixty foreign countries. The ten countries with the largest number of filers accounted for over seventy percent of the foreign applications:

Trademark Applications for 2005 Top Ten Foreign Nation Filers

Germany	8,146
Canada	7,730
United Kingdom	6,273
Japan	4,824
France	4,555
Switzerland	3,346
Italy	2,894
Australia	2,204
Netherlands	1,725
Mexico	1,403
Total	**43,100**

A measure of the importance placed on trademarks is indicated by the amount of annual spending invested to support brands. *Advertising Age* presents annual data showing amounts spent by the top one hundred advertisers. In 2004, the amount spent was over $98 billion. General Motors spent more than any other company, at $3.997 billion. Procter and Gamble took second place, spending $3.920 billion. The top twenty-five ad spenders are presented in Exhibit 1.6.

The top one hundred leading advertisers supported five hundred sixty-nine brands, with $10 million or more of measured media in 2004. Procter and Gamble supported the most brands, with forty-five. The top twenty-five U.S. mega-brands are listed in Exhibit 1.7.

Johnson and Johnson supported the second largest number of mega-brands, with twenty-six. The undisputed king of media was the Verizon Communications brand, with $1.51 billion in spending. This amount was the largest spent on a single brand.

COPYRIGHTS

A copyright is a form of protection provided to authors of "original works of authorship," including literary, dramatic, musical, artistic, and certain other intellectual works, both published and unpublished. The 1976 Copyright Act generally gives the owner of a copyright the exclusive right to reproduce the copyrighted work, to prepare derivative works,

EXHIBIT 1.6   TOP 25 U.S. ADVERTISERS

From 100 Leading National Advertisers (AA, June 27, 2005). Table ranks marketers by their 2004 U.S. spending, the sum of measured media from TNS Media Intelligence and unmeasured estimates by *Ad Age* that include promotion and direct marketing, etc. Dollars are in millions. *SBC acquired AT&T Corp. in late 2005 and changed the SBC moniker to AT&T. The next edition of this Special Report will be published June 26, 2006.

Rank	Marketer	U.S. Ad Spending	% Change
1	General Motors Corp.	$3,997	6.3
2	Procter & Gamble Co.	3,920	17.0
3	Time Warner	3,283	6.8
4	Pfizer	2,957	10.3
5	SBC Communications*	2,687	3.4
6	DaimlerChrysler	2,462	3.2
7	Ford Motor Co.	2,458	11.4
8	Walt Disney Co.	2,242	10.1
9	Verizon Communications	2,197	31.4
10	Johnson & Johnson	2,176	10.9
11	GlaxoSmithKline	1,828	17.0
12	Sears Holdings Corp.	1,823	-10.9
13	Toyota Motor Corp.	1,821	11.1
14	General Electric Co.	1,819	5.5
15	Sony Corp.	1,665	-7.8
16	Nissan Motor Co.	1,540	17.6
17	Altria Group	1,399	1.0
18	McDonald's Corp.	1,389	1.4
19	L'Oreal	1,341	6.1
20	Unilever	1,319	-1.3
21	Novartis	1,285	34.2
22	PepsiCo	1,262	4.3
23	Home Depot	1,256	22.6
24	Merck & Co.	1,250	11.2
25	U.S. Government	1,229	9.4

Reprinted with permission from the "Top 25 U.S. Advertisers," 2006 Fact Book—4th Annual Guide to Advertising Marketing issue of *Advertising Age*, Copyright, Crain Communications Inc., 2006.

to distribute copies or phonographic records, and to perform or display the work publicly.

The copyright protects the form of expression, rather than the subject matter of the work. For example, a description of a machine could be copyrighted, but this would only prevent others from copying the description; it would not prevent others from writing a description of their own,

EXHIBIT 1.7   TOP 25 U.S. MEGABRANDS

From Megabrands (AA, July 18, 2005). Basic data from TNS Media Intelligence. Measured media totals are AA estimates in millions for calendar 2004. *Cingular absorbed AT&T Wireless in 2005 eliminating the AT&T Wireless megabrand. The next edition of this Special Report will be published July 17, 2006.

Rank	Megabrand	U.S. Ad Spending	% Change
1	Verizon	$1,505.9	27.5
2	Ford	948.0	10.9
3	Nissan	901.0	15.2
4	Chevrolet	895.2	29.1
5	Spring	857.4	9.7
6	Cingular*	833.7	34.6
7	Toyota	792.7	5.3
8	Dodge	707.6	22.6
9	Dell Computers	625.0	26.1
10	McDonald's	614.0	-1.0
11	AT&T Wireless*	591.2	-23.4
12	Wal-Mart	578.4	21.3
13	Honda	565.1	16.4
14	Sears	560.9	-13.5
15	Citibank	549.7	117.7
16	Chrysler	540.9	4.7
17	Hewlett-Packard	530.6	23.2
18	Macy's	530.5	-3.7
19	Target stores	523.2	10.7
20	Home Depot	518.3	-5.5
21	GM corporate	508.8	35.0
22	T-Mobile	440.5	26.0
23	J.C. Penney	430.4	0.5
24	American Express	395.6	5.4
25	Best Buy	387.6	13.4

Reprinted with permission from the "Top 25 U.S. Megabrands," 2006 Fact Book—4th Annual Guide to Advertising Marketing issue of *Advertising Age*, Copyright, Crain Communications Inc., 2006.

or from making and using the machine. The Copyright Office of the Library of Congress registers copyrights.

The Library of Congress is the nation's oldest federal cultural institution, and serves as the research arm of Congress. It is also the largest library in the world, with more than 130 million items, on approximately 530 miles of bookshelves. The collections include more than 29 million books and other printed materials, 2.7 million recordings, 12 million photographs, 4.8 million maps, and 58 million manuscripts.[4]

TRADE SECRETS

Under the Restatement of Torts, §757 (1939), "a trade secret may consist of any formula, pattern, device, or compilation of information which is used in one's business, and which gives him an opportunity to obtain an advantage over competitors who do not know or use it. It may be a formula for a chemical compound, a process of manufacturing, treating or preserving material, a pattern for a machine, or other device, or a list of customers."

Trade secrets are defined under the Uniform Trade Secrets Act as "information, including a formula, pattern, compilation, program, device, method, technique, or process that: (1) derives independent economic value, actual or potential, from not being generally known to, and not being easily ascertainable by proper means, by other persons who can obtain economic value from its disclosure or use, and (2) is the subject of efforts that are reasonable under circumstances to maintain its secrecy."

"The Illinois Trade Secrets Act, §765 ILCS 1065/1 et seq. (West 1993), provides that trade secrets are 'information, including but not limited to, technical or non-technical data, a formula, pattern, compilation, program, device, method, technique, drawing, process, financial data, or list of actual or potential customers or suppliers, that: (a) is sufficiently secret to derive economic value, actual or potential, from not being generally known to other persons who can obtain economic value from its disclosure or use; and (b) is the subject of efforts that are reasonable under the circumstances to maintain its secrecy or confidentiality.'

"The New Restatement of the Law Third, Unfair Competition defines a trade secret in Section 39 as follows: '§39. Definition of Trade Secret. A trade secret is any information that can be used in the operation of a business or other enterprise and that is sufficiently valuable and secret to afford an actual or potential economic advantage over others.'

"In addition, it is well established that 'a trade secret can exist in a combination of characteristics and components, each process, design and operation of which, in unique combination, affords a competitive advantage and is a protectable secret.' Also, 'a trade secret need not be essentially new, novel, or unique; . . . The idea need not be complicated; it may be intrinsically simple and nevertheless qualify as a secret, unless it is common knowledge and, therefore, within the public domain.'"[5]

Evaluating Trade Secrets

Important factors a business owner should consider, in determining whether information owned and used by his/her business is a trade secret, include:

1. the extent to which the information is known outside the owner's business;
2. the extent to which it is known by those involved in the owner's business;
3. measures taken to guard the secrecy of the information;
4. the value of the information to the owner or to his/her competitors;
5. the information; and
6. the ease or difficulty with which the information could be properly acquired or duplicated by others.

The principal idea to remember is that a protectable trade secret may not be "within the realm of general skills and knowledge" in one's field of business, and may not be "readily duplicated without involving considerable time, effort or expense."

Upon examining these factors in comparison to the confidential business information of the company, it may be prudent to conduct an intellectual property audit to identify the protectable business information and assess the value to the company of that information, i.e. the value of the trade secrets.

The number of trade secrets is impossible to count. As long as they remain secret, their number will remain unknown. The respect for trade secrets, however, is well demonstrated by a recent attempt to steal a secret formula from the Coca-Cola Company.

Coke and Pepsi are often perceived as bitter enemies, but when PepsiCo received a letter offering Coca-Cola trade secrets, it went straight to its corporate rival. Six weeks later, three people were scheduled to appear in federal court to face charges of stealing confidential information, including a sample of a new drink, from Coca-Cola to sell to PepsiCo. "Competition can sometimes be fierce, but it also must be fair and legal," Pepsi spokesman Dave DeCecco said. "We're pleased the authorities and the FBI have identified the people responsible for this."[6]

The suspects arrested, the day the $1.5 million transaction was to occur, include a Coca-Cola executive's administrative assistant, who is accused of rifling through corporate files and stuffing documents, and a new Coca-Cola product, into a personal bag. Atlanta-based Coca-Cola thanked PepsiCo for its assistance.[7]

CHAPTER 2

Licensing Intellectual Property

To get an idea of the size of the business of licensing, look at statistics gathered by the IRS. While this data cannot completely capture the entire picture, it can provide a reasonable approximation. The IRS has compiled data showing the total amount of royalty income reported by active companies.[1] For 2002, the most recent data available, companies in all the industries covered by the IRS reported a total amount of $115 billion in royalty income. "All Industries" is comprised of the following business categories: agriculture, arts and entertainment, construction, finance, information, insurance, lodging, manufacturing, real estate, remediation, restaurants, retail, support services, transportation, warehousing, and wholesaling.

To get an idea of the revenues associated with this level of licensing, the royalty income (representing payments by licensees) is divided by the most common royalty rate associated with intellectual property (IP) licensing. This royalty rate, which will be discussed at greater length later in this book, is five percent. When the calculation is completed, revenues derived from licensed IP nearly reach an enormous $2.3 trillion. This huge amount does not include revenue generated from licensed IP where no royalty payment is due, such as where companies have cross-licenses allowing each party to use the other's IP without a royalty payment.

Historical information allows for detecting trends in the business of licensing. The IRS gathered the same royalty income as far back as 1994. In 1994 the total amount of royalty income for all industries was almost $50 billion. In just eight years, the business of licensing has more than doubled. Dividing the $50 billion by the same five percent royalty rate indicates that revenue generated by licensed IP was only $998 billion for 1994.

Technology licensing can be gauged by focusing on industries where licensing would be expected to involve technological innovations, not trademarks and copyrights. Shown below is a table showing royalty income for selected manufacturing industries expected to deal in licensed technology.[2]

Royalty Income for Selected Manufacturing Industries (in thousands of dollars)

Industry	2002	1994
Food	1,863,709	3,503,549
Textile	187,943	60,881
Apparel	641,317	647,923
Wood Products	33,659	49,348
Paper	923,410	801,938
Printing	480,625	1,338,563
Petroleum and Coal	665,830	1,153,114
Chemical	20,447,291	6,322,809
Plastics and Rubber	468,199	524,927
Nonmetallic Mineral	359,472	461,634
Primary Metal	579,262	351,842
Fabricated Metal	2,168,144	512,567
Machinery	2,516,092	12,652,490
Computer and Electronic	23,317,357	—
Electrical Equipment	2,245,571	4,044,577
Transportation Equipment	9,405,614	796,936
Miscellaneous	1,995,981	—
TOTAL	68,299,476	33,223,098

Overall, the data shows that technology licensing payments more than doubled, from $33 billion in 1994, to $68 billion in 2002. Assuming a five percent royalty rate as the basis for paying these royalties, revenue generated by licensed technology rose, from $664 billion in 1994, to $1.3 trillion by 2002.

Trademark and copyright licensing can be approximated by focusing on the IRS data compiled for industries where technology is not as often licensed, but where licensing focuses on trademarks and copyrights. For 2002, royalty income totaled $18.7 billion for the accommodations, arts, broadcast, entertainment, internet publishing and services, food, motion pictures, publishing, recordings, and recreation industries. Still, assuming a five percent royalty rate as the basis for the royalty payments, the revenue derived from licensed trademarks and copyrights exceeded $373 billion. While the data does not lie, this level of trademark and copyright-based revenue seems low.

FORCES BEHIND LICENSING

The pharmaceutical industry provides evidence of the reasons behind licensing, which are relatively common for most industries, even though the patented technology of pharmaceuticals and biotechnology companies is unique.

During the past ten years, royalty rates have been pressured upward by several conditions within the pharmaceutical industry:

- New drug discovery has become increasingly difficult.
- It takes more than ten years, and several hundred million dollars, to put a new drug on the market.
- Pharmaceutical companies are under constant pressure to continually obtain or discover promising compounds.
- Internal research and development pipelines are not sufficiently filled with new discoveries and products.
- Pharmaceutical companies need to supplement their research and development deficiencies with licensing activities.
- Pharmaceutical companies are in heated competition to acquire new molecules and technology from any source.[3]

A quick history of healthcare starts with the traditional pharmaceutical companies, that became multinational giants by turning chemicals into medical products benefiting millions of people. The chemical-based products were easy to use and very inexpensive to mass-produce. Then came—initially from university labs—products based on genes and organisms. In many ways these new discoveries were superior to chemical-based products, having fewer side effects; but biotechnology therapies were, and still are, costly to make. They were also sometimes difficult to market because they often must be injected or inhaled. Big drug companies largely left biotechnology to the small companies, created by scientists and venture capitalists. Now the big drug companies are in trouble. They are watching their research pipeline shrink while simultaneously seeing some biotech firms successfully commercialize gene and organism-based products.

Ernst and Young, a consulting and accounting firm, reports that biotech firms are more productive than the old guard. Since 2003, biotech firms have submitted more new drug applications to the Food and Drug Administration than have old-line firms.[4] In response, the old-line drug companies are shifting their focus and exploring biotechnology. Some are spending more internal research dollars on biotechnology. Some are banking on alliances, product licensing deals, or acquisitions of small biotech firms. Some are pursuing multiple initiatives. Glaxo spent $5.2 billion on internal research and development, but says it expects half its new products to come from outside its organization. Patricia Danson, of the Wharton School at the University of Pennsylvania, says that no firm can rely exclusively on its own research and development.[5]

Amgen is the world's largest biotechnology company. Amgen's chief executive, Kevin Sharer, recently told the *Philadelphia Inquirer* that his company no longer subscribes to the "not-invented-here" syndrome. An example of this new attitude is Amgen's recent acquisition of Abgenix for $2.2 billion. The deal will provide Amgen with full rights to the experimental cancer drug Panitumumab, which the companies have been developing together. Real estate, manufacturing facilities, cash, and inventory were never mentioned as anything of importance in this deal. IP was the sole source of value.

Young companies, with promising new technologies and products, are in the driver's seat, as larger companies clamor around them. Inventors are being approached at earlier stages of development, and with larger offers. Pfizer, signed a $1.9 billion deal with Vicuron. This is the biggest deal ever for a drug in the first phase of regulatory approval.

Industry conditions are also allowing inventors to get more than money. The inventors are getting to structure deals any way they want. Nuvelo announced an agreement to sell rights to its new Alfimeprase, an experimental anti-clotting enzyme, to Bayer HealthCare. Nuvelo will receive up to $385 million, plus royalties of between 15 and 37.5 percent of sales outside the United States. The unique feature of this deal is that Nuvelo will retain U.S. commercialization rights.

The pace of IP acquisitions is also increasing. In less than three weeks, Wyeth Holdings completed three deals centered on obtaining access to technology. Wyeth reached a deal with Trubion Pharmaceuticals, to develop and co-market treatments for inflammatory diseases and cancer. Trubion will be paid a $40 million initial fee, and potentially up to $800 million in milestone payments, excluding royalties. Two weeks before the Trubion deal, Wyeth agreed to pay up to $416.5 million to Progenics Pharmaceuticals for rights to an experimental treatment, for constipation and post-operative bowel dysfunction caused by opioid painkillers. The day before the Progenics deal, Wyeth signed a license agreement with Exelixis for development of treatments for metabolic and liver disorders. Wyeth paid an up-front fee of $10 million, and may pay up to $147.5 million for milestones and royalties.[6]

Johnson & Johnson showed the industry a very successful biotech acquisition when it purchased Centocor, the maker of Remicade, a treatment for rheumatoid arthritis, for $4.9 billion in 1999. With Centocor, Johnson & Johnson became (at the time) one of the largest biotechnology companies in the world. Centocor's products, and global leadership in monoclonal antibody technology, enhanced Johnson & Johnson's growth platforms in biotechnology, cardiology and circulatory, gastrointestinal, pain management, and oncology.

Later, in a 2001 acquisition, Johnson & Johnson purchased Alza, and clearly indicated that the driving force behind the $10 billion deal was IP. Patented drugs already on the market, and new technologies from which new and patented products could be developed, drove the deal, which gave J&J several promising new drugs, including Ditropan XL, for treating overactive bladder, and Concerta, a treatment for attention deficit disorder. J&J previously co-marketed, with Alza, two products developed by Alza-Concerta, and the Duragesic skin patch for chronic pain.

In addition, Alza's technologies might lead to new forms of J&J's blockbuster anemia treatment, Procrit, which at the time of the acquisition was slated to face tough competition, from a longer-acting anemia drug, developed by Amgen. Alza's delivery technologies eliminate many typical side effects, by controlling the release of drugs and keeping them at controlled levels in the bloodstream. J&J's acquisition of these delivery technologies can extend the uses and patent life of some of its existing therapies. J&J is best known for its consumer products, such as Tylenol and Band-Aids, but derives sixty percent of its profits from prescription drugs.

In another 2001 deal, Bristol-Myers Squibb (BMS) paid $7.8 billion for DuPont's pharmaceutical unit to gain access to patented products and technologies needed for creating new products. BMS basically acquired a portfolio of commercialized drugs, with $1.5 billion of annual sales, and a pipeline of early-stage research initiatives. At the time of the acquisition, BMS was the world's number five drug maker, with about $13.3 billion in prescription drug sales in 2000, from such medicines as Glucovance, for diabetes, and Taxol, for breast cancer. The acquisition of DuPont Pharmaceuticals provided only a slim roster of medicines, which brought in $1.5 billion in sales in 2000. DuPont products included Sustiva, for treatment of the HIV virus, and Coumadin, for breaking up blood clots. BMS also obtained DuPont's pipeline of experimental drugs, almost all of which are in the early stages of human trials, including treatments for the HIV virus, blood clots, rheumatoid arthritis, solid cancers, and obesity. The move came after U.S. patents expired on Taxol, and the anti-anxiety treatment BuSpar, which allowed cheaper, generic drugs to enter the market and cut away at its market share.

Once again, the acquisition was driven by patented technology, and benefits expected from integrating newly acquired technology into a stagnant entity. Nowhere in these acquisition stories was there any mention of cash, warehouses, buildings, real estate, or other fixed assets. These deals were driven by IP.

LICENSING MOTIVATION

A recent survey of members of the Licensing Executive Society, by the Licensing Foundation, focused on trying to learn more about the motivation for licensing. The primary focus of the survey was to learn about licensing matters regarding corporate IP owners.[7] Response volume allowed enough data to report insights for four distinct business groups, including:

1. Healthcare (including biotechnology, pharmaceuticals, and medical devices)
2. Digital Information Communications and Electronics, or "DICE" (including Internet, software, and telecommunications)
3. Industrial (comprised of companies in transportation, mechanics, food, beverage, energy, chemicals, petrochemicals, polymers, and allied industries)
4. University/Government

Each of the four groups was further carved into large and small companies, and some interesting insights were derived.

For example, respondents were asked to identify—from patents, trademarks, copyrights, know-how, and trade secrets—which were most important for creating a competitive advantage.

- Healthcare companies, both large and small, reported that patents were the most important IP for creating a competitive advantage.
- Large and small DICE companies reported that patents were also the most important IP for creating competitive advantages, with large DICE companies indicating know-how and patents as being equally important.
- Industrial companies, both large and small, reported know-how and trade secrets as most important.
- University and government entities, large and small, indicated patents as most important.

When asked about the most important reasons for developing IP assets, the respondents' answers were varied:

- Large healthcare companies indicated higher profit margins as the reason for developing IP.
- Small healthcare companies reported as the most important reason development and maintenance of partnerships and joint ventures.
- Large DICE companies highly ranked the following reasons for IP development: management of litigation risk, stopping imitation, higher profit margins, and patent bargaining power.

- Small DICE companies ranked the generation of licensing income as the most important reason for developing IP.
- Industrial companies, both large and small, ranked higher profit margins and stopping imitation as the most important reasons for developing IP.
- University and government agencies ranked licensing income as the most important reason for developing IP.

When licensing IP into their organizations, respondents indicated the following goals as most significant:

- Healthcare companies, both large and small, indicated the most significant goals were to compensate for a lack of research and development and to broaden options for future development.
- Large DICE companies indicated minimizing licensing payments as the most significant goal.
- Small DICE companies indicated their most significant goals were to broaden options for future development, and to expand their IP estates.
- Large industrial companies indicated that obtaining options for future development was most significant.
- Small industrial companies cited as most important their options for future development, minimizing licensing payments, expansion of IP estates, and maintaining partnerships and joint ventures.
- Large university and government entities indicated the most important reason they license IP into their organizations was to compensate for a lack of research and development and to develop an industry standard.
- Small university and government entities indicated the maintenance of partnerships and joint ventures as most significant.

When licensing IP out of their organizations, respondents indicated the following goals as most significant:

- Healthcare DICE and industrial companies, large and small, indicated that out-licensing allowed for maximizing licensing revenue.
- University and government entities out-licensed to allow for full exploitation of research and development capabilities.

REASONS COMPANIES ENGAGE IN LICENSING

Degnan and Horton[8] surveyed 428 licensing executives hoping to learn why companies engage in licensing. The majority of respondents (sixty-one percent) indicated that their organization's primary interest in licensing was for the generation of royalty income. Developing a business advantage (fifty-four percent) and maximizing product profits (forty-four percent) were the next highest-ranked reasons for engaging in licensing. The third highest-ranked reason for licensing activities was to increase the company's technical proficiency (thirty-two percent). Improvement of a company's defensive position was the fourth most important reason for licensing (twenty percent).

Degnan and Horton also learned about some of the key factors involved in setting royalty rates. Exhibit 2.1 shows key factors impacting royalty rates when licensing-in technology. It should be noted that the same general pattern was associated with out-licensing. Respondents rated factors affecting royalty rates on a scale of one to five, with five being a very important factor and one being unimportant. Exhibit 2.1 shows the results of that survey.

The three most important factors identified were protection, utility, and exclusivity. Higher royalty rates are associated with property having strong

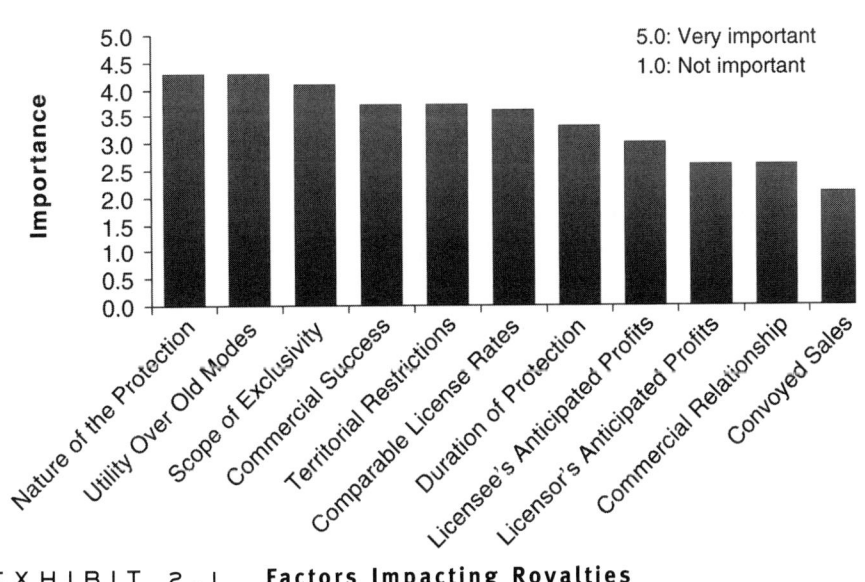

EXHIBIT 2.1   Factors Impacting Royalties

patent protection. In general, people pay more for something stronger, and this certainly applies to licensed technology. Protection was identified as the most important factor, which makes sense. Regardless of any other characteristics and benefits of an invention, if patent protection is considered weak the royalty rate cannot be high.

"Utility over old modes" can be interpreted to mean that licensing executives will pay more for significant enhancements over other technologies than they will for minor enhancements. The more unique or different a licensed technology is, the higher the royalty rate. Higher royalties are also associated with exclusivity, which also makes sense. When a licensor gives exclusive rights, they forego the opportunity to obtain royalty revenue from any other source, so a higher royalty is usually required from a license. Licensees often want exclusivity, to maintain a proprietary advantage. Uniqueness over the competition is difficult to obtain. so when exclusivity is desired, a higher royalty is reasonable.

The only direct evidence of the impact of exclusivity was a deal where DuPont revised a license agreement where that agreement initially conveyed exclusive rights to a licensed invention. Later, the agreement was revised to provide DuPont with only non-exclusive rights, and the royalty rate was reduced. The following story appears in *Royalty Rates for Pharmaceuticals and Biotechnology, Sixth edition*.

> Molecular Biosystems, Inc., (MBI), amended its supply and license agreement with E.I. DuPont De Nemours and Company, which covers proprietary nucleic acid probe technologies owned by MBI. The recently renegotiated agreement was originally established in April of 1986. Previously, DuPont had an exclusive license, but under the new agreement will only retain a non-exclusive right to these technologies. MBI will continue to manufacture nucleic acid probe agents for DuPont, as it did under the previous agreement.
>
> The royalty rate on DuPont's net sales was lowered, from five-and-a-half percent to four percent of net sales, to reflect the change of DuPont's licensing rights, from exclusive to non-exclusive. This represents a reduction in the royalty rate of twenty-seven percent.
>
> MBI is a San Diego company that is recognized as a leading biomedical firm, developing proprietary medical products that diagnose human disease. The company is also a leading developer and supplier of direct, nonradioactively labeled nucleic acid probe products. The company is

also developing diagnostic imaging products, including Albunex, an injectable contrast agent for use in ultrasound imaging.

The next most important group of factors, as indicated by the 1.0 to 5.0 ranking system, includes commercial success, territory restrictions, comparable license rates, and duration of protection.

Commercial success for the technology being licensed is risk-reduction for the licensee. Besides being proven in the laboratory, the technology is proven in the market place, having shown itself to be in demand by consumers. A technology with this characteristic is definitely worth more than a technology which has not addressed this commercial question. Knowing that the market wants a technology makes that technology worth a great deal more, since an important element of risk has been removed.

Territory restriction is a factor included in the second most important group. Limitations to the territory in which a technology can be practiced can impact the profit margins available to the licensee. A large territory provides a large market opportunity. A large potential allows for economies of scale in production and marketing, while limited territories can reduce overall profit opportunity. A larger royalty rate for unrestricted territories is indicated by Degnan's survey.

Comparable license royalty rates are indeed an important factor, and their inclusion in the second group was surprising at first. Comparable royalty rates provide an indication of pricing by showing the price others have paid for similar property. When pricing a home, buyers and sellers look at the price paid for similar homes. Buyers and sellers of technology do the same thing. This factor may be in the second group, and not the first, because the characteristics associated with the factors in the first group must be determined before addressing the royalty rate question. It is important to understand the details of what is being transferred, before any pricing decisions are made. Consequently, licensing executives are interested in many qualitative factors before considering the financial aspects of a transaction.

Also included in the second group is the duration of protection. A higher value is typically associated with something expected to last longer. This is especially important when commercialization of the licensed technology requires up-front investments. These investments may include capital expenditures for manufacturing activities, and/or investments for educating the market about the benefits provided by the new technology. Such investments can be enormous, and when the license term and duration of protection are long, more time exists for recapturing the up-front investment and earnings profit. Conversely, when the duration of protection is short, less time is available for recapturing any up-front investment and risk is higher. Thus lower royalty rates would be expected for shorter durations of protection.

In the third group of factors impacting royalty rates are the licensee's anticipated profits, the licensor's anticipated profits, commercial relationship, and convoyed sales.

Profits are like the previously mentioned commercial success, in that the existence of profits is a reduction of risk for the licensee. The existence of profits also establishes the total amount of economic benefit, to be divided between the licensee and licensor. It makes sense that profit falls into the third group. The previously listed characteristics of the technology need to be identified before the division of profits (determination of a royalty rate) is worth considering.

Also in the third group is commercial relationship. Although not clearly defined, commercial relationship most likely will relate to the competitive relationship between the licensor and the licensee. If the license is between competitors, the level of royalty rate is likely to be higher. When the licensee is a competitor of the licensor, a competitive advantage may be lost to the licensee. This may impact the core business of the licensor, making the licensor demand a higher royalty rate. Surprisingly, this factor is not among the most important.

Also identified as a factor impacting royalty rates are "convoyed sales," or sales associated with the sale of the licensed product, but not covered by the license. A camera may be the licensed product, and accessories, like a flash unit, or telephoto lens, may be sold at the time of the initial camera sale. The flash and lens are convoyed sales. A high probability of selling accessory products enhances the profits of sales that include a "package," where the licensed product and accessories are sold together. The opportunity for selling convoyed items is reported by the survey as the lowest ranked factor. This may be because convoyed sales opportunities are not always common. Since the opportunity for selling accessories is not common, survey respondents do not give it great importance.

Later-stage technology is less risky, and therefore more valuable, than early-stage and unproven technology. Consequently, higher royalty rates are associated with more developed technology. This phenomenon fits well into the Degnan survey results. Later-stage technology has proven itself. Proven success comes in the form of successful, large-scale production, or encouraging market surveys showing desire for the patented invention in a product. Proven success may also be represented by product efficacy. Risk-reduction is a characteristic of a later-stage technology that is desired, and this characteristic leads to a higher royalty rate.

University technology tends to be early-stage technology. This explains statistics which show that royalty rates, where universities are the licensor, are low when compared to other license deals.

Clearly, IP is central to economic activity, and licensing has become a strategic tool for competing in an IP-dominated environment. The remainder of this book will focus on the pricing of licensed IP.

CHAPTER 3

Use of the Twenty-Five Percent Rule in Valuing Intellectual Property

ROBERT GOLDSCHEIDER,* JOHN JAROSZ,**
AND CARLA MULHERN

This chapter is a study by Robert Goldscheider, John Jarosz, and Carla Mulhern. They present the definitive discussion, explaining and proving the broad validity of the famous Twenty-Five Percent Rule for deriving royalty rates.

INTRODUCTION

As the importance of intellectual property (IP) protection has grown, so has the sophistication of tools used to value it. Discounted cash flow,[1] capitalization of earnings,[2] return on investment,[3] Monte Carlo simulation,[4] and modified Black-Scholes option valuation methods[5] have been of great value. Nonetheless, the fairly simple "Twenty-Five Percent Rule" ("Rule") is over forty years old, and its use continues. Richard Razgaitis

---

* Chairman, International Licensing Network.
** Principal, Analysis Group/*Economics*. We would like to thank the following individuals for their hard work and useful comments on earlier drafts of this paper: Jaime Baim, Laura Boothman, Jeff Kinrich, Jennifer Price, Chris Vellturo, and Robert Vigil. The views expressed here are ours and do not necessarily represent those of others at the International Licensing Network or Analysis Group/*Economics*.

31

has called it the "most famous heuristic, or rule of thumb, for licensing valuation."[6]

The Rule suggests that the licensee pay a royalty rate equivalent to twenty-five percent of expected profits for the product that incorporates the IP at issue. The Rule has been primarily used in valuing patents, but has been useful (and applied) in copyright, trademark, trade secret, and know-how contexts as well. Since the Rule came into fairly common usage decades ago, times, of course, have changed. Questions have been raised as to whether the factual underpinnings for the Rule still exist (i.e., whether the Rule has much positive strength) such that it can, and should, continue to be used as a valid pricing tool (i.e., whether the Rule has much normative strength).

In this chapter, we describe the Rule, address some of the misconceptions about it, and test its factual underpinnings. To undertake the latter, we have examined the relationship between real-world royalty rates, real-world industry, and company profit data. In general, we have found that the Rule is a valuable tool, rough as it is, particularly when more complete data on incremental IP benefits are unavailable. The Rule continues to have a fair degree of both positive and normative strength.

HISTORY OF THE RULE

According to some sources, the Rule was formally developed decades ago by one of the authors, Robert Goldscheider.[7] Mr. Goldscheider did, in fact, undertake an empirical study of a series of commercial licenses in the late 1950s.[8] This involved one of his clients, the Swiss subsidiary of a large American company, with eighteen licensees around the world, each having an exclusive territory. The term of each of these licenses was for three years, with the expectation of renewals if things continued to go well. Thus, if any licensee turned sour, it could promptly be replaced. Even though all of them faced strong competition, they were, in fact, either first or second in sales volume, and probably profitability, in their respective markets. Those licenses, therefore, constituted the proverbial win-win situation. In them, the IP rights transferred included a portfolio of valuable patents, a continual flow of know-how, trademarks developed by the licensor, and copyrighted marketing and product description materials. For those licenses, the licensees tended to generate profits of approximately twenty percent of sales, on which they paid royalties of five percent of sales. Thus, the royalty rates were found to be twenty-five percent of the licensees' profits, on products embodying the patented technology.[9]

Mr. Goldscheider first wrote about the Rule in 1971.[10] He noted, however, that in some form it had been utilized by valuation experts prior to that.[11] For example, in 1958, Albert S. Davis, general counsel of Research Corporation, the pioneer company in licensing university-generated technology, wrote:

> If the patents protect the licensee from competition, and appear to be valid, the royalty should represent about twenty-five percent of the anticipated profit for the use of the patents.[12]

A form of the Rule, however, existed even decades before that. In 1938, the Sixth Circuit Court of Appeals, in struggling with the problem of determining a reasonable royalty, heard expert testimony to the affect that

> ... ordinarily, royalty rights to the inventor should bear a certain proportion to the profits made by the manufacturer, and that the inventor was entitled to a 'proportion ranging from probably ten percent of the net profits to as high as 30 percent,' which should be graduated by the competitive situation.[13]

Regardless of its origins or authorship, the concept has aided IP valuators for many years.

EXPLANATION OF THE RULE

In its pure form, the Rule starts with an estimate of the licensee's expected profits, for the product that embodies the IP at issue. Those profits are divided by the expected net sales, over that same period, to arrive at a profit rate. That resulting profit rate, say sixteen percent, is then multiplied by twenty-five percent, to arrive at a running royalty rate. In this example, the resulting rate would be four percent. Going forward—or calculating backwards, in the case of litigation—the four percent royalty rate is applied to net sales, to arrive at royalty payments due to the IP owner. The licensee/user receives access to the IP, yet the price it pays (i.e., the royalty) will still allow it to generate positive product returns.

The theory underlying this rule of thumb is that the licensor and licensee should share in the profitability of products embodying the patented technology. The a priori assumption is that the licensee should retain a majority (i.e., seventy-five percent) of the profits because it has undertaken substantial development, operational, and commercialization risks, contributed other technology/IP, and/or brought to bear its own development, operational, and commercialization contributions.

Focus of the Rule is placed on the *licensee's* profits, because it is the licensee who will be using the IP.[14] The value of IP is, for the most part, dependent upon factors specific to the user (e.g., organizational infrastructure).[15] IP, like any other asset, derives its value from the use to which it will be put.[16]

Focus also is placed on *expected* profits, because the license negotiation is meant to cover forthcoming, and ongoing, use of the IP.[17] It is the expected benefit from use of the IP that will form the basis for the licensee's payment of an access fee. Past, or "sunk," costs typically should be ignored because a decision is being made about the future.[18] That is, what future price results in the product being a sound investment? Any product, in which the projected marginal benefits exceed the projected marginal costs, should be undertaken.

Focus is placed on *long-run* profits, because access to IP often will afford the user more than just immediate benefits.[19] Focusing on a single month, or single year, typically will not properly represent the forthcoming, and ongoing, benefits of the IP. In many instances, it takes some period of time for a new company, or new product, to obtain its operational efficiencies and a steady state. Furthermore, up front investments often need to be amortized over the economic life of a product, not just its starting years, in order to properly evaluate the economic returns for the product.

Finally, the Rule places focus on *"fully-loaded"* profits, because they measure the accounting returns on a product. Gross profits represent the difference between revenue and manufacturing costs. Gross profits, however, do not account for all of the operating expenses associated with product activity. Those costs include marketing and selling, general and administrative, and research and development expenses. Some of those costs are directly associated with product activity, others are common across product lines.

Fully-loaded profits account for the fact that a variety of non-manufacturing overhead expenses are undertaken to support the product activity, even though they may not be directly linked to certain volume or activity levels. Such costs are often driven by product activity. Failure to take into account these operating expenses may lead to an overstatement of the returns associated with the sales of a product.

According to Smith and Parr:

> Omission of any of these [overhead] expenses overstates the amount of economic benefit that can be allocated to the IP. In a comparison of two items of IP, the property that generates sales, captures market share, and grows, while using less selling and/or support efforts, is more valuable than the one that requires extensive advertising, sales personnel, and administrative support. The economic benefit generated by the property are most accurately measured after considering these expenses.[20]

According to Parr:

> The operating profit level, after consideration of the non-manufacturing operating expenses, is a far more accurate determinant of the contribution of the IP. The royalty for specific IP must reflect the industry and economic environment in which the property is used. Some environments are competitive and require a lot of support costs, which reduce net profits. IP that is used in this type of environment is not as valuable as IP in a high-profit environment where fewer support costs are required. A proper royalty must reflect this aspect of the economic environment in which it is to be used. A royalty based on gross profits alone cannot reflect this reality.[21]

Fully loaded profits may refer to either pretax profits or operating profits. Pretax profits are calculated as revenue minus 1) cost of goods, 2) non-manufacturing overhead expenses, and 3) other income and expenses. The historical relationships underlying the Rule, however, have in fact been between royalty rates and *operating profits*.[22] The latter is revenue minus 1) cost of goods sold, and 2) non-manufacturing overhead. Not subtracted out are other income and expenses. In many cases, these two measures of profit are quite similar; in other cases, they are not. Given that the value of IP is independent of the way in which a firm or project is financed,[23] from a theoretical point of view, the operating profit margin is the correct measure to use.

Suppose that firm A and firm B each have one piece of identical IP, and each manufactures and sells one product which embodies that IP. The only difference between the firms is that firm A is heavily financed by debt and firm B is not. Firm A would then have significant interest expenses to deduct from its operating profits, resulting in pretax profit levels below operating profit levels. Firm B does not have any interest expense to deduct. Thus, on an operating profits basis, firm A and firm B would have equivalent profit margins; but, on a pretax basis, firm B would be considerably more profitable.

Application of the Rule to operating profits would result in the same royalty rate in the case of firm A and firm B, whereas application of the Rule to pretax profits would result in a lower royalty rate for firm A. Since the underlying IP, and the products embodying it, are identical for both firms, one would expect to obtain the same resulting royalty rate. Thus, application of the Rule to operating profits would yield the appropriate results.

ILLUSTRATION OF THE RULE

IP, like any asset, can be—valued using three sets of tools. They are often referred to as the income approach, the market approach, and the cost approach.[24] The income approach focuses on the returns generated by the user, owing to the asset at issue. The market approach focuses on the terms of technology transfers covering comparable assets. The cost approach focuses on the ability, and cost, to develop an alternative asset that generates the same benefits.

The Rule is a form of the income approach. It is particularly useful when the IP at issue comprises a significant portion of product value, and/or the incremental benefits of the IP are otherwise difficult to measure.

IP is often priced based on the enhanced revenue, and/or reduced costs, that it generates versus the next best alternative.[25] Holding all else constant, the extent of that excess or incremental value may form the upper bound for the appropriate price.[26]

The Rule can be—applied when the licensee reports product line revenue, and operating profit data, for the product encompassing the IP. It need not be the case that the IP at issue is the only feature driving product value. In fact, underlying the Rule is the understanding that a variety of factors drive such value. That is why only a portion of the profits—twenty-five percent—is paid in a license fee, which is why the appropriate profit split may be much less than twenty-five percent of product profit.

The Rule also can be—applied when the licensee does not report profits at the operating profit level. (In fact, there are very few instances in which firms report *product* profits at such a level.) As long as product revenue, and costs of goods sold, are reported (i.e., gross margins are available), the accountant or economist can—allocate common (or non-manufacturing overhead) costs to the product line in order to derive operating profits. The illustration in Exhibit 3.1 shows how the Rule is applied.

A patent may enhance or improve product revenue through increased prices—though that may occur with a reduction in volume[27]—or through increased volume. The second column in Exhibit 3.1 illustrates the impact of a revenue-enhancing patent. Applying the Rule to the expected operating profits results in a royalty rate of 9.1 percent.

A patent may also reduce product costs. Exhibit 3.2 illustrates that applying the Rule to such expected operating profits results in a royalty rate of ten percent.

Valuators and courts who use the Rule occasionally *split* the expected or actual cost (i.e., incremental) savings associated with the IP at issue.[28] According to Degnan and Horton's survey of licensing organizations, that base a royalty payment on projected cost savings, almost all of them provide for the licensee paying 50 percent or less of the projected savings.[29] The apparent reasoning is that such incremental benefits should be shared.

Splitting the cost savings seventy-five/twenty-five, however, may not be consistent with the Rule. In Exhibit 3.2, the incremental, or additional, cost savings are $10. Multiplying that amount by 25 percent results in a running royalty rate of 2.5 percent ($10 × 25%/$100), which is one-

EXHIBIT 3.1   25 PERCENT RULE ILLUSTRATION—REVENUE SIDE

	No Patent	Revenue Enhancing Patent	25 Percent Rule
Revenues	$100	$110	
Cost of Sales	$40	$40	
Gross Margin	$60	$70	
Operating Expenses	$30	$30	
Operating Profits	$30	$40	($40*25%)/ $110=9.1%

EXHIBIT 3.2 25 PERCENT RULE ILLUSTRATION—COST SIDE

	No Patent	Cost Reducing Patent	25 Percent Rule
Revenues	$100	$100	
Cost of Sales	$40	$30	
Gross Margin	$60	$70	
Operating Expenses	$30	$30	
Operating Profits	$30	$40	($40*25%)/$100=10%

sixteenth of the new "product" profits, rather than one-quarter. Applying the Rule to *incremental* savings, or benefits, results in a running royalty that is lower than the rate dictated by the Rule. It may undercompensate the IP owner. The Rule, in its pure sense, should be applied to fully-loaded operating profits, not to already computed incremental benefits.

Several courts have implicitly recognized the problem of splitting incremental benefits. In *Ajinomoto*, the district court wrote:

> Although the 'licensing rule of thumb' dictates that only one-quarter to one-third of the benefit should go to the owner of the technology . . . given [defendant's] relatively low production costs, and its belief that the sale of [the product] would increase [convoyed sales], the court concludes that [defendant] would have been willing to share all of the benefit with [plaintiff] and that [plaintiff] would have settled for nothing less.[30]

Furthermore, in *Odetics,* the federal circuit court noted that "one expects [an infringer] would pay as much as it would cost to shift to a non-infringing product."[31] And in *Grain Processing,* the federal circuit court adopted the lower court's reasoning, that an infringer "would not have paid more than a three percent royalty rate." The court reasoned that this rate would reflect the cost difference between infringement and non-infringement.[32]

To the extent that incremental benefits (i.e., cost savings) have already been calculated, any profit split applied to those may not be consistent with the Rule. In theory, the licensee should be willing to accept a royalty that is close to one hundred percent, rather than twenty-five percent, of the cost savings.

APPLICATION OF THE RULE

The Rule is used in actual licensing and litigation settings. Over the past three decades, a variety of commentators have noted its widespread use.[33] In their survey of licensing executives, published in 1997, Degnan and Horton found that roughly twenty-five percent (a sheer coincidence) of licensing organizations used the Rule as a starting point in negotiations.[34] They also found that roughly fifty percent of the organizations used a profit sharing analysis—of which the Rule is a variant—in determining royalties.[35]

A dramatic employment of the Rule occurred in the early 1990's, in the course of negotiations between two major petrochemical companies, respectively referred to as "A" and "B". A was a leading manufacturer of a basic polymer product ("X"), with annual sales of over $1 billion. Its process ("P-1") required the purchase from B of an intermediate compound ("Y") in annual volumes of over $400 million. A owned a patent, which would expire in seven years, on its P-1 process to manufacture X.

A developed a new process ("P-2") to make X, and decided to switch all its production of X to the new process, essentially for cost reasons, but also because P-2 was more flexible in producing different grades of X. P-2 did not involve the need to purchase Y from B. Rather than simply abandon P-1, however, A decided to offer B the opportunity to become the exclusive worldwide licensee of P-1. The argument was that such a license could be profitable to B because it was a basic producer of Y, which A had been purchasing at a price containing a profit to B. Meaning B could thus manufacture X on a cost-effective basis. Another attraction of such a license was that it could compensate B for the loss of its sales of Y to A.

B was interested in such a license for P-1, and offered to pay a five percent running royalty on sales of X made in accordance with P-1. A decided to test the reasonableness of this offer by applying the Rule. A understood the market for X, past and present, and had what it considered to be realistic projections for the future. A had made such a study because it intended to remain in the market for X, utilizing P-2. A was also able to calculate pro-forma profitability to B by subtracting B's margin on its sales of Y to A for use in P-1.

This analysis revealed that B should be able to operate as a licensee, under A's P-1 patent, at an operating profit of forty-four percent. A shared its fully documented analysis with B and asked, "Please tell us if we are wrong." If not, A would expect to receive an eleven percent royalty, according to the Rule, based on B's sales of X using A's patented P-1 process, rather than the five percent offered.

Following a study of A's work product, B reluctantly agreed with A's conclusion. B accepted these terms because they believed they could still make a thirty-three percent operating profit under the license, which was higher than B's normal corporate operating profit rate. In fact, over the remaining life of its P-1 patent, this additional six percent royalty amounted to added profit of several hundred million dollars to A.

In *Standard Manufacturing and DBP v. United States*,[36] the U.S. Court of Claims employed a two-step approach to determining a reasonable royalty. The first step involved an estimation of an initial, or "baseline," rate. The second step entailed an adjustment upward or downward, depending on the relative bargaining strengths of the two parties, with respect to each of the fifteen factors described in *Georgia-Pacific v. U.S. Plywood*.[37]

The *Standard Manufacturing* court found application of the Rule to be an appropriate method for determining the baseline royalty rate. In support of its use of the Rule, the court cited defendant's expert, Robert Goldscheider's, considerable practical experience with the Rule.[38] The court also noted that a number of other federal courts had recognized that the Rule is a rule of thumb typically used in the licensing field.[39] For example, the Rule has been useful in situations where a party analyzes its own IP, for management or tax reasons, or as part of a merger, acquisition, or divestiture. The Rule has been employed as follows:

- the remaining economic life of the property being valued, which may be shorter than the remaining legal life of any patents which may be part of the analysis, is estimated;
- the operating profit rate expected during each of such years is projected, and twenty-five percent (or another rate considered appropriate in accordance with the Rule) is applied to each of the annual figures;
- a discounted cash flow analysis is performed, using an appropriate discount rate, to convert future flows into a current year, lump sum amount.

The rationale for this appraisal methodology is that the plus or minus twenty-five percent apportionment is the price of a reasonable royalty, which the appraising party would be willing to pay for a license for the property at that point in time, assuming that it *did not* own it.

The Rule, whether used in litigation or non-litigation settings, provides a fairly rough tool, to be augmented by a more complete royalty analysis. The precise split of profits should be adjusted depending on the circumstances of each case, and the relative bargaining positions of the two parties.[40] If a licensor comes to the bargaining table armed with a relatively strong arsenal of assets, it may be entitled to twenty-five percent, or perhaps more, of the pie. Correspondingly, a weak arsenal of assets supports a lower split. In determining the appropriate split of profits, the factors established in *Georgia-Pacific* are quite helpful.[41] In fact, many of the courts that have used the Rule in litigation have done so in the context of evaluating *Georgia-Pacific* factor number thirteen—"the portion of the realizable profit that should be credited to the invention, as distinguished from non-patented elements, the manufacturing process, business risks, or significant features or improvement added by the infringer."

JUSTIFICATION FOR THE RULE

The Rule, based on historical observations, provides useful guidance for how a licensor and licensee should consider apportioning the benefits flowing from use of IP. Somewhat untenable, and unrealistic, is guidance that either the licensor or licensee is entitled to all of the returns. No bargain would be reached. Though a fifty/fifty starting split may have the ring of a win-win situation, the evidence suggests otherwise.

Richard Razgaitis has identified six reasons why a twenty-five/seventy-five starting split makes sense.[42] First, "that's the way it is." Numerous licensors and licensees have agreed to a twenty-five/seventy-five split, so it is, according to Razgaitis, the industry norm. Second, typically seventy-five percent of the work needed to develop and commercialize a product must be done by the licensee. Third, "he who has the gold makes the rules." Licensees have considerable leverage because of the numerous investment alternatives open to them. Fourth, a three-times payback ratio is common. Such is obtained by a licensee, retaining seventy-five percent of the return by investing twenty-five percent. Fifth, technology is the first of four required steps of commercialization. The others are: making the product manufacturable, actually manufacturing it, and selling it. Finally, the ratio of research and development costs to profits is often in the range of twenty-five to thirty-three percent.

CRITICISMS OF THE RULE

Despite, or perhaps because of, its widespread use, the Rule has been criticized in several ways. First, it has been characterized as a "crude tool," and as "arbitrary." According to Paul Schaafsma:

> A typical 'rule of thumb' ... is for the licensor to command twenty-five percent of the profit. While this ... attempts to link the value of the patent to the profitability of commercial exploitation, because it does not relate to the value and degree to which the patent can exclude substitute products, and therefore command a patent profit, it is little better than [an] 'industry norm.' ... Patented products add to economic profit the patent profit tied into the ability of the patent to further exclude substitutes. ... the portion of the total profit can vary greatly, even within a given industry. Adding these values together, and multiplying by an arbitrary fraction to derive the value of a patent, is an exercise in arbitrary business analysis.[43]

According to Mark Berkman:

> [The Rule does] not take into account specific circumstances that will determine the actual value of the patent at issue. No consideration is given to the number, or value, of economic alternatives, or the incremental value of using the patented technology over other viable alternatives.[44]

Richard Toikka has questioned whether, in litigation contexts, the Rule is reliable, specifically in relation to *Daubert v. Merrill Dow Pharmaceuticals*,[45] and *Kumho Tire Co. v. Carmichael*.[46]

The Rule, however, is one of many tools. Ultimately, royalty rates are often higher or lower than twenty-five percent of fully-loaded product profits, depending upon a host of quantitative and qualitative factors that can, and should, affect a negotiation or litigation. Even critics of the Rule have conceded that, despite its crudeness, it retains "widespread endorsement and use."[47] Part of that is due to its simplicity, and part is due to self-fulfilling prophecy (i.e., because of its simplicity, it has become a norm, and because it is a norm, it is used over and over again). Moreover, the Rule is not ever intended to be used in isolation. There are a variety of other tools that should be employed in any valuation assignment.

A second criticism is that the Rule is "indefinite." That is, should twenty-five percent be applied to gross profits, operating profits, or some other measure of profits? According to William Lee

> the Rule is sometimes a little indeterminate as to whether it refers to twenty-five percent of net profit or twenty-five percent of gross profit (if you represent the prospective licensor, then of course you apply the twenty-five percent against anticipated gross profit; if you represent the prospective licensee, you contend that the twenty-five percent applies to net profit!). Note that the indefiniteness as to whether the Rule speaks to net profit or gross profit brings it somewhat in line with the rule of thumb of one-third to one-quarter of profit as a reasonable royalty, as expressed in [some publications].[48]

In fact, there is no indefiniteness. The Rule is based on historical observations of the relationships between *royalty rates and operating margins.*[49] That is, rates often are twenty-five percent of *operating* margins, and it is anticipated operating margins, according to the Rule, against which the profit-split figure should be applied. Applying it to another level of profits may be valid, and useful in certain contexts, but such an application is not grounded in the concepts and facts surrounding the Rule.

Third, some analysts believe that there is no indefiniteness, and that, in fact, twenty-five percent is meant to be applied to a licensee's *gross* profits.[50] (Gross profits, again, represent the difference between revenue and cost of goods sold. No deduction for non-manufacturing overhead costs is included.) Some analysts criticize that application because gross margin ignores a host of other relevant costs. Such analysts have concluded that while the Rule is simple, popular and easy to understand, it should be avoided.[51] Focusing on gross profits, they say, ignores too many important factors.[52]

This criticism is specious, however, because the Rule is an allocation, or splitting, of *operating* profits. Explicit consideration is given to all of the costs, including non-manufacturing overhead, needed to support a product or driven by the product. The Rule is *not* properly applied as a split of gross profits.

Furthermore, in their survey of licensing executives, Degnan and Horton found that royalty rates tend to be ten to fifteen percent of *gross profits.*[53] In other words, royalty rates divided by *gross* margin is substantially lower than twenty-five percent.

In *Procter and Gamble v. Paragon Trade Brands*,[54] the court cited testimony that the Rule "is not really even useful as a general guide for deriving an appropriate royalty rate."[55] In part because of that, the court wrote that it "will consider the [twenty-five percent] rule of thumb analysis in determining the royalty rate, [but] this approach will not receive substantial weight."[56] Nonetheless, in its final royalty analysis, the court did rule that "the [twenty-five percent] rule of thumb analysis provides an additional confirmation of the reasonableness of a royalty rate of two percent."[57]

Fourth, it has been asserted that the Rule is inappropriate for use in those instances where the IP at issue represents a small fraction of the product's resident value. The authors are sympathetic to the criticism. However, both the concepts underlying the Rule, as well as the empirics supporting it, recognize the flexibility of the Rule. The precise split should be adjusted depending on a host of factors, including the relative contribution of the IP at issue. Relatively minor IP often should, and does, command a split of profits that is lower than relatively important IP.

A final criticism of the Rule is that it provides a rough, or imprecise, measure of incremental benefits. A complete and accurate incremental analysis is preferred, and none of the authors disagrees. Often, the Rule is an adjunct to other valuation methods. And it is particularly useful when helpful data on incremental value are either unavailable or limited. The Rule is a starting point to apportioning the profits. William Lee, both a critic and proponent of the Rule, has noted

> . . . in most instances, the rule of thumb of approximately one-quarter to one-third of the licensee's anticipated profit to go to the licensor is a good starting place for negotiations. Whether or not anticipated profit is expressed during negotiations, the effect of royalty on profitability should certainly be in the minds of the negotiators on both sides. My experience, and apparently the experience of others, tends to show that most successful licensing arrangements end with royalty levels in this range. However, like all rules of thumb, circumstances alter cases.[58]

EMPIRICAL TEST OF THE RULE

To test the validity of the Rule, we attempted to compare royalty rates from actual licensing transactions with the expected long-run profit margins of the products that embody the subject IP. We were able to gather royalty rate data from thousands of actual licensing transactions.[59] Because of the confidentiality of these licenses, along with a lack of access to expected or actual product profit rates, we were unable to undertake a direct comparison of product profit and royalty rates. We therefore examined profit data for two surrogates—licensee profits and "successful" licensee profits.

With the first proxy, we examined profits for those firms in each industry that were involved in licensing transactions. We used those profit rates as a proxy for expected long-run *product* profits.

With the second proxy, we examined "successful" licensee profits. We defined as "successful" those licensees in the top quartile in their respective industries, in terms of profitability. Presumably, these may more accurately reflect the kind of profit rates that are generated by products that embody valuable IP.

For both proxies, we compared *median* industry royalty rates to weighted average profit rates. Although we considered comparing median royalty rates to *median* profit rates, for some industries median profit rates differed substantially from weighted average profit rates due, at least in part, to the presence of a significant number of small, start-up firms earning negative profit margins. Given that the negative margins earned by start-ups may not be indicative of expected long-run profits, we examined weighted average profit margins, which gives these negative profit margins relatively less weight.

ROYALTY RATES

To obtain information regarding royalty rates observed in actual licensing transactions, we used information provided by RoyaltySource.com, a searchable database of IP sale and licensing transactions, containing information spanning the late 1980s to the present. From RoyaltySource, we obtained summaries of all available licensing transactions, involving the following fifteen industries:

- Automotive
- Chemicals
- Computers
- Consumer Goods

- Electronics
- Energy and Environment
- Food
- Healthcare Products
- Internet
- Machines and Tools
- Media and Entertainment
- Pharmaceuticals and Biotechnology
- Semiconductors
- Software
- Telecom[60]

These licenses involved a variety of payment terms, including lump-sum, fee per unit, and running royalties on sales. For ease of comparison, we confined our analysis to the 1,533 licenses that involved running royalties on sales.[61]

Exhibit 3.3 shows, on an industry-by-industry basis, the information we obtained from RoyaltySource. We have reported minimum, maximum and median royalty rates. The median royalty rate across all industries was 4.5 percent, though median rates ranged from a low of 2.8 percent to a high of 8.0 percent.

INDUSTRY PROFITS

We obtained financial information for the fifteen industries included in our analysis from Bloomberg. The Bloomberg database provided financial data for the years 1990 through 2000, for 6,309 companies included in the fifteen industries under consideration. Exhibit 3.4 reports the average operating profit margin for each of the industries.

LICENSEE PROFITS

Because total industry profits are not a particularly close match to royalty rates covering a limited number of companies, for our first analysis, we examined profitability data for only those companies that were identified

EXHIBIT 3.3   LICENSED ROYALTY RATES
(LATE 1980s–2000)

Industry	No. of Licenses	Minimum Royalty Rate	Maximum Royalty Rate	Median Royalty Rate
Automotive	35	1.0%	15.0%	4.0%
Chemicals	72	0.5%	25.0%	3.6%
Computers	68	0.2%	15.0%	4.0%
Consumer Goods	90	0.0%	17.0%	5.0%
Electronics	132	0.5%	15.0%	4.0%
Energy & Entertainment	86	0.5%	20.0%	5.0%
Food	32	0.3%	7.0%	2.8%
Healthcare Products	280	0.1%	77.0%	4.8%
Internet	47	0.3%	40.0%	7.5%
Machines/Tools	84	0.5%	25.0%	4.5%
Media & Entertainment	19	2.0%	50.0%	8.0%
Pharma & Biotech	328	0.1%	40.0%	5.1%
Semiconductors	78	0.0%	30.0%	3.2%
Software	119	0.0%	70.0%	6.8%
Telecom	63	0.4%	25.0%	4.7%
Total	1,533	0.0%	77.0%	4.5%

EXHIBIT 3.4   INDUSTRY PROFIT RATES
(1990–2000)

Industry	No. of Companies	Wtd. Avg. Operating Margin
Automotive	100	5.0%
Chemicals	126	11.1%
Computers	459	6.9%
Consumer Goods	544	11.0%
Electronics	425	8.8%
Energy & Entertainment	767	12.2%
Food	240	7.3%
Healthcare Products	433	14.8%
Internet	781	−13.5%
Machines/Tools	174	7.9%
Media & Entertainment	360	10.6%
Pharma & Biotech	534	16.4%
Semiconductors	207	17.4%
Software	534	18.8%
Telecom	627	14.2%
Total	6,309	10.4%

EXHIBIT 3.5 LICENSEE PROFITS (1990–2000)

Industry	No. of Companies	Licensee Wtd. Avg. Operating Margin
Automotive	4	6.3%
Chemicals	6	11.6%
Computers	20	8.0%
Consumer Goods	23	16.2%
Electronics	30	8.8%
Energy & Entertainment	14	6.6%
Food	6	7.9%
Healthcare Products	80	17.8%
Internet	14	1.0%
Machines/Tools	8	9.4%
Media & Entertainment	3	−304.5%
Pharma & Biotech	76	25.4%
Semiconductors	16	29.3%
Software	19	33.2%
Telecom	28	14.1%
Total	347	15.9%

as licensees in the licensing transactions database. Exhibit 3.5 reports weighted average operating profit margins for each of the industries.

ROYALTY RATES AND LICENSEE PROFITS

A comparison of royalty rates and licensee profits provides some support for use of the Rule as a tool for analysis. Across all fifteen industries, the median royalty rate, as a percentage of average licensee operating profit margins (as shown in Exhibit 3.6) was 26.7 percent. Excluding the media and entertainment and Internet industries, the range among the remaining industries varied, from eight and one-half percent for semiconductors, to 79.7 percent for the automotive industry.

In spite of the variation across industries, the majority of industries had ratios of royalty rates to licensee profit margins of twenty-one to forty percent. Exhibit 3.7 shows a distribution of these ratios across industries.

EXHIBIT 3.6 ROYALTY RATES AND LICENSEE PROFITS

Industry	Median Royalty Rate	Average Operating Profits	Royalty as % of Profit Rate
Automotive	5.0%	6.3%*	79.7%
Chemicals	3.0%	11.6%	25.9%
Computers	2.8%	8.0%	34.4%
Consumer Goods	5.0%	16.2%	30.8%
Electronics	4.5%	8.8%	51.3%
Energy & Entertainment	3.5%	6.6%	52.9%
Food	2.3%	7.9%	28.7%
Healthcare Products	4.0%	17.8%	22.4%
Internet	5.0%	1.0%	492.6%
Machines/Tools	3.4%	9.4%	35.8%
Media & Entertainment	9.0%	−304.5%*	−3.0%
Pharma & Biotech	4.5%	24.5%	17.7%
Semiconductors	2.5%	29.3%	8.5%
Software	7.5%	33.2%	22.6%
Telecom	5.0%	14.1%	35.5%
Total	4.3%	15.9%	26.7%

* Fewer than 5 observations in data set.

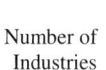

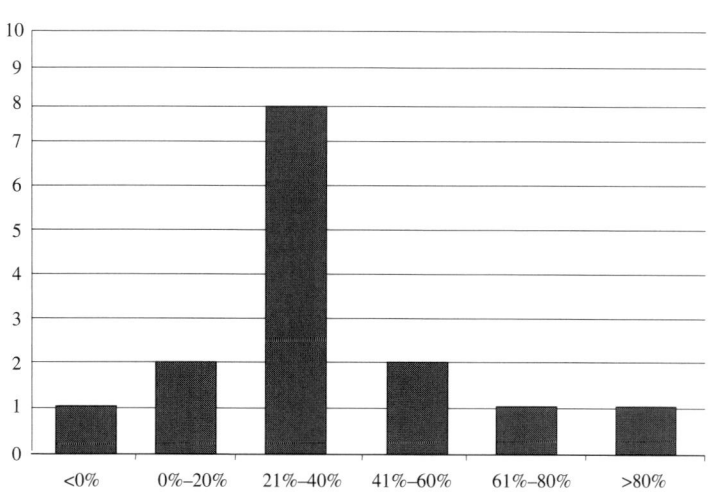

EXHIBIT 3.7 Distribution of Profit Splits–Licensee Profits

Successful Licensee Profits

We also examined profitability data for "successful licensees." We defined those to be licensees with profit rates in the top quartile for each industry. We used these profit rates as a further-refined surrogate for projected product profit rates.

Royalty Rates and Successful Licensee Profits

A comparison of royalty rates and successful licensee profits appears to, again, provide some support for use of the Rule. As shown in Exhibit 3.8, the median royalty rate as a percentage of average operating profits was 22.6 percent, across all industries. Excluding the media and entertainment industry, for which only limited data were available, the ratios range from a low of 7.8 percent, for the semiconductor industry, to a high of 48 percent, for the Internet industry.

Exhibit 3.9 reports the ratio distribution across industries and shows

EXHIBIT 3.8   ROYALTY RATES AND SUCCESSFUL LICENSEE PROFITS

	Median Royalty Rate	Average Operating Profit	Royalty as % of Profit Rate
Automotive	5.0%	11.3%*	44.1%
Chemicals	3.0%	12.0%	25.0%
Computers	2.8%	8.3%	33.3%
Consumer Goods	5.0%	18.4%	27.1%
Electronics	4.5%	13.1%	34.3%
Energy & Entertainment	3.5%	9.2%	38.1%
Food	2.3%	14.2%	15.8%
Healthcare Products	4.0%	18.5%	21.6%
Internet	5.0%	10.4%	48.0%
Machines/Tools	3.4%	9.6%	35.0%
Media & Entertainment	9.0%	−13.5%*	−66.7%
Pharma & Biotech	4.5%	25.8%	17.4%
Semiconductors	2.5%	31.9%	7.8%
Software	7.5%	25.1%	21.4%
Telecom	5.0%	14.5%	34.5%
Total	4.3%	18.8%	22.6%

* Fewer than 5 observations in data set.

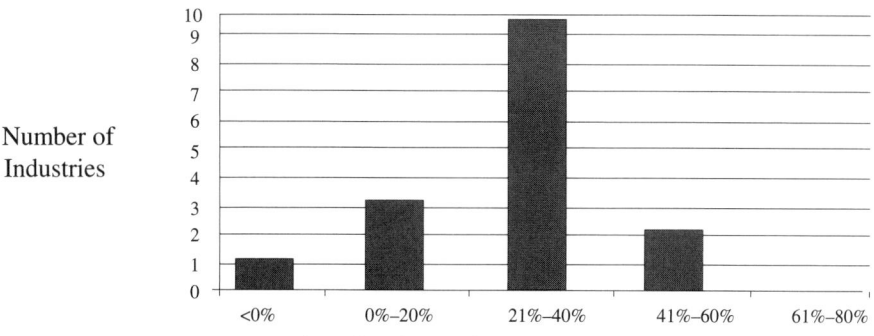

EXHIBIT 3.9 **Distribution of Profit Split-Successful Licensee Profits**

that, again, the majority of industries have ratios of royalty rates to successful licensee profit margins in the twenty-one to forty percent range.

CONCLUSIONS

An apportionment of twenty-five percent of a licensee's expected profits has become one, of many, useful pricing tools in IP contexts.[62] Our empirical analysis provides some support for its use.

A comparison of royalty rates, with two proxies, for expected long-run product profits (namely, licensee profits and "successful" licensee profits), yields royalty-to-profit ratios of twenty-seven and twenty-three percent, respectively.

Although the data generally support the Rule, there is quite a variation in results for specific industries. As this variation makes clear, the Rule is best used as one pricing tool, and should be considered in conjunction with other quantitative and qualitative factors that can, and do, affect royalty rates.

CHAPTER 4

Royalty Rate Guidelines

Industry guidelines focus on the general rates that others are charging, for intellectual property (IP) licensed within a specific industry. Investment risks, net profits, market size, growth potential, and complementary asset investment requirements are assumed as being reflected, but are absent from direct consideration. The use of industry guidelines places total reliance on the ability of others to correctly consider, and interpret, the many factors affecting royalties.

Examples of general guidelines are presented in Exhibit 4.1. They provide interesting information, but do not help determine a specific royalty rate, for a specific IP, because the ranges presented are rather broad. These guidelines can, however, provide an order of magnitude.

The high-end royalty rates associated with pharmaceuticals is due to the high profit margins many medical therapies can command.

The following guidance is from Patent to Profit (www.frompatenttoprofit.com), a company focused on helping inventors turn their ideas into commercial products, generating royalty income.

Toys	5% to 10%
Software	15% to 20%

Tools	3% to 7%
Automotive	2% to 5%
Baby Goods	5% to 7%
Michael Jordan	17.5%

EXHIBIT 4.1   ROYALTY RATE GUIDELINES

Industry	Royalty Rate
Electronics	0.5–5%
Machinery	0.33–10%
Chemical	2–5%
Pharmaceutical	2–10%

Source: 1998, Dr. Michael Gross, CASRIP Newsletter (V413), Actual Royalty Rates in Patent, Know-How and Computer Program License Agreements. This article discusses the "remuneration guidelines" of the German Law Relating to Inventions Made by Employees.

In Germany, there exists the "Law Relating to Inventions Made by Employees." This law determines that inventions made by employees belong to them. Only by a special act, and in conjunction with a special remuneration, can they become the property of the employer. The most usual method to calculate the inventor's remuneration is the so-called "license analogy." The inventor receives a certain percentage, based on the net sales made by the employer, of a reasonable royalty. Added to the Law Relating to Inventions Made by Employees are renumeration guidelines, which provide examples of reasonable royalties[1]:

Electronics	0.5–5%
Machinery	0.33–10%
Chemical	2–5%
Pharmaceutical	2–10%

Analysis Group, a national economic consulting firm, studied 2,279 license deals, for fifteen different industries (based on data from RoyaltySource.com). The average royalty rate, for the industries studied, ranged from three to nine percent, averaging five percent. Looking at the graph in Exhibit 4.2, you can see that the average royalty rate for ten of the industries is very similar, at four to five percent. Only three industries, internet, media and entertainment, and software, have an average rate above five

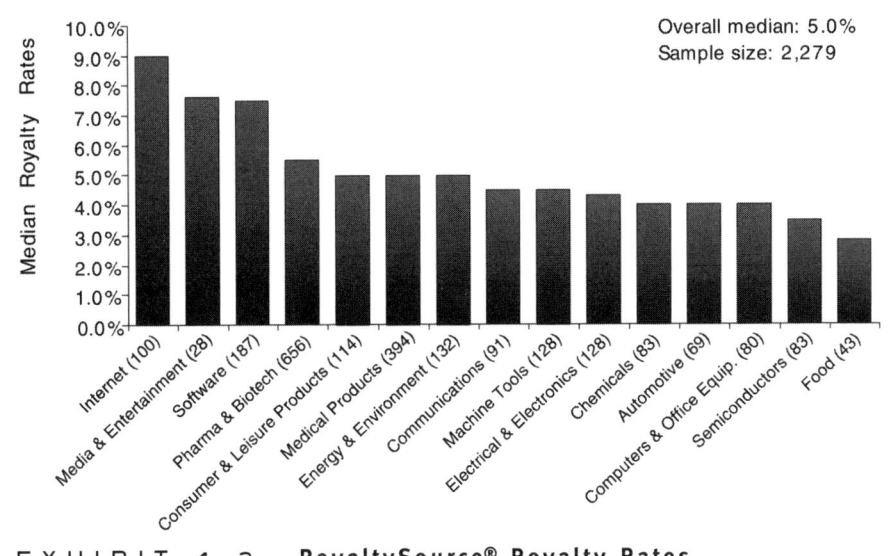

EXHIBIT 4.2 RoyaltySource® Royalty Rates

Overall median: 5.0%
Sample size: 2,279

Bar chart categories (with counts): Internet (100), Media & Entertainment (28), Software (187), Pharma & Biotech (656), Consumer & Leisure Products (114), Medical Products (394), Energy & Environment (132), Communications (91), Machine Tools (128), Electrical & Electronics (128), Chemicals (83), Automotive (69), Computers & Office Equip. (80), Semiconductors (83), Food (43)

percent. Only two industries, semiconductors and food, have average rates below five percent. Low profit margins in these industries are the likely reason for these below-average rates.

These averages and general guidelines are terrific, but must be approached with caution. For example, the average royalty rate for pharmaceuticals and biotechnology, for the six hundred fifty-six deals studied, was approximately five percent. Remember that within this average are licenses involving untested new molecules, along with licenses involving successfully commercialized inventions. Untested inventions might involve a royalty rate in the low single digits, while inventions past phase III trials represent technology that could command royalty rates of fifteen to twenty percent. This wide range may not exist for all fifteen industries, but surely a range does exist, and relying solely on the average could be a mistake, for many of the industries (see Exhibit 4.2).

More guidance about royalty rates is provided in the frequency distributions presented below.

ROYALTY RATES FOR TECHNOLOGY, THIRD EDITION

Published by Intellectual Property Research Associates (IPRA, Inc.), *Royalty Rates for Technology, Third Edition,* contains more information about technology pricing than any other publication. The book represents over a decade of research. Included in its pages is information about technology royalty rates, license fees, and milestone payments. The information in the book has been collected from reliable sources, from September 1990 through May 2003, and is considered to represent a comprehensive collection of technology pricing information (a new edition is expected to be released in 2007). Information in this report is categorized by the following industries:

Industries

Aeronautics	Construction	Glass	Semiconductors
Agriculture	Electrical	Household Products	Sports
Automotive	Electronics	Internet	Steel
Chemistry	Entertainment	Mechanical	Toys
Communications	Financial	Medical	Waste Treatment
Computer Hardware	Food	Natural Resources	
Computer Software	Franchises	Photography	

Exhibit 4.3 summarizes royalty rates across all the industries covered in the book. The royalty rates are grouped by rate, as a percent of sales, and graphed by the frequency of their appearance. Excluded from this graph are instances where royalty rates are specified on a per unit basis. Generally, royalty rates range between one and forty percent of sales, but the vast majority of royalty rates are ten percent of sales, or less.

Unlike the Analysis Group study of RoyaltySource data, a distribution of royalty rates is presented, but guidance is not provided for specific industries.

The most frequent royalty rates are five and ten percent of net sales. A cumulative analysis of the rates reported in the book provides the following insight:

28% of the royalty rates are 3% or less
36% of the royalty rates are 4% or less
58% of the royalty rates are 5% or less
62% of the royalty rates are 6% or less
66% of the royalty rates are 7% or less
70% of the royalty rates are 8% or less
73% of the royalty rates are 9% or less
87% of the royalty rates are 10% or less

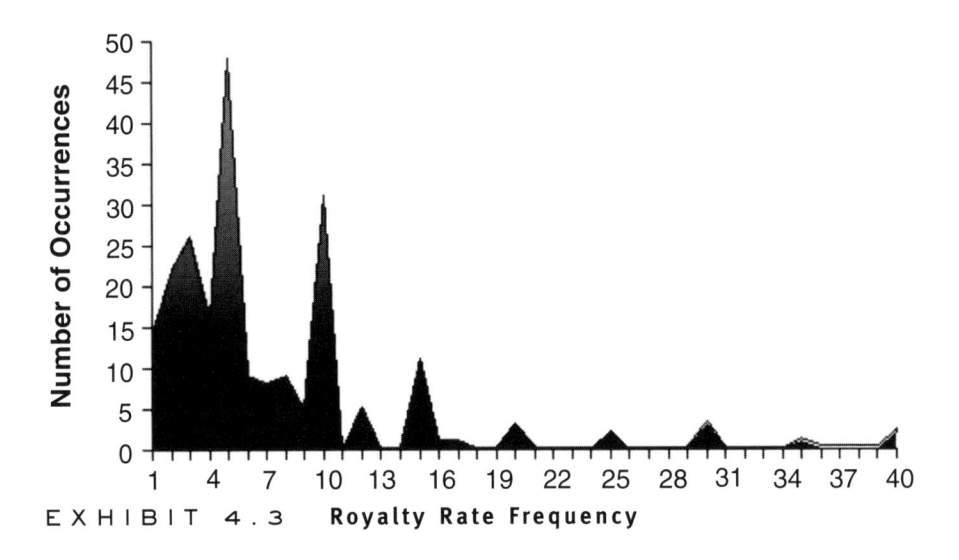

EXHIBIT 4.3 Royalty Rate Frequency

ROYALTY RATES FOR TRADEMARKS AND COPYRIGHTS, THIRD EDITION

Also published by IPRA, is *Royalty Rates for Trademarks and Copyrights, Third Edition*, which provides a guide to royalty rate information for trademarks and copyrights, based on real-world transactions. The information in this book represents data collected from reliable sources, from September 1990 through December 2003, and is considered to represent the most comprehensive collection of trademark and copyright pricing information. The information contained in the book is organized by industry, as follows:

Airline	General Merchandise
Apparel	Internet Domain Names
Architecture	Medical
Art	Movies
Automotive & Boats	Music
Celebrities	Party Goods
Communications	Publishing
Corporate Names	Restaurants and Hotels
Electronics	Sports
Food & Beverage	Toys
Franchises	University Names
Furniture	

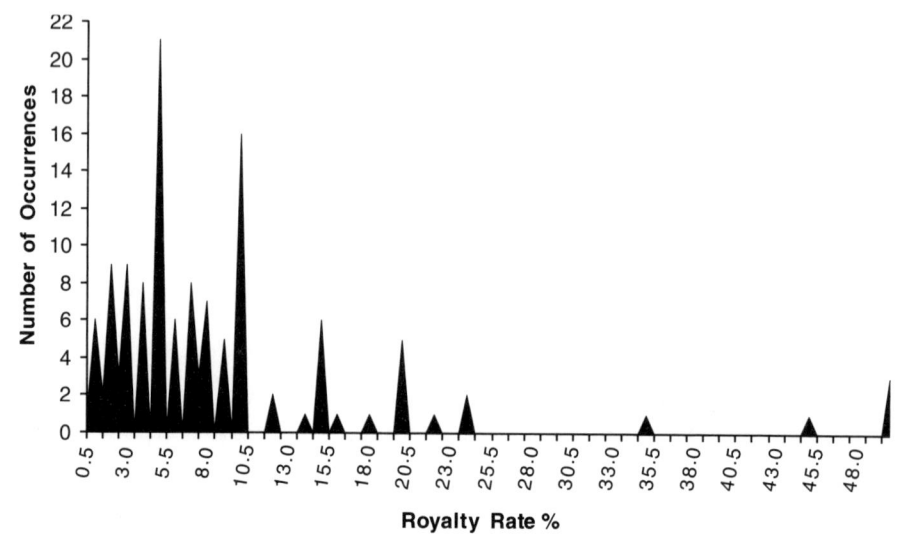

EXHIBIT 4.4 Trademark Royalty Rate Frequency

Exhibit 4.4 summarizes royalty rates, across all the industries and products covered in the book, by the number of times the rate was mentioned throughout the book. The royalty rates reported in the book are grouped by rate, and graphed by the frequency of their appearance, providing the following distribution. Only royalties expressed as a percentage of sales are included in Exhibit 4.4. The most commonly reported royalty rates are, once again, five and ten percent of net sales.

ROYALTY RATES FOR PHARMACEUTICALS AND BIOTECHNOLOGY, SIXTH EDITION

Royalty Rates for Pharmaceuticals and Biotechnology, Sixth Edition, is also published by IPRA, and focuses on the royalty rates associated with biotechnology and pharmaceutical intellectual property transfers. Exhibit 4.5 graphs the royalty rate data, collected between September 1990 and December 2005, found throughout the "License Agreement" section of the book. Only royalty rates, presented as a percent of sales, are included in the graph below. For license agreements containing more than one rate, rates are represented with equal weight in the graph.

Exhibit 4.5 clearly shows that the majority of royalty rates are in the mid

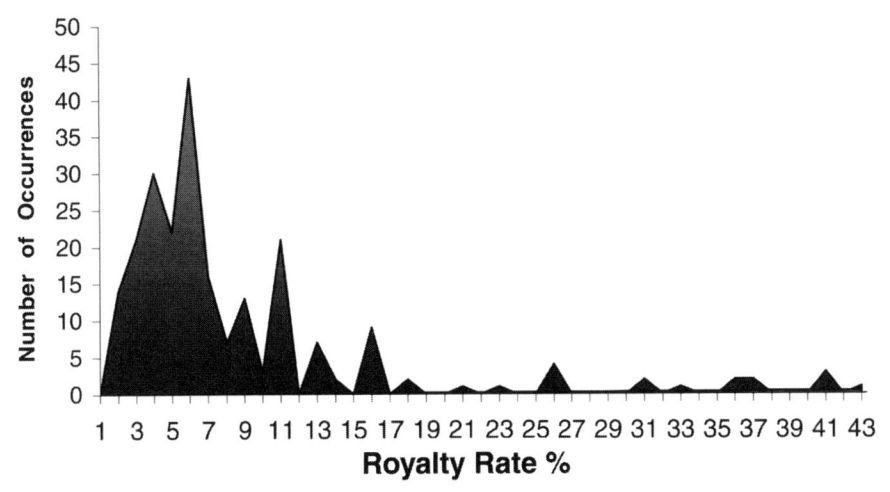

EXHIBIT 4.5 Licensing Agreement Royalty Rate Frequency

to low single digits. In Exhibit 4.6, all license fees found in the "License Agreement" section of the book are presented.

Early-stage technology has typically commanded royalty rates, and license fees, that are relatively low. The risky nature of developing pharmaceutical and biotechnology, coupled with the long lead-time between

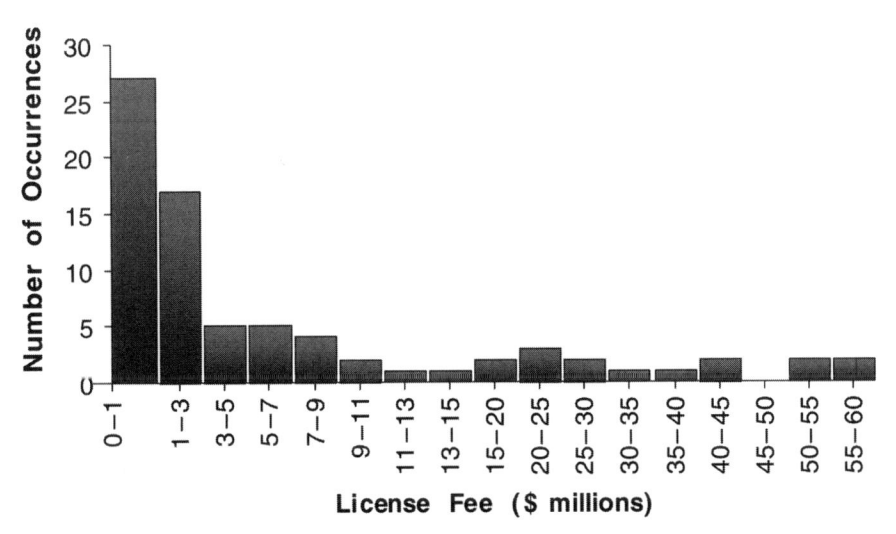

EXHIBIT 4.6 Distribution of License Fees

discovery and commercialization, provides significant downward pressure on royalty rates and license fees. However, when clinical trials and/or regulatory hurdles are passed, a successful, commercialized therapy, available for licensing, will command double-digit royalty rates and enormous license fees.

The remainder of this book will attempt to provide more details, so that readers can get behind the averages and guidelines.

CHAPTER 5

Comparable Licenses

When it comes time to consider the price to pay for a license, comparable licenses are an important factor to consider. The amount for which independent parties licensed similar intellectual property (IP) can provide an indication of a reasonable royalty. Market transactions, considered useful for deriving reasonable royalties, are usually between unrelated parties where IP is the focal point of the deal. Transactions most often cited, as useful indications for reasonable royalties, are license agreements, which disclose the compensation terms for other licenses involving the IP being studied. As an alternative, an analysis of licensing transactions involving *similar* IP is often relied on for deriving reasonable royalties.

Many aspects of market transactions should be studied closely before a specific transaction can be discerned as representing a reasonable royalty, for comparison purposes. The remainder of this chapter considers the appropriateness of using comparable license agreement royalty terms as a proxy for a subject case.

INTERNAL LICENSES ARE OFTEN SELF-SERVING

Multinational corporations often transfer IP to foreign subsidiaries. Parent companies often own keystone IP, while their subsidiaries hold licenses allowing them to use the property. These licenses are referred to as "internal," or "inter-company," licenses. In the past, these have not typically been reliable market transactions for deriving reasonable royalties. Many of the royalty terms in these types of transactions were structured to shift income into jurisdictions with lower income tax burdens. Hence, the royalty rate did not reflect the economic contribution of the IP as much as they reflected the differential corporate income tax rates, between a multinational corporate parent and a foreign subsidiary. Internal licenses were missing a fundamental element, because the royalty terms were not established by arms-length negotiation, where each party to the transaction argued their self-interests. Many other self-serving issues clouded royalties specified in internal licenses.

This is beginning to change. International taxing authorities are looking at transfer pricing issues, and IP is getting closer scrutiny. Many corporations are commissioning studies to use as the basis of their IP pricing. These studies are based on market transactions, and the investment rate-of-return analyses explored later in this book. Such studies are not common, as the IRS does not closely scrutinize many companies. As more corporations set internal transaction pricing in line with third-party transaction pricing, internal licenses may become useful indications of royalty rates.

RELEVANT TIME PERIOD

The price paid for a stock in the past is an interesting notation, but has little to do with a current pricing analysis. The same is true when corporations engage in mergers and acquisitions. The prices at which businesses are exchanged seldom relate to amounts at which prior transactions were consummated. When considering the purchase of an investment real estate property, a lot of analysis goes into determining the price to offer. Included are considerations of prevailing interest rates, inflation, rental income, operating expenses, property taxes, and income taxes. All of these considerations are analyzed, from the perspective of quantifying future expectations about profits and return on investment. Very little, if any, consideration is given to the price at which the property has historically changed hands. Manhattan Island was purchased from the original owners for $24 worth of novelty trinkets, though this price may be justified by the questionable title conveyed by the seller.

Historic transaction prices are interesting footnotes, but not usually relevant for current transaction pricing. It's no different for IP. A reasonable royalty must be based on future expectations, that both the licensee and licensor individually possess, and which eventually converge as negotiations reach a conclusion. Reasonable royalties must be determined with an eye to the future.

FINANCIAL CONDITION OF BOTH LICENSING PARTIES

When one of the parties in a license transaction is desperate to complete it, the amount paid for the license is clouded. A nearly bankrupt licensor may not have enough time to shop for the best offer, and could leave a significant amount of money on the negotiating table. On the other hand, a manufacturing company with obsolete technology may find itself going out of business without access to new technology. A fair and reasonable royalty is best determined in an environment where both of the negotiating parties are on equal footing. Both parties should have the option to walk away from the deal. When ancillary forces are compelling one of the negotiating parties to capitulate to the demands of the other, then a fair and reasonable royalty may be not indicated.

RELEVANT INDUSTRY TRANSACTIONS

Some licenses may involve property that is similar to a specific property under negotiation, but the property is licensed for use in a different industry. To be useful for deriving a fair market royalty, a proxy royalty rate must have been negotiated for similar property used in a similar industry. Each industry has its own set of unique economic forces. Some are highly competitive, like consumer electronics. Others are oligopolies. Some industries are sensitive to interest rates, like construction, while others, such as automotive, are under strong pressure from foreign producers. Others are only regionally competitive, like gravel quarries.

All of these factors drive the profitability and growth prospects of the industry participants. These factors also impact the amount of economic benefit that IP can contribute to a commercial operation, which directly relates to the royalties that can be considered reasonable.

INTERNATIONAL TRANSACTIONS

In developing nations, where IP protection is weak, the amount paid for a license would likely be far less than in developed nations, where IP rights are respected and enforced. A low rate in developing nations reflects that exclusive use of the property may not be realistic, regardless of what the license agreement says. A low royalty in some countries might also reflect differences in governmental regulation, inflation, and general economic conditions. As such, license agreements in different countries might possess different royalty rates for the same IP, none of which may be relevant for a specific case, depending on the country in which the technology in question is being licensed.

NON-MONETARY COMPENSATION

Compensation for the use of IP can take many different forms. Sometimes cash alone is the basis of licensing compensation; the licensee makes a cash payment and no further payments are required. Lump sum payments, with additional running royalties, are another example of license compensation. Running royalties alone are another example. Sometimes the licensor gets a royalty and also an equity interest in the licensee's company; sometimes the licensor gets only an equity interest. License agreements can also call for the licensee to share technological enhancements, as grant-backs, with the licensor. In return, the licensee might demand a lower royalty rate because a portion of the licensor's compensation will be in the form of access to enhancements of the original property. For similar license agreements to be used as a proxy for derivation of a fair market royalty, the form of license compensation should be on a like-kind basis.

EXCLUSIVITY

Regarding the aspect of exclusivity, what should the basis of reasonable royalties be? Typically, higher royalty rates are associated with license agreements that provide the licensee with exclusive rights to use the IP. An exclusive right to use a keystone IP places the licensee in a superior position. If the IP provides highly desirable utility, premium prices can be demanded for the product. Competitors cannot counter with the same product without risking infringement, and the exclusive licensee will earn superior profits. Such an arrangement is worth higher royalty payments. DuPont once negotiated a license involving worldwide, exclusive rights to a drug patent. Later, the agreement was renegotiated to a non-exclusive basis. As a result, the royalty dropped by twenty-seven percent. Good

PACKAGE LICENSES

Licenses don't always grant use of one specific item of IP. Several patents may be granted as a group, with one royalty rate specified as compensation for all of the property. Sometimes patents and trademarks are licensed together, for a single royalty. Sometimes they are licensed separately. A problem of comparability arises, however, when licenses used for comparison cover not only a similar patent, but also grant use for other property not pertinent to the subject analysis.

COMPARATIVE ANALYSIS SUMMARIZED

Comparative analysis of similar technology licenses can be very useful for negotiating royalty rates, but many aspects of the license agreement must be analyzed for a royalty provision to be a useful proxy. In a perfect world, useful proxy licenses for establishing a fair market royalty would:

1. not be an internal license between a parent corporation and a subsidiary;
2. have been negotiated at a date that is reasonably relevant to the date of the subject analysis;
3. have been negotiated between two independent parties, neither of which were compelled to complete the transaction because of financial distress;
4. involve similar IP, licensed for use in the same industry in which the fair market royalty is desired
5. transfer license rights for use of similar IP, into a country having similar economic conditions as the country in which the fair royalty is desired;

6. involve similar IP, with similar, remaining-life characteristics;
7. require similar complementary asset investment requirements, for commercial exploitation;
8. specify royalty terms unclouded by non-monetary components of compensation;
9. include comparable aspects of exclusivity;
10. include royalty terms freely negotiated and unencumbered by governmental regulations;
11. specify royalty terms not clouded by undefined amounts indirectly attributed to other assets in the deal.

CHAPTER 6

Technology Royalty Statistics

This chapter provides specific royalty rate information for selected industries.

AUTOMOTIVE

The auto industry is highly competitive, with Japanese and other imports currently crushing the market share and profits of General Motors, Ford, and DaimlerChrysler. Light trucks and sport utility vehicles (SUVs) are the chief revenue source for the U.S. market, but the imports have responded with excellent offerings of their own, like Toyota's Tundra, its first full sized truck. While U.S. manufacturers struggle to maintain market share through price cuts, marketed as cash-back rebates, and incentives like zero percent financing, Japanese companies are gaining market share without such strategies.

Innovation in this industry is being driven by consumer demand for more features, and the emergence of demand for hybrid vehicles, that run on a combination of electric and combustion engines. The race is also on to develop engines that use no petroleum products, such as hydrogen-powered engines.

The U.S. strategy for cost control involves manufacturing vehicles that share common body platforms, allowing for multiple vehicle types to be produced on fewer production lines. Efficiency and cost controls are expected to improve margins. However, common vehicle platforms allow for fewer unique automobiles to be produced, leaving an opening for foreign producers to fill this gap.

Profit potential for U.S. manufacturers is extraordinarily burdened by under-funded pension benefits. GM's pension shortfall is estimated at nearly $20 billion, an amount nearly equal to all of GM's equity market value. The low profit margins in the industry provide downward pressure on the royalty rates that can be paid in license agreements.

Battery Terminals

In a press release, Exide Corporation revealed that the U.S. District Court of Delaware ruled against the company in a patent infringement action brought by GNB Battery Technologies. Exide said the court had held that Exide infringed a battery patent issued to GNB. The patented invention involved a dual-terminal configuration associated with connecting the battery to cars and trucks. The court assessed $3.6 million in damages, and $1.65 million in prejudgment interest. Exide said it plans to appeal, adding that neither party manufactures batteries embodying the technology disclosed in the patent. Exide also said the amount awarded was slightly more than one percent of the damages sought by GNB.[1] This licensing and court decision information shows low royalty rates for this industry.

Transaxles

In the early 1990s, Mercedes Benz AG of Germany entered into a ten-year agreement with Ssangyong Motor Company of Korea. Under terms of the agreement, Ssangyong was to produce small trucks, vans, mini-buses, diesel engines, and transaxles using Mercedes Benz technical inputs. The deal called for Ssangyong to invest almost $1 billion to build the necessary manufacturing plants. Initially, eighty thousand trucks, vans and other vehicles were to have been produced, with plant production capacity to increase to one hundred thousand units after 1996, at which time Ssangyong was to begin producing cars licensed by Mercedes Benz. Royalties and fees that were to have been paid to Mercedes Benz included: an eighty million mark down payment, made in four installments, over a thirty-eight month period; a fixed payment of sixty million marks, to be paid in six installments, following the down payment; and a running royalty charge of two percent of sales, per unit. Ssangyong had been producing jeeps, and specially equipped vehicles and trucks. The company planned to upgrade its jeeps with up-to-date, low-pollution diesel engines, to be introduced under the agreement.[2]

Manufacturing Technology

Japan's number two automaker, Nissan Motor Company, agreed to sell to Samsung Group the manufacturing technologies that the South Korean conglomerate needed to build a new auto business from scratch. Nissan, and about seventy of its Japanese partsmakers, agreed to supply Samsung with state-of-the-art technology to build a car similar to Nissan's popular Maxima. The move is a radical departure for Japanese manufacturers, who have tended to transfer only older technologies abroad; Nissan's transfer of leading-edge technology could create a future global rival. The deal apparently didn't go down easily within Nissan, who had spurned Samsung's overtures four years earlier before capitulating two years later. By then, Nissan's financial position had soured. They had accumulated a heavy debt load, following deep losses for the previous two years amid Japan's prolonged recession. The Samsung agreement gave Nissan a desperately needed cash infusion. Samsung's plans cost billions. In addition to $1.9 billion in research and development plans unveiled by the company, a manufacturing plant in the Korean city of Pusan was expected to cost $5.7 billion. Samsung's hefty research and development budget was required to keep pace with plans that called for the first cars to roll off assembly lines by 2003.

In order to accomplish its goals, Samsung hoped to have its own models designed by 1998. The speedy start-up was helped along by Nissan technical advisors, who assisted three hundred fifty researchers on Samsung's own car and engine designs. Samsung hoped to have its own models by 2003, without Nissan's support, and expand annual production from an initial sixty-five thousand to half a million units. The deal called for Samsung to pay royalties to Nissan that included: $190 million down payment, running royalties of one and six-tenths to one and nine-tenths percent of the factory price of each unit sold; and $676 million, as part of a joint development of new models.[3]

Self-Dimmable Rearview Mirrors

Research Frontiers announced that Glaverbel SA extended the scope of its license agreement relating to self-dimmable automotive rearview mirrors. Glaverbel is now permitted to manufacture and sell self-dimmable rearview mirrors worldwide. Research Frontiers will receive royalties equal to five percent of net sales by Glaverbel. Self-dimmable rearview mirrors using Research Frontiers' proprietary suspended particle device (SPD) technology will automatically reduce glare and eyestrain from approaching car headlights. Self-dimmable rearview mirrors using SPD technology do not have the yellow tint normally associated with most electrochromic mirrors, and are expected to be cheaper, and faster. In addition, Glaverbel's SPD mirror, with its virtually instantaneous reaction time, will feature "real-time" switching, in which the mirror can automatically adjust to an infinite number of intermediate levels of glare reduction, rather than merely switching from light to dark.

CHEMICALS

Base chemicals are the leading source of revenue for the U.S. chemical manufacturing industry. The industry has benefited from the good economic conditions within the plastics and coating sectors, resulting in strong demand for ethylene and titanium dioxide. The industry produces raw materials, used by companies in a great variety of industry sectors. Consequently, the chemical industry experiences cycles directly linked to the general economy. The increasing price of hydrocarbons continues to be problematic for manufacturers and end-users.

Chemical manufacturers are very focused on increasing the efficiency of their operations, to improve yield and reduce employee costs. In addition, e-commerce has brought about supply chain improvements. Chemical manufacturers are using e-commerce to improve the efficiency of their procurement processes. Buyers and sellers are increasingly connecting their respective planning systems through online marketplaces. E-commerce increases the speed, and quality, of procurement activities, and reduces operational expenses. Cost savings result, but all industry participants can enjoy the same savings.

Leading companies in the United States include BASF, Bayer, Dow Chemical, DuPont, Huntsman Corporation, and ExxonMobil. Profits are slim, and so are royalty rates.

Flame-Retardant Products

United Fire Technology (UFT) entered into a license agreement with Yuanchen for the Far East territories of Taiwan, Hong Kong, Thailand, Indonesia, Malaysia, the Phillipines, and Singapore. Yuanchen projects the Far East market to substantially exceed $1 billion in the next ten years. The license agreement provides for a $500,000 set-up, training, and license fee, with a minimum initial order of $500,000 for raw materials. UFT will earn a three percent royalty on all retail sales within the licensed territories. It is anticipated that the flame-retardant products will become mandatory for all commercial businesses, including hotels, nightclubs and retail outlets. UFT products include environmentally safe fire extinguishing products, substantially superior to current products, for all four classes of fire. Recent tests proved the extinguishing products to be over ten times more effective than current products. Their flame-retardant formulations will "fire-proof" fabrics to over two thousand degrees Fahrenheit, while a cigarette burns at four hundred degrees.[4]

Fuel Reactor Technology

Hydro Environmental Resources (HER) and Allied Energy entered into a non-exclusive worldwide license agreement that gives Allied the right to market, and manufacture, HER's ECHFR system. The ECHFR is a fuel reactor that produces clean-burning hydrogen gas, at low pressure, from any water source. HER's ultimate objective is to build, market, and operate a stationary power site, using an ECHFR system capable of supplying power for a city of approximately three thousand people. HER plans to market the ECHFR technology in areas underserved by conventional power companies, including Indonesia, China, the Philippines, Malaysia, the Middle East, and parts of Central and South America. Allied agreed to pay HER a one-time fee of $500,000 and 1.5 million shares of Allied's common stock, upon the successful completion of a demonstration test using the HER reactor. Allied has also agreed to pay HER a royalty of five percent of net sales for products manufactured by Allied, and eight percent of net sales for products manufactured by HER. Allied has the right to grant sublicenses to third parties, if the terms and conditions are approved by HER.[5]

Fuel Technology

Unocal Corporation sued Valero Energy for patent infringement, claiming that Valero has been making cleaner burning gasoline, using Unocal's patents, without a license agreement. Unocal said it was seeking damages from Valero, which it says has refused to discuss a license agreement, for willful infringement of two of Unocal's five fuel patents. Included in the suit were refineries owned by Ultramar Diamond Shamrock, which Valero bought last year. Unocal sought damages triple the five and three-quarter cents-per-gallon royalty rate, as imposed in earlier cases, and a mandatory license for court ordered royalties, for future infringements by Valero. Unocal is involved in the exploration and production of crude oil and natural gas in fourteen countries. In 2001, Unocal produced one-hundred-seventy thousand barrels of petroleum liquids, and two billion cubic feet of gas, per day. Unocal also has a geothermal operations group that provides steam, for the generation of electricity, to power plants.

COMMUNICATIONS EQUIPMENT AND SERVICES

Mobile phones are the equipment segment of this industry's primary source of revenue, but broadband in the United States has created a large demand for DSL modems. The industry is characterized by a high degree of product obsolescence, as new products are constantly introduced, with new technologies and features. This keeps sales volume high, as consumers trade up to the new devices. This same condition also requires continuous research and development expenditures. Examples of product evolution include the inclusion of cameras into cell phones. Most recently, cell phones have been combined with PDA and email capabilities.

To remain competitive, industry participants must commit to continuous new product introductions, which require continuous research and development spending, which in turn pressures profit margins. These costs, coupled with increasing costs for labor and energy, have driven communications equipment manufacturers to relocate some of their production to areas of low cost labor and energy, such as China. Cost savings result, but they are not proprietary to any specific company.

The industry is sensitive to economic conditions, as interest rates and consumer credit ratings determine the ability of consumers to spend for upgrades. The concern over the links between radiation, cancer, and the use of cellular phones—whether unfounded or not—is making it somewhat difficult for communications companies to extend network capabilities, in terms of constructing new phone masts. The potential for network expansion is still considerable, so any hindrance to its development will pose a serious revenue threat for equipment manufacturers.

Leading companies in this industry in the United States include Alcatel, Cisco, Lucent, Motorola, Nokia, Nortel, and Siemens.

In communications services, the major source of revenue has been the voice services sector, although increasingly stringent legislation has placed pricing pressures upon long distance phone calls, detracting from margins. The growth of digital networks has given a boost to the market, although companies are still competing to define an industry standard for a wireless format in the United States, with the competition among networks acting only to stunt the overall development of the market. Industry participants are challenged to differentiate their products in the marketplace, with slim profiles, video and vast amounts of minutes and further challenged by the fact that many consumers are still unwilling to part with the extra money for the provision of third generation (3G) services.

The industry has an enormous amount of overcapacity. Wholesale prices reflect this condition, and the builders of the systems are facing slim profit margins, as they service debt associated with creating capacity that is largely unused. This situation has also stalled industry participants' ability to spend even more, to build new systems based on 3G technology.

Leading participants in the communications services market include AT&T, Cingular, MCI, Sprint, and Verizon.

Third-Generation Wireless Technology

The Universal Mobile Telecommunications System (UMTS) Intellectual Property Association (IPA), which includes the world's major telecommunications-equipment makers, has proposed a maximum five percent royalty for the licensing of patents essential to the making of various types of 3G mobile communications equipment. Seeming to have found a compromise acceptable to most of its constituents, the UMTS IPA is presenting the 3G Patent Platform as the commercial enabler for 3G systems. The 3G patent platform went into effect on March 1, 2000.

Qualcomm disagreed with the proposed 3G patent arrangements. The alternative is a free-for-all, as happened in GSM, with a multitude of bilateral agreements. That would make UMTS technology very expensive to acquire. Proponents of 3G cellular telephony are setting up an independent company to oversee IP claims for 3G technology, but the move is already drawing fire from some observers, who say the effort lacks the clout of a full patent pool or licensing agency. The debate comes as the industry grapples with how best to handle patent claims, from multiple companies, on technologies destined for wide deployment. Independent consultants—largely attorneys and accounting firms—are assuming what appears to be a growing role in areas such as licensing administration, patent evaluation, and royalties collection. Indeed, hiring outside experts, to sort through the tangled web of IP rights essential to emerging standards, has become a trend. In this climate, the 3G Patent Platform appears to be following an uncharted path. It will be set up as a new, nonprofit company called NewCo that is neither a patent pool nor a licensing agency. Rather, the group will oversee the task of licensing administration and patent evaluation, which it plans to outsource."[6]

Under the 3G Patent Platform scheme, the licensees will pay royalties directly to the companies holding the corresponding licenses. Patent holders and licensees are free to negotiate deals to meet their business requirements. All licenses, whether obtained through the 3G Patent Platform or by separate negotiation, are made between the patent holder and the licensees. In this way, the 3G Patent Platform aims to create a voluntary, industry-led process that simplifies IP rights, and cuts the cost of patents, in hopes of gaining a bigger market for the platform. According to industry sources, a lesson was learned from GSM phones. Today, twenty percent of the cost of a second-generation GSM handset pays for IP rights, due to the lack of a joint licensing program.

Video Patent Pool

The Denver-based MPEG LA is an independent agency that has established a successful IP model for MPEG-2 video patent pooling. By getting a clean bill of health from the U.S. Department of Justice, which ruled in June 1997 that the agency is not anti-competitive, MPEG LA is believed to have shown the way for commercializing complex, cross-industry standards. The business models for MPEG LA and the 3G effort are markedly different. Since 3G royalty payments are arranged between licensees and licensors, no fee is taken out of the royalty revenues. At MPEG LA, it is the licensing administrator's responsibility to collect royalties, and to bring companies holding essential IP to the joint licensing program. Because MPEG LA earns its fee according to the amount of money it successfully collects from technology users, it is more financially motivated to succeed in patent pooling. MPEG LA, and the new 1394a (IEEE Standard for a High Performance Serial Bus), are using the same fee structure. The licensing administrators get ten percent of what they collect from licensees, for collected royalties up to $75 million annually. The cut drops as annual royalties rise. For example, administrators get five percent for collected yearly royalties between $75 million and $250 million, and only two and one-half percent for royalties above $250 million a year.[7]

Code Division Multiple Access Technology

Qualcomm and China Unicom have agreed to a framework agreement, but no contracts or license agreements have been signed. The reported royalty rate that Qualcomm would receive from China Unicom, in exchange for Qualcomm's Code Division Multiple Access (CDMA) technology, is five and one-quarter percent of sales. Qualcomm was founded in 1985 and developed the CDMA technology, which is now used in wireless networks and handsets around the world. By making efficient use of the radio frequency spectrum, CDMA allows more people to use airwaves simultaneously, without static or interference. The telecommunications industry is now migrating to CDMA2000 technology. China Unicom operates one of the largest cellular communications companies in China. Based in Hong Kong, China Unicom conducts business in twenty-one provinces, and numerous municipalities, throughout the country, providing nationwide radio paging, international and domestic long distance telephone services, data communications, which include Internet and IP telephony services, and other related value-added services.[8]

Wideband Code Division Multiple Access Technology

NTT DoCoMo, Ericsson, Nokia, and Siemens say they have agreed to license products that use W-CDMA, at a cumulative royalty rate below five percent. So far, Japanese manufacturers Fujitsu, Matsushita/Panasonic, Mitsubishi Electric, NEC, and Sony have expressed interest in cooperating on the new royalty rates. More than one hundred ten operators are currently using the standard in their products. The companies say the single-digit rate keeps the payments proportional to the number of essential Intellectual Property Rights (IPR) patents owned by each company.

Unlike CDMA, which was patented by San Diego-based wireless giant Qualcomm, W-CDMA was developed by the 3G Partnership Project (3GPP), and is the radio access standard proposed for UMTS services (the European version of IMT-2000). The standard was developed as a 3G technology to support very-high-speed multimedia services, such as full-motion video, Internet access, and video conferencing. Qualcomm currently sets its royalty rates at five to six percent of equipment costs, for it's own flavor of 3G technology, CDMA2000. Both are viable alternatives to the GSM wireless standard that dominates Europe.[9]

COMPUTER HARDWARE

Profit margins are under pressure in the personal computer industry, as low-margin machines are now capable of running comprehensive applications without notable loss in performance. New technologies, and new features, are filtering into all price-points of PCs, bringing the industry dangerously close to commoditization. Competition is heated in this industry. Prices are being forced down, and while sales volume is increasing, profit margins are under pressure. Many companies, including Dell, have the majority of their production processes in countries with low-cost labor and energy. These measures only allow price competition to continue along, with slim profits.

Computer manufacturers in the United States have begun to make distinctive products, by combining PC and consumer electronics applications into their new products, creating multimedia-enabled computers. These PCs exploit the massive growth of digital music and film, resulting from the growth of MP3 and DVD platforms. These enhanced machines are selling at higher price-points, and generating better profits, but they have yet to dominate any company's business model. Another strategy to enhance profits involves getting consumers to purchase accessory products when they buy a new PC. These accessories include printers, software upgrades, extended service plans, and other items. Dell's website is very adept at coupling accessory products with PC sales. Overall, profit margins are under pressure, and so are royalty rates.

Information about recent computer technology licenses is rare, but data have been discovered, showing the low-single-digital royalty rates that pervade the industry.

Macintosh Enhancement

Wells American Corporation licensed exclusive worldwide rights to manufacture and sell certain personal computer hardware from Northeast American Enterprises. Under this agreement, Wells introduced the MegaMac CPU Performance Extender in 1990. This enhancement board increased the clock speed of the Apple CPU—from between 8 and 30 MHz to 50 MHz—and enhanced other operating attributes of disk drives and memory management. The agreement called for a running royalty of five percent of net sales.[10]

Computer Architecture

Dell Computer licensed XT class, AT class, and microchannel architecture in 1988, from IBM. The royalty rate varied, depending on the type of computer involved. XT and AT computers were associated with royalties as high as three percent of net sales. Microchannel design computers had a royalty rate of five percent of net sales. As IBM's market share deteriorated, they expanded their computer technology licensing and licensed a number of Taiwanese clone-makers, who paid two percent of net sales on AT and XT computers sold outside the United States. For products sold inside the United States, the rate was three percent.[11]

PS/2 Computers

Computer Automation Systems (CAS) designs and manufactures custom, rack-mount, and industrial computer applications, primarily for the telecommunications industry. The company offers in-house engineering, to provide innovative, customized hardware and software applications, to meet non-standard customer specifications and requirements. In addition, CAS provides computer system integration assemblies, and test services of electronic products, to OEM's and nationwide electronics distributors. CAS also specializes in the development of National Equipment Building Standards (NEBS) certified, Sun and Intel microprocessor-based, fault-tolerant systems for the telecommunications industry. NEBS is a telecommunication industry design standard for manufacturing telecommunications applications equipment. Currently, all of CAS's manufacturing and engineering is conducted out of its Texas facility.

CAS could potentially derive an enormous amount of royalty income, by licensing a patent that covers the technology used in IBM's new personal computer line, the Personal System/2 (PS/2). IBM licensed the patent technology from CAS after discovering that the technology developed for its PS/2 computer line was similar to a 14-year-old patent held by CAS. CAS believes that companies will need to obtain a license to produce legal copies of the PS/2 line, or add-on boards, for the IBM machines. George Pratt, CAS chairman said, "We don't believe either class of potential licensees can produce PS/2 clones, or microchannel compatible add-ons, without infringing on our patents." Michael Murphy, editor of the California Technology Stock Letter, estimates that the royalty payments will average between $8 and $10 for each clone machine. It is likely, however, that IBM will pay royalty fees that are considerably lower. Licenses from CAS will require advance royalty payments of between $25,000 and $300,000.[12]

Modem Standards

3Com Corporation is a pioneer in the computer networking industry, and believes it is the only networking company that offers a unique blend of practical and innovative technology, which provides its channel partners and customers with high-value, practical-to-use solutions. 3Com's competitive strengths include a strong balance sheet, an industry-leading IP portfolio, distributor and customer relationships, and brand identity. 3Com signed an exclusive licensing agreement with the inventor, who made the 56K modem possible, in hopes of moving the industry closer to a uniform standard. 3Com claims that it holds the exclusive license to the

IP of independent inventor, Brent Townshend, who developed the fundamentals behind the new generation of high-speed modems.

Companies using the technology will have to pay a royalty of $1.25 for each 56K modem sold, and $9 for each head-end port. The modems typically retail for about $150, indicating a 0.8 percent royalty rate, at the retail level. The head-end ports, which are used by Internet service providers, cost between $350 and $450 each, indicating a royalty rate between 2.0% and 2.6% at the retail level. Townshend's work was groundbreaking, and he allowed the company to build on his technology, to create a fundamentally different approach from the way modem communications had been handled before. Townshend developed the concept that information could travel faster from the server to the client than from the client to the server. His idea was to connect the server, or Internet service provider, to the digital part of the network and the client, or personal computer user, to the analog part of the network. Previous modems were slower, because both the server and the client sides were connected to analog networks. The 56K modems allow Internet users to download information at about twice the speed of previously available modems.

3Com also said it will license its own patents, to other modem makers, for a one-time fee of $100,000, or at a running royalty, capped at $150,000. The company said licensing its own, and Townshend's, IP would move the industry closer to a uniform standard for the new high-speed modems. 3Com's U.S. Robotics unit has been selling its "x2" 56K modems, while Rockwell International is marketing its K56 Flex modem chipsets. Since the two systems are incompatible with each other, the industry is seeking to define a standard that would make all the modems compatible.[13]

Modems

Hayes Microcomputer Products was granted additional damages, and attorney's fees, in the long-standing patent dispute with Everex Systems, Ven-Tel, and OmniTel. The rulings were issued three months after a San Francisco jury found that the patent was valid, enforceable, and willfully infringed by the defendants. The total award to Hayes from these defendants stands at approximately $10 million. In late January, a jury found that the infringement by Everex, Ven-Tel, and OmniTel was willful. As such, Judge Samuel A. Conti said, "these willful infringers must not be allowed to have infringed a valid patent for five or six years, and then only have to pay a one and three-quarter percent royalty to the owner of the valid patent." The judge then decided, "this is particularly the case where, as here, it is undisputed that Hayes offered defendants an opportunity to license the patented technology, at terms similar to those offered by Hayes to many other competitors, and defendants did not even bother to respond." Judge Conti also noted that the defendants "clearly adopted, early on, a strategy of long-term, expensive litigation—while continuing to sell products which they were on notice might very well be infringing—rather than making any attempt to deal with Hayes directly." The patent involved in this lawsuit, known as the "Heatherington '302 patent" (for the modem with improved escape sequence), was issued to Hayes on October 22, 1985. The escape sequence mechanism has been used by Hayes for the past decade, in every one of its products. Since the first product was shipped in June of 1981, all modem manufacturers who have truthfully made a claim that their modems are Hayes compatible have used the same escape sequence mechanism.[14]

COMPUTER SOFTWARE

Strong sales of low-priced PCs have allowed this industry to experience solid growth for software and programming products. The majority of software sales still involve operating systems, but security systems sold by McAfee and Symantec have greatly contributed to fueling growth in the industry. The computer gaming sector also has provided significant income, though escalating development costs, and increasing competition, could stunt future growth and profitability. Future growth for this industry is directly regulated by PC sales.

Leaders in the United States include Microsoft, IBM, Symantec, McAfee, Oracle, and Computer Associates. Microsoft dominates the market for PC operating systems, with its Windows XP platforms and its Office suite of programs.

Apple Operating System

Apple and Mac cloners are wrestling over Mac OS 8 and Rhapsody licenses. The makers of Mac clones are annoyed that Apple's proposed OS fee structure is designed to steer them toward entry-level, high-volume markets with low profit margins. Apple is apparently pushing a sliding scale, which lowers the cost to license the Mac OS for low-end machines, while increasing fees dramatically for the fastest CPUs. Current Apple agreements include several fees. Cloners pay for the use of Mac logic board designs; these royalties reportedly range from about $5 for entry-level models, to $150 for Tsunami-based systems. The cost of Mac OS 7.6 depends on the number of CPUs sold, and averages about $50. Licensees must also purchase, from Apple, the actual Mac ROMs, which cost about $35. The new fee structure reportedly is an attempt by Apple to prevent cannibalization of its sales.

Sources said Apple's proposed OS fee schedule is based almost solely on system performance. The charges for high-speed models, aimed at Apple's core, high profit, markets, would be higher than those for low-cost machines. Apple's suggested prices reportedly range from less than $10 per machine, to more than $500; the license for a very high-performance system, with multiple processors, could reach $1,000. In addition, Apple reportedly is requesting a fee for Mac ROMs on future machines, where ROMs would be optional.[15]

Decision and Data Mining

Nestor, and its wholly-owned subsidiary Nestor Traffic Systems (NTS), licenses its patented intelligent software solutions for decision and data-mining applications in realtime environments. Nestor products employ proprietary, neural network predictive models, and other algorithms, to convert existing data and business experiences into meaningful recommendations and actions. Nestor has designed and developed software products that can bring additional value, through proprietary software and information-management knowledge. Nestor has granted an exclusive license to NTS, for application of its technology in the field of traffic management applications. Under the license, NTS owes Nestor a royalty equal to ten percent of gross profit (gross revenues less third-party costs of sales) realized from products using the technology covered by the license. The license requires minimum annual royalties, to retain exclusive rights, starting at $125,000 in 2001, then increasing to $1 million per year in 2005.

In 2001, Nestor ceased direct product development, sales, and support in the fields of fraud detection, financial risk management, and CRM.

Through license agreements entered into with ACI and ReD, co-exclusive development, sales, and support rights were granted to these resellers in fraud and risk management. Non-exclusive rights in the field of CRM were granted to ReD. In addition, all expenses associated with development, support, and sales of these products were transferred to these parties. Nestor's PRISM® fraud detection solutions help financial institutions detect and prevent fraudulent payments, manage merchant risks, and identify illicit account usage (money laundering). The fraud detection products are used by many of the world's largest financial institutions, and represented approximately eighty-seven percent of Nestor's 2001 revenues. Nestor has licensed its PRISM software technology to ACI, for fifteen percent on sales.[16]

Windows OS Code

In 2003, Microsoft changed its licensing program, for competitors to use its code to make server products that interoperate with its flagship, Windows OS. The licensing changes were part of an antitrust settlement with the U.S. government. As part of its deal with federal authorities, Microsoft agreed to let third-party developers obtain licenses, and implement Microsoft's protocol technology, in their own server products, to improve interoperability with Windows. Microsoft agreed to slash its advance royalty rates in half—from $100,000 to $50,000—and to set up a new royalty rate structure, based on the licensee's product revenue. The plan is to charge between one and five percent of revenue as a royalty. Royalty rates on Microsoft protocol technology, used in embedded hardware products, will now range from five-tenths of one to two and one-half percent.[17]

Microsoft also extended the scope of the licenses, without any increase in the royalty rate. In addition to Windows 2000, Windows XP, and future operating systems, the licenses cover communications with any Windows legacy client, such as Windows 95 and Windows 98.

CONSTRUCTION

Low interest rates have fueled demand for new homes and home improvement projects. Raw materials are, therefore, in great demand, with concrete products leading the way as the industry's major revenue contributor.

Technological innovation in this industry has most recently been driven by the demand for energy efficiency, though many different technologies have been introduced, into what were once commodity products. Profits in this industry, and royalty rates, are sensitive to economic conditions and interest rates.

Leading companies in this industry include Cemex, Hanson, Lafarge, Rinker, USG Corporation, and Vulcan Materials. Among the raw materials produced by these companies are concrete, roofing systems, and gypsum board.

Paving

Integrated Paving Concepts has reached a five-year agreement with Aydogdu Insaat ve Ticaret of Istanbul, for the licensing of StreetPrint Pavement Texturing, and the distribution of StreetPrint tools, templates, and StreetBond coatings in Turkey, North Cyprus, Azerbaijan, Uzbekistan, Turkmenistan, Kazakhstan, and Georgia. In a press release, Integrated Paving said the agreement calls for an initial licensing fee of $50,000, minimum template purchases of $400,000 in the first three years, plus additional purchases in years four and five, as well as minimum purchases of $2.95 million in surfacing products, or ten percent royalty payments over the five-year period. Within the scope of the renewable agreement, Aydogdu Insaat will try to sub-license the use of StreetPrint to qualified asphalt paving companies in these countries, and will seek initial license fees, and royalties, or product purchase commitments.[18]

Polyvinyl Chloride Pipe Products

Lucky-Goldstar Group, of South Korea, signed a $10 million contract with Sinar Mas Group, of Indonsia, to make polyvinyl chloride products. A 50-50 joint venture was formed, called P.T. Sinar Lucky Plastics Industry, launched with $3 million of investment capital. A plant built in Indonesia produces polyvinyl chloride pipe, providing Indonesia with construction materials for water supply and sewage facilities. Lucky-Goldstar will provided the manufacturing, production, and facilities design technology, while Sinar pays a running royalty of two and one-half percent of net sales, over a five year period.[19]

ELECTRONICS

The market for electronic instruments and controls primarily consists of all sales of electronic instruments and controls, used in the automotive industry, industrial processes, medical equipment, and portable consumer goods. Challenges for this industry include high levels of continuing research and development expenses, rapid product obsolescence, and product commoditization. Of course, profit pressures result. Efforts to offset profit pressures include offshore manufacturing, restructuring, and supply chain optimization. Leading industry participants in the United States include UQM Technologies, Emrise Corporation, Avnet, Emerson, Johnson Controls, and Agilent.

Rapid product obsolescence causes a number of problems, including excessive inventory of obsolete products and continued research and development funding, to keep pace with new technologies being introduced. Offshore manufacturing is a common response, and most manufacturing is conducted where low labor and energy costs help control overhead.

DVD/Video Players

Philips, Pioneer, and Sony began patent licensing for DVD/Video players and discs, and DVD/ROM drives and discs. The three companies decided to start licensing their patented technologies, following the market introduction of DVD/Video and DVD/ROM products. Pioneer and Sony each have authorized Philips to execute the licensing program. Philips, Pioneer, and Sony are members of the DVD Consortium, and strong supporters of the DVD format.

Continued discussions within the DVD Consortium, regarding the licensing of their patents in a single license (to provide the industry with the benefit of a one-stop-shop licensing program), have not been conclusive. To avoid further undesirable delay, Philips, Pioneer, and Sony have decided to move forward, in the best interest of consumers, the DVD system and its future licensees. Licenses will be available to all interested parties—with a royalty of three and one-half percent for the player, and five cents for the disc—for those patents which they consider to be essential for DVD/Video and/or DVD/ROM.

Detection Monitoring

Fiberchem licensed its fiber-optic chemical sensor technology to Sippican, for use in environmental markets in the areas of ocean, ground, and surface water detection and monitoring. Fiberchem will also continue to market the technology, in the same markets, under its own label. Sippican agreed to pay a licensing fee of $25,000, and an additional $500,000 in sensor research and development funding, in three payments. These payments included $100,000 in 1991, followed by $200,000 in both 1992 and 1993. In addition, Sippican agreed to a five percent royalty on its gross sales of Fiberchem-developed products, along with a three percent royalty on accessories made for use with a Fiberchem sensor. Fiberchem manufactures sensors for both its own product lines and those of the licensee. Sippican is a privately owned corporation, located in Massachusetts, specializing in oceanographic instrumentation. It has annual sales of approximately $30 million.

Flat Panel Display Technology

SI Diamond Technology, through its subsidiary Applied Nanotech (AN), entered into a worldwide, non-exclusive license agreement with a large, Japanese display manufacturer. The license covered all owned and assigned patents of SI Diamond and AN, relating to carbon films, carbon nanotubes, and electron emission technologies, for the manufacture and sales of flat panel displays. AN will receive an up-front payment of $500,000, and a two percent running royalty, on product parts manufactured by the licensee. The running royalty will be paid by the licensee once the licensee's parts sales exceed $100 million. Additionally, AN will conduct research and development for the licensee, in the field of hydrogen sensors, for a total payment of $400,000. SI Diamond Technology is based in Austin, Texas, and is a holding company for three subsidiaries, AN, Electronic Billboard Technology (EBT), and Sign Builders of America (SBOA). EBT develops and produces products for the business and consumer markets, using liquid crystal display technology. AN conducts the research and development for flat panel displays, utilizing carbon nanotube (field emission display) technology. SBOA manufactures high-quality signage, for a broad range of consumers, throughout the United States.

Remote Metering

Atrix International manufactures and markets a modular device, called the R3 copy control system, that can be installed on a copy machine to remotely read, record, or report a number of specific events, and automatically transmit data to a central computer, on a standard telephone line. This product serves a market which the company believes is generating approximately $100 million in sales annually. The company also sells two software packages, which enhance the sales and reporting capabilities of the R3 system.

WinTrax-TR is a transactional-based software system for the legal, public relations, and copy center markets. WinTrax-PNP is a notebook software package, allowing the user to automatically retrieve, format, and report data from R3 modules. Atrix has entered into a non-exclusive license agreement with American Innovations (AI), of Austin, Texas. The agreement grants AI a non-exclusive license to make, use, or sell its licensed products, under the Atrix patent, for remote metering. In consideration for the license, AI has agreed to pay Atrix a five and one-half percent royalty, on all net sales made by AI, from the date they received notice until the expiration of the patent. Atrix has patent license agreements with Scientific Atlanta, Monitel, Interactive Technologies, Schlumberger, and now AI.

FOOD AND BEVERAGE

Food processing is one of the largest manufacturing sectors in the United States. The largest sectors of the industry, as measured by value, are meat, dairy, fruit and vegetable preservation, and specialty foods. Other niche sectors include bakeries and tortilla manufacturing, grain and oilseed milling, sugar and confectionary, animal food manufacturing, and seafood products.

Food companies are facing rising criticism that they are contributing to obesity in children. Reducing fat and sugar content in foods, and insuring that products are intelligently marketed, is a significant challenge faced by this industry. The leading industry participants in the United States include Archer Daniels Midland, Bunge, Kraft, and Tyson.

Mineral Water

Clearly Canadian Beverage Corporation produces and markets Clearly Canadian®, a line of natural mineral waters, and flavored, sparkling water beverages. The company announced it had exercised its right to terminate its royalty and distribution agreement with Camfrey Resources, effective 1992. In connection with the termination of the agreement, the company was required to pay a "royalty termination allowance," equal to five times the average annual royalty paid during the previous two years of the current agreement. Based on this royalty buy-out formula, the company paid $22,900,478 to Camfrey to terminate, and as a result, is no longer required to pay any royalties to Camfrey. Previously, the company was required to pay twenty-five cents per case on sales of Clearly Canadian® products outside of Canada (★). Clearly Canadian's profitability had been enhanced by twenty-five cents per case by terminating the Camfrey royalty. The company funded the payment of the royalty termination allowance through the liquidation of short-term investments, which were held for this purpose. Through distribution agreements, Clearly Canadian is sold throughout the United States, Canada, Japan, Great Britain and Ireland.

Packaging

Advanced Oxygen Technologies (AOT) incorporated (DE is a popular state for incorporations) in 1981 under the name Aquanautics Corporation, and was, from 1985 until May 1995, a development-stage specialty materials company, producing new oxygen-control technologies. AOT entered into a definitive agreement with W.R. Grace to sell its proprietary oxygen-control technology. The deal called for $335,000 in cash plus a two percent royalty for the next twelve years, on sales of products incorporating the company's technology. This technology removes residual oxygen from packages, contributing to overall freshness of food and beverages. Specific applications include crowns and closures for bottled foods and beverages, bag-in-box packaging, bags, plastic films, and coatings for cans and aseptic packages.

Eggs

A new line of eggs, with increased polyunsaturated fats, was licensed at a royalty of five cents per carton of a dozen. Sales of egg byproducts require a royalty of one cent per pound. Vitafort International is a company that designs nutritionally enhanced food and beverage products, and then develops integrated processing and marketing procedures. They granted the license for the new line of eggs to Nulaid Food, an egg producer on the West Coast. Under the agreement, the eggs are to be sold under the Vitafort name.

MEDICAL EQUIPMENT

An aging U.S. population drives strong growth for the medical equipment and supplies industry. Supplies form the largest part of the industry, while the home healthcare market, for disposable medical supplies, grows rapidly as consumers explore self-treatment and preventive medicine. Cardiology and diagnostics equipment accounts for another substantial portion of annual revenues. Other important segments in this industry include orthopedic products, laboratory equipment, ophthalmology, and respiratory products.

The strongest demand for disposable supplies involves pre-filled inhalers and syringes, angioplasty supplies, nucleic acid diagnostics, tissue sealants, and adhesives. Rising demand for all things medical is driven by the increasing U.S. population, which brings about an increase in the number of diseases and disorders that require professional medical treatment. As they transition through their lifecycles, BabyBoomers impact various industries, and medical equipment is getting its turn.

In additional to technological innovation, competition has encouraged brand-building to gain market share. Technological innovations include the introduction of products which combine treatments, such as drug coated stents, which combine a medical device with a pharmaceutical therapy. Combination products are expected to drive greater licensing, and partnering, by industry participants.

This industry can be characterized as having a strong and steady demand for products, not subject to economic cycles. The major industry participants in the United States include Boston Scientific, GE HealthCare, Henry Schein, Johnson and Johnson, Medtronic, Stryker, Siemens, and Zimmer. Profits in this industry can be quite healthy, which allows for strong royalty rates.

Breast Cancer Detection

Scantek Medical signed a licensing agreement allowing Health Technologies International (HTI) to assemble, market, and sell its BreastAlert™ medical device in Chile and Singapore. Scantek received a twenty percent stake—four hundred thousand shares—of HTI, plus licensing fees of $250,000 in the first quarter of 1997, at least $100,000 in royalties for that year, and a minimum of $400,000 in royalties beginning in the year 2000. HTI also agreed to pay Scantek a one hundred percent markup on product cost for Scantek's services in operating its manufacturing line, and HTI will pay all royalties exceeding the minimum level, up to fifteen percent of the company's net sales. Scantek's BreastAlert is a non-invasive test used by physicians to detect breast disease, including breast cancer. Scantek develops products and devices to help doctors in the diagnosis and early detection of disease.

Cancer Screening

AccuMed International (AI) and Ampersand Medical announced they had settled all past disputes relating to a prior license agreement by agreeing to a new patent and technology license agreement. The new agreement gives Ampersand access to AI technology, and patent rights relating to computerized microscopy, for use in Ampersand's point-of-care systems for cervical and ovarian cancer screening. Ampersand will pay AI an unspecified up-front fee, and a running royalty of four percent of Ampersand sales. AI also received additional shares of Ampersand stock as part of the deal. AI was incorporated in California in 1988 as Alamar Biosciences. They design and build two product lines: AcCells™ computer-aided microscopes, which help medical experts examine human cells, and AcCell-Savant® electronic imaging systems, which produce digital images of microscopic specimens.

Catheter

SciMed Life Systems entered a broad agreement to settle patent litigation in a patent infringement case filed by Advanced Cardiovascular Systems (ACS) and Eli Lilly. Under the agreement, SciMed agreed to pay $48 million in cash, and ACS granted SciMed a worldwide, non-exclusive license to make, use, and sell existing and future products under certain U.S. and corresponding foreign patents. The company also received a worldwide non-exclusive license (until November 1993) to make and sell its Express, catheter product under U. S. patents. SciMed, ACS, and Eli Lilly entered into covenants not to sue each other on existing, and certain future, products. SciMed agreed to pay $28 million in 1992, then make $10 million payments annually in 1993 and 1994. Royalties to be paid for the non-exclusive licenses equalled seven-and-a-half percent of net sales, under two separate licenses. A royalty rate equal to twenty percent of net sales was required for the non-exclusive license on the Express catheter.

Digital Scanner

Austin Medical signed a non-binding letter of intent to pay Longport $1 million, over four years, for the right to sell Longport's digital scanner. Longport agreed to accept in exchange a ten percent royalty on scanner revenues, and a monthly fixed-lease payment for each scanner from Austin Medical.

Laser Finger-Perforator Technology

Cell Robotics International (CRI) manufactures, markets, and sells a sophisticated, laser-based medical device, and a scientific research instrument. CRI's key targets include the clinical and diabetes care markets, for the Lasette, and the scientific research market for the Cell Robotics Workstation. CRI, and Ohio-based GEM Edwards, announced an agreement to rapidly introduce laser finger-perforator technology, by CRI, into the diabetic care market. This new product utilizes CRIs proprietary technology, with an erbium yttrium aluminum garnet (Er: YAG) laser, to painlessly penetrate the skin for the purpose of obtaining blood samples.

This technology has numerous applications, for both the general public and health care professionals. CRI's laser perforator is especially useful for individuals with diabetes, who must test their glucose levels as many as ten times per day. An individual with diabetes currently obtains readings by sticking their finger with a stainless steel lancet, placing a drop of blood on a reagent strip, and inserting the strip into a blood glucose monitor. The laser perforator replaces the lancet, and makes the process virtually painless, encouraging more frequent blood glucose monitoring. Such procedures are necessary to allow individuals with diabetes to adjust their diets, activity levels, and insulin dosages. Close monitoring of blood glucose levels has been clinically proven to help prevent the long-term affects of the disease, such as blindness, amputation, kidney failure, and even death.

The market for all diabetic home monitoring products reached $1.2 billion in 1994. GEM Edwards, one of the leading distributors of products to the diabetes supplies market, signed a letter of intent to obtain the exclusive license to manufacture and distribute CRI's laser finger-perforator in the United States. Under the agreement, GEM will pay CRI a fifteen percent royalty for the first twenty-five hundred finger-perforators produced each year, and ten percent for any additional units sold. CRI will be the sole supplier, to GEM, of the laser crystal for the finger-perforator. As part of the agreement, GEM has guaranteed the production of twenty-five hundred units. GEM projects U.S. sales of $4.5 to $6 million in the first year, $10 to $12 million in the second, and $20 million in the third. Based on those projections, the agreement would yield a royalty income of over $3 million, with sales of crystals projected at $2 million. GEM will pay for the product development and FDA submittal. The product is to be manufactured by Quatro of Albuquerque, under a separate agreement with GEM. CRI retains the rights to international markets.

Laser Hair-Removal

Palomar Medical Technologies is exclusively focused on the use of lasers, and light-based products, in dermatology and cosmetic procedures, with an emphasis on laser/light-based hair-removal, and research and development relating to that and other cosmetic laser/light based products. The company was organized in 1987 to design, manufacture, and market lasers, delivery systems, and related disposable products for use in medical procedures. In order to spread risk and bolster operating assets, Palomar has pursued an acquisition program, acquiring companies in its core laser business, as well as others, principally in the electronics industry. By the beginning of 1997, the company had more than a dozen subsidiaries. At the same time, having obtained FDA clearance to market its EpiLaser® ruby laser hair-removal laser system, Palomar was well positioned to focus on what it believed was, at that time, the most promising product in its core laser business.

On April 27, 1999, the company sold all of the issued and outstanding common stock of Palomar's Star Medical Technologies subsidiary to Coherent, for $65 million, paid in cash, and an ongoing seven and one-half percent royalty on the LightSheer product line. The purchase price was paid to the stockholders of Star, in proportion to their holdings of Star capital stock. Under the agreement, Coherent will pay an ongoing royalty of seven and one-half percent on the sale of any products that incorporate certain patented technology, or use certain patented methods, on an exclusive basis, from Massachusetts General Hospital (MGH). Portions of these royalty proceeds are remitted to MGH. In addition, Palomar has licensed its hair-removal technology to Asclepion-Meditec for a royalty of seven and one-half percent on revenue. The company believes the successful introduction and marketing of new products is critical to their long-term success. Broad market acceptance of laser/light-based hair-removal, and specific acceptance of the SLP1000™ diode laser system, EsteLux™ light-based system, and the Q-Yag 5™ Q-Switched ND.

PHARMACEUTICALS AND BIOTECHNOLOGY

Massive innovation and capital investment characterize this industry. Blockbuster therapies, with annual sales over $1 billion, can generate incremental profits nearing ninety percent of sales. The patented technology of pharmaceuticals and biotechnology companies is very unique. It requires a huge investment in research and development, for products that won't generate any revenue for many years, with a high probability of failure before commercialization can begin. However, when successful, these products deliver extraordinarily high profit margins, and billions of dollars in annual revenue. Market risk is not as significant a problem in this industry, as in others. As an example, if a cure for cancer is developed, the market will embrace the product.

During the past ten years, royalty rates have been pressured upward by several conditions within the pharmaceutical industry:

New drug discovery has become increasingly difficult.

It takes twelve to fourteen years, and several hundred million dollars, to put a new drug on the market.

Pharmaceutical companies are under constant pressure to continually obtain, or discover, promising new compounds.

Internal research and development pipelines are not sufficiently filled with new discoveries and products.

Pharmaceutical companies need to supplement their research and development deficiencies with licensing activities.

Pharmaceutical companies are in heated competition to acquire new molecules and technology from any source.[20]

In 2004, the global drug therapy market was $550 billion.[21] The United States is the world's dominant market, representing forty-five percent of global sales; Western Europe comprises twenty-six percent, and Japan represents eleven, while the rest of the world represents the remaining eighteen.

Major biotech firms include Amgen, Biogen Idec, Chiron, Genentech, and MedImmune. The largest traditional pharmaceutical companies include Pfizer, GlaxoSmithKline, Johnson and Johnson, AstraZeneca, Novartis, Amgen, and Wyeth. Sales of biotechnology products are growing at double-digit rates, while traditional pharmaceutical companies have recently experienced only single-digit growth.

Challenges to industry participants include generic (off-patent) products, and over-the-counter (OTC) products. As patent protection expires, competitive companies produce equivalents to branded predecessors, but at significantly discounted prices. This increases the pressure for the development of new, patented products to replace the high profit, off-patent products lost to generic producers. As a result, pharmaceutical and biotechnology companies spend more on research and development, as a percentage of sales, than any other industry.

The pharmaceutical and biotechnology industry has yielded a substantial number of royalty guidelines, as reported in Exhibit 6.1 below, based on data gathered by David Weiler of RoyaltySource, who compiled the data shown from a survey of four hundred fifty-eight Pharmaceutical and Biotechnology license agreements.[22] Remember, the average royalty rate across all industries was previously reported to be five percent of sales. For pharmaceuticals and biotechnology, the average is significantly higher, at seven percent.

458 Deals	*Rate*
Average Royalty	7%
Median Royalty	5%
Maximum Royalty	50%
Minimum Royalty	0%

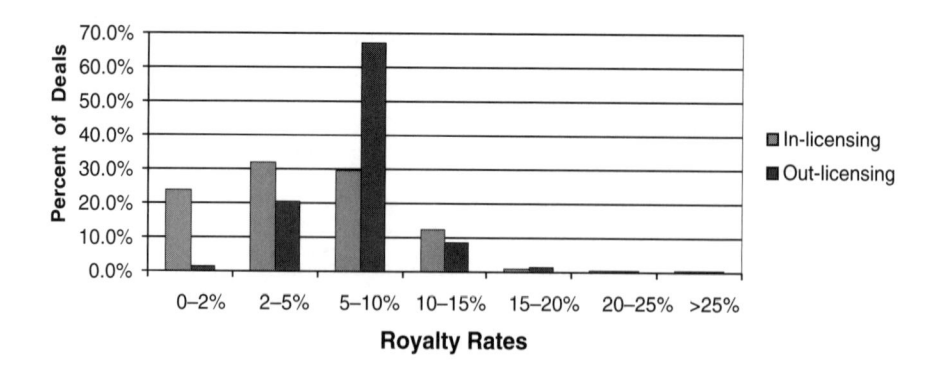

EXHIBIT 6.1 Royalty Rate Distribution for Pharmaceuticals

Rate	0-2%	2-5%	5-10%	10-15%	15-20%	20-25%	>25%
In-licensing	23.6%	32.1%	29.3%	12.5%	1.1%	0.7%	0.7%
Out-licensing	1.3%	20.7%	67.0%	8.7%	1.3%	0.7%	0.3%

In another survey, Degnan and Horton compared royalty rates in the pharmaceutical industry with non-pharmaceutical technology transfers.[23] They found that for all categories of invention, pharmaceutical inventions yielded higher royalty rate ranges (see Exhibit 6.2).

Category	Non-Pharmaceutical	Pharmaceutical
Revolutionary	10–15%	5–10%
Major Improvement	5–10%	3–7%
Minor Improvement	2–5%	2–3%

Information about average royalty rates by development stage is provided by Medius Associates,[24] which confirms previous discussions, relating higher royalty rates and risk reduction. As new compounds successfully pass through clinical trial phases, risk of failure lessens, and royalty rates rise, as shown in Exhibit 6.3.

Development Stage	Royalty Rate
Pre-clinical	0–5%
Phase I	5–10%
Phase II	8–15%
Phase III	10–20%
Launched Product	20%+

EXHIBIT 6.2 **PHARMACEUTICAL AND BIOTECHNOLOGY LICENSE DEALS (FEE PRESENTED IN THOUSANDS OF DOLLARS)**

Technology Description	Fee	Royalty	Licensor/Licensee
Adenocard, Heart Disease Treatment	$0	25%	Medco Research/Fujisava
Alzheimer's Diagnostic Test Techn.	$45	5%	Cornell University/Biopharamceutics, Inc.
Antiviral Composition and Methods	—	5%	State University of NY/Biopharmaceutics
Option for Contraceptive Regime	$157	3%–5%	Gynex/Organon
Cough Medicine	—	7%	P&G/Upjohn
Cypress Stem Cells Research	—	3%	University of Arizona/Cryo-Cell
Dermatology Product	$100	15%	DermaSciences/Trans CanaDerm
Diabetes Treatment	$9,000	10%	Ajinomo/Sandoz
DNA Binding Invention	—	4%	Princeton University/OnocorPharm, Inc.
Genetic Research	—	8%	Genetic Therapy/National Institute of Health
Hepatitis A Vaccine	$2,500	15%	Medeva/American Biogenetics
Influenza Drug	—	6%	Biota/Glazo
MichellamineB/Tropical Vine Leaves	—	3%–5%	University of Yaunde/National Cancer Inst.
Neupogen for Chemotherapy	—	3%	Amgen/Memorial Sloan-Kettering Cancer
Nucleic Acid Probe Technology	—	4%	Molecular Biosystems/DuPont
Oral Contraceptive	$175	30%	Gynex/Organon Group
Hypoix Tumor Cell Radiosensitizer	—	10%	Roberts Pharma./Dupont-Merck
Diagnostic Test Kit Technology	$110	6%	Disease Diagnostics/Meridian Diagnostics
Spirulina		8%	Spirulina Research/Cynatech
Wart Removal Products	$1,300	6%	Taumura/Bradley Pharmaceuticals
Water-Jel Burn Dressings	—	5%	Trilling Medical/Pfizer

Source: *Royalty Rates for Pharmaceutical & Biotechnology, 6th Edition, IPRA, Inc.* (www.ipresearch.com)

Another study relating development stage to royalty rates shows, once again, that the earlier the stage, the lower the royalty rate. Higher stages of development are associated with higher royalty rates (see Exhibit 6.4).

Royalty Rate by Stage of Development Pharmaceutical Industry

Stage	Rate
Process, Formulation or Software Technology	0–2%
Pre-Clinical Compounds	2–5%
Early-Stage Clinical Compounds	5–10%

Source: McGavock, et. al. 1991.

More focused guidance is available from Mark G. Edwards, of Recombinant Capital, at www.recap.com. Shown below, in Exhibit 6.5, are average royalty rates for different stages of development.

Average Royalty by R&D Stage

R&D Stage	Rate
Discovery	6.4%
Lead Molecule	8.1%
Pre-Clinical	11.3%

Harold A. Meyer III, CEO of patent law firm Novelint, suggests these guidelines for royalty rates:

- A raw idea is worth virtually nothing, due to an astronomical risk factor.
- A patent pending, with a strong business plan, may be worth one percent.
- An issued patent may be worth two percent.
- A patent with a prototype, such as a pharmaceutical with pre-clinical testing, may be worth two to three percent.
- A pharmaceutical, with clinical trials, may be worth three to four percent.
- A proven drug with FDA approval may be worth five to seven percent.
- A drug with market share, such as one pharma distributing through another, may be worth eight to ten percent.[25]

From a survey conducted by Rose Ann Dabek, a distribution of royalty rates for pharmaceuticals was developed. Exhibit 6.6 shows the percent of reported royalty rates for in-licensing and out-licensing.[26]

In "Patent and Technology Transfers in a Biotechnology Context" the following royalty rates were reported for a variety of products.[27]

Product	Royalty Rate
Research Reagents (e.g. expression vector, cell culture, media supplements)	1–5%
Diagnostics Products (e.g. monoclonal antibodies, DNA probes)	1–5%
Therapeutic Products (e.g. monoclonal antibodies, cloned factors)	5–10%
Vaccines	5–10%
Animal Health Products	3–6%
Plant/agriculture Products	3–6%

Richard Cox conducted a survey to determine the sharing of royalties among different entities when universities license-out technology.[28] Results are shown in Exhibit 6.7.

Royalty Recipient	Average Share
Inventors	36.90%
Inventor's department	20.90%
Inventor's college	13%
Inventor's research account	16.30%
University/institution	48.10%
Research foundation	33.80%

As previously stated, averages and guidelines miss instances when royalty rates are outside narrow ranges. Exhibit 6.2 summarizes pharmaceutical deals with rates that range from three to thirty percent.

SEMICONDUCTORS

The semiconductor industry is capital-intensive and cyclical. Recent gains have been driven by demand for wireless, and process-based, electronic goods. Microprocessors and chipsets form a substantial part of the semiconductor market. Integrated circuits and memory chips, however, have experienced slow growth, because of the availability of more competitive products, principally from Taiwanese manufacturers.

Due to the capital-intensive nature of the industry, with only large players having the financial muscle to invest large sums of money, there has been significant consolidation in recent years. Most of the smaller players have moved to less competitive areas, or have been acquired. Even the larger players are facing significant pressure on margins, driving them to outsource manufacturing.

Leading participants in the U.S. semiconductor industry include Infineon Technologies, Intel, Samsung, ST Microelectronics, and Texas Instruments. Competition is strong, with the top five players sharing approximately one-third of the global market. Intel leads the industry, with a global market share of over thirteen percent.

Profit margins have eroded because of over capacity in the industry. Most participants in the semiconductor industry added capital and substantial capacity, anticipating high demand, but Asian competition added more capacity, which lead to price erosion and profit pressure.

Innovation in the industry comes from industry participants building greater functionality into chips. This is intended to yield better performance and system management. Companies have started making chips that enable virtualization, network security, and data mining, leading to greater collaboration between the semiconductor, data storage, and computer security industries. Product design has become the primary focus of the major players in this market. To control costs, and reduce capital requirements for manufacturing, many companies in the industry are turning into fabrication-less (fabless) manufacturing companies, with many manufacturing functions outsourced.

High-Bandwidth Chip Connection Technology

Rambus officials disclosed, during testimony in *Rambus v. Infineon Technologies*, that Rambus charged licensees a royalty rate of approximately three and one-half percent on DDR DRAM, and a royalty rate of three-fourths of one percent on SDRAM. Further testimony disclosed that Rambus had signed royalty agreements with a number of companies under these terms, one of which was Samsung.

Rambus, based in California, designs, develops, licenses, and markets high-speed, chip-to-chip interface technology. Chip-to-chip interface products can be grouped into two categories, memory interfaces and logic interfaces. The company's two memory interface products are the Rambus dynamic random access memory (RDRAM) and Yellowstone. Other products currently offered are Rambus Redwood Interface, and Rambus RaSer™. Rambus Redwood is a parallel bus interface product, offering data rates of 400 MHz to 6.4 GHz. The logic interface product, RaSer™, is a high-speed serial link for chip-to-chip communications.

Samsung is a leading producer of CDMA cell phones, LCD and CRT monitors, DRAM memory chips, and microwave ovens. The company has worldwide electronic product sales of $27 billion, over sixty-four thousand employees in eighty-nine facilities, and a global network in forty-seven countries.

Lightning Resistance

Aritech reported in 1990 that it licensed certain U.S. patents, pertaining to a lightning-resistant, magnetic contact switch used in electronic security products, burglar alarm system components, and equipment and intrusion-detection systems. Artitech was granted an exclusive worldwide license, for three percent of net sales.

Manufacturing

Integrated Process Equipment Corporation (IPEC) announced that it proffered a letter of intent to acquire the Precision Materials Operation (PMO) from Hughes Danbury Optical Systems (HDOS), a subsidiary of Hughes Electronics Corporation. PMO will be operated as a wholly-owned subsidiary of IPEC. The purchase price for PMO was $20 million, payable in cash and subject to adjustment for inventory fluctuations, and a royalty of three and one-quarter percent of net sales, for a period of five years after the closing. In addition, IPEC will pay HDOS a one-time, contingent payment of $2 million, if net sales during the three years following the closing exceed $173 million. The contingent payment is payable in cash, or IPEC common stock, at IPEC's option. PMO, to be renamed IPEC Precision, will provide capability for Adaptive Planarization Technology, using an advanced plasma concept, called PACE, and revolutionary metrology, to be used for online, Chemical Mechanical Planarization (CMP) measurement.

These technologies are also to be used to produce equipment, for ultra-flat and silicon-on-insulator (SOI) wafers, for next-generation CMP. IPEC plans to sell wafer-polishing, Performance Optimized Production Station (POPS) equipment through this subsidiary. IPEC Precision will integrate metrology into other IPEC products, such as CMP tools. Metrology provides the ability to measure five hundred to two thousand points on a wafer in less than one minute, a thousand-fold improvement over current systems. POPS can perform all of the steps, from wafer-grinding through final polishing and, combined with IPEC's silicon wafer-polishing, this will allow IPEC to offer a complete, raw wafer production system.

IPEC designs, manufactures, markets, and services semiconductor processing equipment for CMP, and cleaning, of advanced integrated circuits. IPEC's wholly-owned subsidiary, Westech Systems, is a leading supplier of CMP systems. Athens Corporation, another IPEC subsidiary, is a leading manufacturer of on-site, ultra-high purity chemical reprocessing systems, and is a manufacturer of automatic chemical and mixing distribution systems for the semiconductor industry.

Pentium II Processor

Intel has granted its first license, giving another company the rights to develop chipsets supporting Intel's closely-guarded Pentium II microprocessor technology. Under a restricted agreement, Taiwan's Via Technologies may build, and sell, specific core-logic chipsets, incorporating the P6 bus, which connects to the Pentium II through a "Slot 1" connection. In exchange for the P6 patent license, Via must pay a per-unit royalty, and will license certain undisclosed patents to Intel. The agreement proves Intel's earlier contention, that it would license the bus patents for "fair value." But analysts aren't sure whether similar deals will be signed by Acer Laboratories and Silicon Integrated Systems (SIS), Via's primary competitors in the chipset market. The controversy surrounding the P6 bus began in March, when Acer announced its Aladdin Pro 2 chipset.

At the time, Intel representatives stated that none of the companies who had announced P6-based chipsets had done so under license from Intel. After government antitrust investigators reportedly began looking into whether Intel's Slot 1 interface inhibited competition, Intel representatives did an about-face, indicating that Intel had already granted a P6 license, to an undisclosed number of third-party companies. According to analysts and industry sources, the Via license, and other deals, were delayed for a difference of opinion between Intel and the chipset vendor, regarding the "fair value" of the agreement. In essence, Intel asked for sufficient royalties to bring prices of Intel-manufactured chipsets, and those made by third parties, to about equal. The vendors argued that OEMs would then have no incentive to buy from a third party, other than Intel. Other sources were more specific, reporting that Intel at least initially, asked for royalties of $4 to $5 per chipset. Intel declined to comment, on both the terms of the license and what royalties it negotiated. Via has stated that they should still be able to sell the chipsets at a competitive price, even with the royalty payments.

Power Conversion

IXYS is a leading company in the design, development, manufacture, and marketing of high-power, high-performance power semiconductors. The company's power semiconductors improve system efficiency, and reliability, by converting electricity at relatively high voltage into the finely regulated power required by electronic products. IXYS focuses on the market for power semiconductors capable of processing greater than five hundred watts of power. IXYS was found to infringe Harris Semiconductor patented technology related to IGTB (integrated gate bipolar transistor) chips, used to switch electrical currents, and help control power, in a wide variety of electronic equipment. Markets served include medical equipment, automobiles, and communications systems. Damages were awarded based on a royalty of nine and-one-quarter percent of sales.

Thin Film Ferroelectric Technology

Ramtron International is a fabless semiconductor company, focused on creating widespread use of its proprietary memory technologies, through both direct product sales and licensing activities, with the world's leading semiconductor manufacturers. The company was incorporated under the name Amtec Securities in 1984. Its name was changed to Ramtron International in 1988. Ramtron designs, develops, and markets two types of specialty semiconductor memory products; non-volatile ferroelectric random access memory (FRAM™) devices, and high-performance enhanced dynamic random access memories (Enhanced-DRAM). Ramtron's FRAM™ products are developed and marketed by Ramtron, while the company's Enhanced-DRAM products are developed and marketed through its subsidiary, Enhanced Memory Systems (EMS). Ramtron's recently acquired, wholly-owned subsidiary, Mushkin, focuses on meeting the growing aftermarket demand for high-performance DRAM memory products, through e-commerce Internet sales, and operates under the aegis of the company's Enhanced-DRAM business unit.

Racom Systems licensed certain confidential, and proprietary, thin-film ferroelectric technology from Ramtron. The technology covers minimum physical dimensions of 1.2 microns, utilizing a storage cell comprised of two transistors and two capacitors which, when applied to a separate base semiconductor technology, can be used for the manufacture and production of nonvolatile, random access semiconductor memory devices. Racom has agreed to pay a royalty of one to two percent of net sales.

SIMMs

A patent infringement case for SIMMs (single inline memory modules) ended with an award of damages based on royalties of two and three-quarters to four percent. At the center of the case were Wang's SIMMs, designed to be mounted vertically, or at an angle, on circuit boards, to increase memory while conserving space.

WASTE MANAGEMENT

Solid waste management accounts for the majority of the industry's revenue, with wastewater treatment also generating significant revenue. Recycling is also emerging as a key function of the U.S. waste disposal industry. Costs to establish new recycling methods can be substantial, but once the costs are funded, companies reap substantial benefits, and ultimately enhance profit margin growth. Industry participants are challenged by increasingly stringent environmental legislation.

Innovation is expected to transform the industry. The introduction of bioreactor landfill technology is set to provide significant environmental and economic benefits. The technology is capable of revolutionizing landfills, from waste repositories to waste treatment systems.

The industry is the subject of extensive, constantly evolving, legislative pressure, in the form of environmental, health, safety, and transportation laws. New regulations are increasing company liabilities, and compliance costs, cutting into margins and presenting future risk of civil penalties.

Key players are publicly owned companies, including Waste Management, Allied Waste Industries, and Republic Services.

Recycling of Asphalt Roofing Debris

ReClaim is the nation's leading recycler of asphalt roofing debris, and currently operates facilities in New Jersey. The company entered into a license agreement for the operation of a facility in Tampa, Florida. ReClaim indicated that the licensee, ReClaim of Tampa, intends to build a $5 million recycling facility, though financing has not yet been arranged. The Tampa site is the first of several new recycling facilities that ReClaim hopes to build during the next two years, with one each slated for the northeast, southeast, west, northwest, and central regions.

The company envisions geographic and market benefits from this strategy, as it allows national distribution outlets for the firm's recycled product line, as well as plant locations in diverse climatic regions. A ten-acre Tampa industrial site, located near I75 in Northeast Hillsborough County, has been acquired by the Tampa licensee. The licensing agreement is for a period of twenty years, and calls for a $250,000 license fee, with royalty fees of up to six percent of sales. In addition, the licensee intends to engage ReClaim to manage the new facility, on a cost-plus basis.

This is the first licensing contract offered by ReClaim. The Tampa site will represent a major production increase for ReClaim's recycled product line. Currently, ReClaim's leading patented recycled product is RePave™, a permanent, pothole patch, sold in packaged form. The Tampa recycling plant would manufacture and distribute RePave™ in bulk quantities also. Additionally, the Tampa license would produce hot mix finished asphalt using ReClaim's patented formula, which incorporates the company's Multi-Functional HMA Modifier.

Used Oil Recovery

Interline Resources has formed a joint venture company, with Whelan Environmental Services of Birmingham, England, to construct a $2.2 million used oil re-refinery in Stoke, England. The used oil re-refinery, with a capacity to process twenty-four thousand gallons of used oil per day, will be the first re-refinery in the United Kingdom. Interline will own forty percent of the joint venture, called Interline UK, and Interline will receive a royalty of six cents per gallon of used oil processed by the re-refinery. The joint venture will sell the re-processed oil as a lubricating base oil, and for other uses.

Interline's construction division, Gagon Mechanical, will build the re-refinery at its Sandy, Utah, location, then supervise installation of the plant at the site in Stoke. Whelan will contribute $750,000 to the joint venture, and has already commenced site improvements at Stoke. The joint venture company has also been appointed as Interline's marketing agent in the Netherlands, Belgium, Portugal, and Spain. As marketing agent, the joint venture will pursue licensing agreements for Interline with companies in these countries. The agreement includes the construction of one re-refinery, but leaves open the possibility of building additional plants in the United Kingdom.

Interline licenses a proprietary technology for used oil re-refining, and for cleaning contaminated hydrocarbons. Besides the end product of a lubricating base oil, the finished product can be sold as a diesel extender, and a clean-burning industrial fuel, and the by-products from the Interline re-refineries are environmentally safe. The first re-refinery utilizing this technology is being constructed in Dubai. The oil re-refining division of Interline has previously signed exclusive licensing agreements with Western India Group for ten Middle and Far Eastern countries, and with Quaker State Resources for the United States, Canada, and Mexico.

Tire Recycling

Titan Technologies and Skoda Klatovy, a wholly-owned subsidiary of the giant Czech Republic conglomerate Skoda, concluded an agreement with the Environmental Solution Agency (ESA) of Fort Meyers, Florida, for the erection of the first one-hundred-ton-per-day tire recycling plant, in Traiskirchen, Austria. Titan anticipates initial revenue, exclusive of its $1.5 million royalty, by this summer. Thereafter, Titan will receive $2.5 million, from each plant sold by ESA, including a marketing markup and initial license fee. Each plant will also pay a five percent royalty fee on the sale of byproducts, and tipping fees.

ESA has already identified over sixty serious customers in the burgeoning new European market. Under the agreement, Skoda Klatovy agreed to perform all necessary preliminary engineering, in tandem with Titan's engineers, to bring the plant into compliance with European Community industrial and environmental standards; in addition, it agreed to provide a full, one-year warranty of the Titan facility. The plant in Austria will be managed and operated by a joint venture, led by ESA and Semperit/Conti's recycling subsidiary. Semperit/Conti is the largest private employer in Austria, and the oldest tire manufacturer in the world. Semperit/Conti is a wholly-owned subsidiary of Continental Tire, the world's third-largest tire manufacturer, and will guarantee the venture enough scrap tires each year to keep the new plant operating at its full, one hundred ton capacity.

CHAPTER 7

Trademark and Copyright Royalty Statistics

APPAREL

The apparel and accessories industry is a mature business in the United States. Women are the primary driving force for this industry, and represent the major source of revenue. Consumers, particularly women, are willing to pay extra to differentiate themselves in terms of fashion. This allows manufacturers to produce huge collections of apparel and accessories, for a wide spectrum of price points. Major players within the United States include Coach, Jones Apparel, Liz Claiborne, VF, and Polo Ralph Lauren. These manufacturers attract customers by promoting an array of established brands.

Changing consumer tastes are a continuing challenge for the industry. This drives demand for new product, but also generates uncertainty in terms of production planning, forecasting, inventory management, production systems, and distribution. Another challenge is introduced by the continuing threat from counterfeit products.

Economic conditions can greatly impact sales and profits for industry participants. During downturns, consumers reduce spending on discretionary luxury items. As income is reduced, consumers focus their spending on essentials. Money for new clothes and accessories is often not part of their strained budgets. The industry is also impacted by seasonal fluctuations, because apparel products and accessories are frequently given as gifts, resulting in substantial seasonal fluctuations in sales and operating profits.

Everlast™

The Everlast trademark reminds everyone of boxing gloves, trunks, and headgear. Its distinctive curved lettering is now appearing on other forms of sports clothing and sporting goods, bringing to the market a locker room feeling of strength, and no-nonsense athleticism. USA Classic has been licensing the Everlast trademark for use on a wide variety of non-boxing sporting goods, and paying the licensor six percent of sales.

Lotto™

Lotto is an Italian company, and owns the trademark to the Lotto brand name. The Lotto brand name adorns mens', womens', and childrens' athletic shoes, apparel, and accessories. Aarica Holdings designs, manufactures, and distributes athletic footwear, apparel, and accessories in Mexico, for U.S. and European brands. Aarica is the exclusive distributor of the L.A. Gear and Lotto brands in Mexico. In 1998, Lotto and Aarica entered into a license agreement, whereby Lotto granted Aarica an exclusive license to use technical information, and the Lotto trademark, for manufacturing, packaging, and distribution of products in the Mexican market. The specific products covered by this ten-year agreement are to be agreed upon seasonally. In consideration for this license, Aarica agreed to pay Lotto a semi-annual royalty, equal to five percent of net sales.

Disney

Disney licensed the use of a portfolio of its characters to Sun Green River, a Japanese manufacturer, for use on swimwear and suspenders in Japan. Disney will get a ten percent royalty on the wholesale price of the garments.

Ralph Lauren and Polo

Ralph Lauren and Polo Ralph Lauren Corporation were involved in a dispute with their largest licensee, Jones Apparel, over the designer's department store apparel line. Lauren wanted Jones to give back the license at the end of 2003, while Jones maintained that it had until 2006. Jones annual sales amounted to approximately $1 billion, and the licensed apparel accounted for over fifty percent of revenue. In 2002, Jones sold $548 million of the Lauren brand, and $37 million of the Ralph Casual collection. Jones licenses from Ralph Lauren three product lines: Polo Jeans, Lauren, and Ralph. Currently, the Polo Jeans line is not part of the dispute. Jones pays seven percent of sales on all three lines.

In the 1980s, fashion designers like Ralph Lauren raced to sign up licensees to manufacture and distribute branded clothing, bed linens, towels, and other furnishings. Currently, designers want more control over their brands, so they are buying back their licenses. In 2000, Polo spent $200 million to buy back its European licensees; in 2003, they spent another $70 million to acquire their Japanese licenses, with plans to produce the lines itself.

Jones is a $4 billion company—the second-largest publicly traded clothing-maker in the United States. Approximately twenty-five percent of its sales come from the licensed Ralph Lauren lines. To stay profitable, Jones must have a strong-selling, well-known brand as leverage with its retailing customers. If Jones loses the Ralph and Lauren lines, but keeps the Polo Jeans line, it contractually cannot replace the lost lines with competing designers.

ARTWORK

Licensed artwork is a broad category, not including original works of art, such as oil paintings. The type of artwork discussed here adorns almost every conceivable product, including paper towels. Royalty rate information for this category is scarce, but some data have been found, as presented below.

- Greeting cards and gift wrap: two to five percent
- Household items such as cups, sheets, and towels: three to eight percent
- Fabrics and apparel such as tee-shirts, caps, and decals: two to ten percent
- Posters and prints: ten percent or more
- Toys and dolls: three to eight percent[1]

Textile Patterns

Leon B. Rosenblatt Textiles won damages against a licensee for failure to pay royalties A federal judge in New York City ordered a corporate principal to personally pay $56,685, in damages and attorney fees, for breach of contract and willful copyright violation (*Leon B. Rosenblatt Textiles v. Griseto*). The judge entered a default judgment and fee award, after the officer's repeated failure to appear in court and produce tax returns. Leon B. Rosenblatt Textiles licensed Nicholas Griseto's company to sell copyright-protected textile patterns, for a three percent royalty. After Rosenblatt was not paid, it sued Griseto in the Southern District of New York, for copyright infringement and breach of contract.

After defense counsel withdrew, Griseto appeared pro se and a default was entered against him. Griseto failed to comply with orders to produce copies of personal and corporate income tax returns. He also failed to appear at a status conference, and a scheduling conference. The judge granted Rosenblatt a default judgment, rejecting Griseto's assertions that he was not notified of the conference dates.

The judge found bad faith in his failure to disclose the tax returns and awarded: $8,737 in contract damages, based on unpaid royalties on actual sales; $8,737 for willful infringement, for knowingly selling copyrighted patterns without paying royalties; $2,888 in interest; and $38,330 in attorney fees. While the attorney fees were awarded under the Copyright Act, a substantial portion of that amount could also have been awarded as a sanction, for failing to comply with discovery orders, and for missing court ordered conferences.

Food

Food processing is one of the largest manufacturing sectors in the U.S. The largest sectors of the industry, as measured by value, are meat, dairy, fruit & vegetable preservation and specialty foods. Other niche sectors include bakeries and tortilla manufacturing, grain and oilseed milling, sugar and confectionary, animal food manufacturing and seafood products.

Food companies are facing rising criticism that they are contributing to obesity in children. Reducing fat and sugar content in foods and ensuring that products are intelligently marketed is the challenged faced by this industry.

The leading industry participants U.S. include Archer Daniels Midland Company, Bunge, Kraft Foods, and Tyson Foods.

Andretti™

Mario Andretti and AWG entered into a non-transferable, non-sublicensable, worldwide license agreement in 1997, to use the "Andretti" name on wine. In exchange, AWG will pay Andretti a royalty, equal to five percent of the gross revenue, from sales of wine products bearing his name. In addition, AWG agreed to an annual payment of either two percent of profits, or $150,000 dollars (whichever is lower), on all wine sales. The term of the agreement is perpetual.

Mario Andretti is one of the most decorated racecar drivers of all time. Born in Italy in 1940, Andretti moved to the United States, and began his racing career, in 1959. He was an incredibly versatile driver, winning open car, drag racing, and stock car events. In 2000 he was awarded "Driver of the Century" by *Racer* magazine. In his illustrious career, he won the Indy Five Hundred, the Daytona Five Hundred, and driver of the year—in three different decades. AWG is a company formed for the production and marketing of wine, initially under the Andretti name.

Big League Chew

Big League Chew is a shredded bubble gum product that lets kids pretend they are using chewing tobacco, just like their professional baseball heros. The gum is shredded and comes in a foil pouch. The product was developed by Yankee ex-pitcher Jim Bouton, partly because he disliked the taste of chewing tobacco. Amurol, a subsidiary of Wrigley Company, pays royalties ranging from two and one-half to five percent on sales, to manufacture and distribute the product.

Dannon/YoCream®

Dannon Company and YoCream International entered into a license agreement in 2001, giving YoCream a non-transferable, non-assignable license to use the co-brand name "Dannon/YoCream" for the marketing, manufacture, and sale of soft frozen yogurt in the United States. In exchange for the co-brand, YoCream agreed to pay Dannon four percent of net sales of product sold under the co-brand. The license runs for five years, with the option to renew if mutual agreement is reached one year prior to the expiration of the agreement.

Dannon is a subsidiary of the Danone Group, a worldwide leader in water and fresh dairy products. In 2003, Danone had approximately $16.88 billion dollars in sales, and employed a worldwide work force of approximately ninety-five thousand employees. YoCream International makes, markets, and sells frozen yogurt, sorbet, frozen custard, smoothie, and ice cream products in a variety of non-fat, low fat, and premium flavors. These products are distributed to yogurt shops, fast food chains, discount club warehouses, convenience stores, restaurants, hospitals, school districts, food distributors, military installations; and various other businesses and outlets. The company's primary brand is YoCream®, and many of its products fall under that trademark.

Condiment Names

Sugar Foods is a specialty packager and distributor of serving size portions of condiments, including lemon juice, mustard, relish, mayonnaise, and salad dressing. The company has expanded its business by differentiating its products through the licensing of trademarks displayed on the individual packages. The company has licenses to use the Sunkist, Vlasic, French's, and Tobasco brand names. A typical contract with a trademark owner runs for ten years, with options to renew. Most of the time no up-front fee is paid. Sugar Foods pays for the products used in preparing the packages, plus a royalty fee between three and five percent of sales.

PERSONAL CARE

In the U.S. personal and household products industry, slow growth indicates a mature market. Cosmetics and fragrances are the largest sectors of this industry. The maturity of the market is reflected in the high level of competition, and difficulties manufacturers face in differentiating products and raising prices. The rise of the retailing giants like Wal-Mart, and the increased popularity of private-label products, have further increased negative price pressure within the market. Profit pressure results. In order to boost profits, leading companies have resorted to acquiring additional market share through acquisition, and have also implemented a variety of cost-cutting measures.

Leading participants in the U.S. personal and household products industry include Avon, Colgate-Palmolive, Gillette, Procter and Gamble, and Unilever. The world's largest consumer products company was recently created when Procter and Gamble spent nearly $60 billion to acquire Gillette.

Convenience, health, and sensory improvements are driving forces in product development, with emphasis on health and sensory benefits. In order to achieve a competitive advantage, manufacturers are releasing new combination products, such as shampoo that includes vitamin enrichment and soothing fragrances.

Hawaiian Tropic®

Tanning Research Laboratories and American Water Star (AWS) entered into a license agreement in 2003, granting AWS an exclusive license to sell, market, and produce flavored water with the Hawaiian Tropic® brand within the United States and Canada. In exchange, AWS paid a royalty rate of four percent of invoice sales from the bottled flavor water. Upon signature of the agreement, AWS agreed to pay an advance of $25,000, credited toward the first royalty payment, with following payments scheduled as follows: a minimum royalty payment for the first year of $40,000; a minimum royalty payment for the second year of $120,000; and a minimum royalty payment for the third year of $200,000. The initial term of the contract is three years, with the option to renew for another three-year period.

Tanning Research Laboratories is the originator of Hawaiian Tropic® tanning lotion. The private company, based out of Ormand Beach, Florida, began with founder Ron Rice producing tanning products out of his garage in 1969. Hawaiian Tropic® tanning lotions were the first to use designer fragrance and the first to offer lotions higher than SPF fifteen in the mass marketplace. Hawaiian Tropic® branded products include tanning oils and lotions, sun and wind screens, skin moisturizers, moisteners for tan preservation, shampoos, hair conditioners, hand and body lotions, clothing, and other accessories.

AWS is a public holding company for different entities and brands within the beverage industries. AWS beverage products are sold primarily to distributors, who in turn sell to different outlets. Originally named American Career Centers, the name was changed in 2002 to AWS to reflect the significant transformation, from acquiring technical career training centers to the bottling and distribution of water.

Tapazole®

Eli Lilly and Jones Medical Industries signed a license agreement in 1996 that gave Jones the exclusive right to market and sell Tapazole® in the United States. The license also allows the right to use intellectual property, defined as the copyright, trademarks, and marketing materials, associated with Tapazole®. In exchange, Jones agreed to pay $26,010,000, in three equal payments, with the first payment due at execution, and subsequent payments to occur at 90 day intervals. In addition, Jones agreed to pay a royalty of 15 percent of sales for ten years. The term of the agreement is perpetual, unless the license agreement is breached.

Eli Lilly specializes in the discovery, development, manufacture, and sale of pharmaceutical products, for fields that include neuroscience, endocrinology, oncology, cardiology, immunology, and veterinary. Jones was founded in 1981, and is a manufacturer and marketer of drugs, vitamins, and food supplements.

Vidal Sassoon

In 2003, Vidal Sassoon sued Procter and Gamble claiming that they deliberately sabotaged the sales of Vidal Sassoon products in favor of other products they owned. With the acquisition of Richardson-Vicks, Procter and Gamble acquired the Vidal Sassoon license, which carried a one and one-half percent royalty on sales. Vidal Sassoon is claiming that the marketing giant is favoring its other hair care products, including Pantene, Clairol, Herbal Essence, and Nice 'n Easy.

PUBLISHING

The book publishing industry is facing forces that increase their business risk and pressure their profit margins. Factors impacting the industry are as follows:

- Big publishing houses complain that they are forced to pay huge amounts of money to attract, or keep, proven stars, while increases in book sales are not keeping up with the growing advances.
- The largest book publishers are predominantly owned by conglomerates, which view publishing as a contributor to the bottom line.

- Publishers are criticized for offering popular books, that will sell, as opposed to books that contribute to cultural advancement.
- Independent publishers and bookstores are struggling to compete with the well-financed publishing houses.
- Internet publishers are competing with old-line publishers, by offering royalties of up to fifty percent of the price at which digital books are sold.

The results of these compounding factors include tumbling profits. A book that doesn't immediately perform well is often abandoned. Sales in most book categories have been flat or are declining, and returns from booksellers have reached unprecedented lows.

To save money, publishers are cutting back on the number of titles released. Many publishers are reducing the number of titles they will print, some by as much as twenty-five percent. These moves, however, don't decrease overhead, production, and promotion costs. With fewer titles in the marketplace, it becomes even more urgent for each book to succeed during its initial release. Getting manuscripts that meet such demands requires even more spending on advances, for "event" books by well-known authors. As a result, celebrity-books have become a common offering among publishers, as have seven-figure advances. The ceiling for royalties in this industry is generally reported at fifteen percent. While rumors abound that this ceiling is being cracked, many publishers have successfully held fast to this standard. Holding the line on advances is another story.

Prosecutor Marcia Clark commanded a high price for writing her side of the O.J. Simpson case, signing a $4.2 million book deal that puts her among the likes of Colin Powell and Newt Gingrich. Penguin U.S.A. emerged on top after a spirited, three-day, eight-way bidding war for Clark's book.

Former President Bill Clinton's book deal for "My Life" got him between $10 and $12 million from Knopf. Extensive marketing included appearances by the former president on *60 Minutes, The Oprah Winfrey Show, Today, Good Morning America, Larry King Live,* and *The Charlie Rose Show.*

Senator Hillary Rodham Clinton donated proceeds from her book, *It Takes A Village* to children's causes around the country. The first-installment provided about $750,000, which was divided among childrens' hospitals and other programs mentioned in her book. The bulk of the money was given to the National Association of Childrens' Hospitals and related institutions.

Johnnie Cochran, trial attorney for O.J. Simpson, was reportedly paid $3.5 million by Ballantine for his book, *Journey to Justice.* The book sold only half of its five-hundred thousand initial copies.

Former House Speaker Newt Gingrich turned down a $4.5 million advance from Harper Collins for two books. He told a news conference the controversial deal would have been used by critics of the Republican program in the new Congress. Instead of accepting the offer, Gingrich said, in a letter to his Republican colleagues, that he would take only a $1 advance, plus royalties on sales. Gingrich defended the book deal as perfectly ethical, saying it would have been appropriate had he been a rank and file member of the House. He said the $4.5 million sum had been offered in an auction between publishing houses, in which two had offered more than $4 million. HarperCollins had contracted for a two-book package for *To Renew America* and *The Democracy Reader. To Renew America* would have a first printing of seven-hundred-fifty thousand copies. Gingrich's $4.5 million advance would have been the second-highest for a politician; former President Ronald Reagan received $7 million in 1989, for his autobiography and a book of speeches.

RESTAURANTS

In one year, the restaurant industry generated sales of $511 billion. This came out of nine hundred twenty-five thousand locations, serving more than seventy million meals and snacks. The industry employs over 12.5 million people, the majority of which are paid an hourly wage. Other key factors include the following:

Restaurant-industry sales were forecast to advance over five percent in 2006, and equal four percent of the U.S. gross domestic product.

- The overall economic impact of the restaurant industry was expected to exceed $1.3 trillion in 2006, including sales in related industries, such as agriculture, transportation, and manufacturing.

- Every dollar spent by consumers in restaurants generates an additional $2.34, spent in other industries allied with the restaurant industry.
- Every $1 million in restaurant sales generates thirty-seven jobs for the nation's economy.
- In 2003, average unit sales were $755,000 at full-service restaurants, and $606,000 at limited-service restaurants.
- In 2004, the average household expenditure for food away from home was $2,434, or $974 per person.
- More than seventy percent of eating-and-drinking establishments are single-unit, independent operations.
- Eating-and-drinking establishments are mostly small businesses, with seventy percent having fewer than twenty employees.[2]

The industry is very competitive, especially among "white tablecloth" establishments that compete for discretionary spending dollars.

Ruth's Chris Steakhouse

Under Ruth's Chris franchise program, each franchise arrangement consists of an area development agreement, and a separate franchise agreement, for each restaurant. Their new form of area development agreement grants exclusive rights to a franchise, to develop a minimum number of restaurants in a defined area, typically during a five-year period. Individual franchise agreements govern the operation of each restaurant opened. Each has a twenty-year term, with two renewal options for ten additional years each, if certain conditions are met. The agreement requires franchisees to pay a five percent royalty on gross revenue, plus a one percent advertising fee, applied to national advertising expenditures.

Capital Grille Steakhouse

Rare Hospitality owns and operates various restaurants and Capital Grille steakhouses. Their franchise agreements grant rights for individual restaurants, and are either for a term of ten years—with a right of the franchisee to acquire a successor franchise for an additional ten-year period, if specified conditions are met—or for a period of twenty years. The agreement provides for a franchise fee of $60,000 which is reduced for subsequent franchises acquired by the same franchisee, and is payable in full upon execution. It also specifies royalties to Rare Hospitality, with respect to each restaurant, of four percent of gross sales; it requires the franchisee to expend, on local advertising, during each calendar month, an amount equal to at least one and one-half percent of gross sales. If Rare Hospitality establishes an advertising fund, franchisees must contribute an additional one-half percent of gross sales to that fund, up to four and one-half percent of the restaurant's gross sales, for the duration of the market, regional or national advertising campaign.

Benihana Japanese Restaurants

Benihana's current, standard franchise agreement provides for payment of a non-refundable franchise fee, ranging from $30,000 to $50,000 per restaurant, and royalties from three to six percent of gross sales.

CHAPTER 8

Profit Differentials and Royalty Rates

Converting intellectual property (IP) into revenues, profits, and value still requires a framework of integrated complementary business assets. These assets are needed to produce the product, package it, sell it, distribute it, collect payments, and implement the many other business functions required for running a business. Companies that create IP, and then license it to others, are still not free of the fundamental need for complementary assets. While licensors may not need to acquire and use complementary assets, successful commercialization of the licensed IP is still dependent on the licensee organizing such assets.

BUSINESS ENTERPRISE FRAMEWORK

Shown below is the composition of a typical business enterprise, as comprised of working capital, fixed assets, intangible assets, and IP. It represents the collection of asset categories that all companies use, to participate in an industry and generate profits.

$$\text{Business Enterprise} = \text{Working Capital} + \text{Fixed Assets} + \text{Intangible Asset} + \text{IP}$$

Working capital is the net difference between the current assets and current liabilities of a company.[1] Current assets are primarily composed of cash, accounts receivable, and inventory. Current liabilities include accounts payable, accrued salary, and other obligations due for payment within twelve months. The net difference between current assets and current liabilities is the amount of working capital used in the business.

Fixed assets include manufacturing facilities, warehouses, office equipment, office furnishings, delivery vehicles, research equipment, and other tangible equipment. This asset category is sometimes referred to as "hard assets." The amount of funds invested in this category can vary greatly for different companies, dependent on the industry in which they participate. As an example, huge investments in manufacturing assets are needed by companies participating in the automotive, aerospace, paper, semiconductor, and telecommunications industries. In other industries the manufacturing asset investment requirement is lower. Arguably, assemblers of electronic consumer goods fall into this category. Also in this category are insurance brokers, computer software publishers, manufacturers of cosmetics, and many business service companies.

Intangible assets and IP are the *soft* assets of a company. Generally, IP is created by law; such as the provision in the U.S. Constitution that established the patent system. Trademarks, patents, copyrights, and trade secrets are examples. Intangible assets are of a similar nature. They often do not possess a physical embodiment but are, nonetheless, very valuable to the success of a business. Customer lists, distribution networks, regulatory approval know-how, clinical trial know-how, and good manufacturing practices are examples.

All of the assets of the business enterprise contribute to the revenue and profit-generating capability of the business. The equity, and long-term debt values, represent the basis by which all other assets of a company are acquired, whether by purchase or internal creation. They are also the underlying basis for the value of the business as depicted below.

Business Enterprise Value = Value of Equity + Value of Long Term Debt

The equation above also shows that the value of the business enterprise equals the value of the aggregate asset categories. The value of the enterprise is equal to the value of the equity, and the long-term debt, of the company. The sum of these two components is also referred to as the

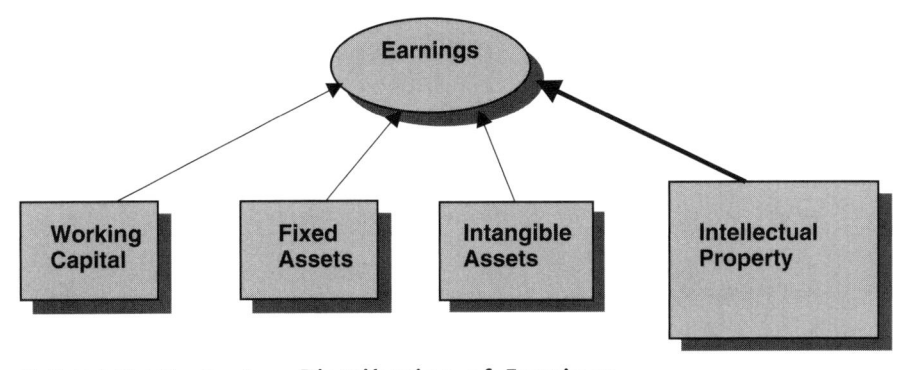

EXHIBIT 8.1   Distribution of Earnings

"invested capital" of the company. All of the assets comprising the business enterprise contribute to the commercialization of IP, by allowing for the creation and delivery of products or services, which generate revenue and profit. The ability of a company to sustain earnings makes it a valuable investment.[2] Estimating the portion of earnings attributed to specific IP can quantify the relative value of IP.

Exhibit 8.1 shows how the profits of an enterprise can be allocated to the different asset categories that comprise the enterprise. The amount of profits enjoyed by an enterprise is directly related to the existence of the different asset categories. Companies lacking any one category of assets would have different profits, because the earnings of a business are derived from exploiting its assets. The amount of assets in each category, along with the nature and quality of the assets, determines the level of earnings the business generates. For pharmaceutical and biotechnology companies, IP is the largest contributor. Exhibit 8.2 presents a more detailed illustration of a typical business enterprise framework.

Some of the key IP and intangible assets, specific to pharmaceutical and biotechnology companies, include

- Patented drugs and therapies on the market
- Patented drugs and therapies in the pipeline
- Established trademarks
- Clinical trial data and information
- Scientific databases
- Patent applications

Business Enterprise Framework

Business Enterprise = Working Capital + Fixed Capital + Intangible Assets & Intellectual Property

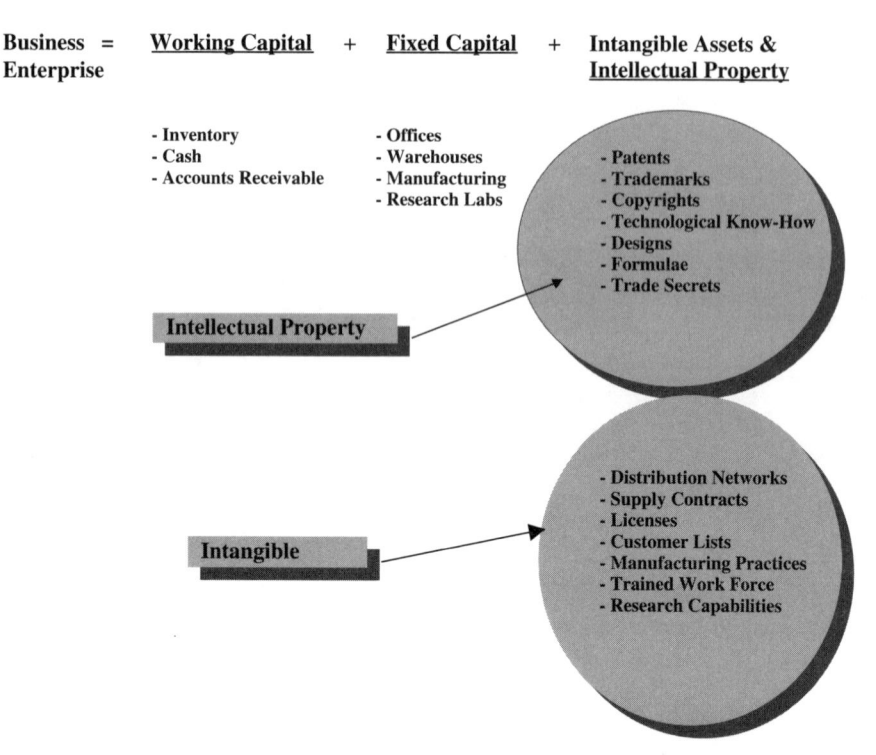

Working Capital
- Inventory
- Cash
- Accounts Receivable

Fixed Capital
- Offices
- Warehouses
- Manufacturing
- Research Labs

Intellectual Property
- Patents
- Trademarks
- Copyrights
- Technological Know-How
- Designs
- Formulae
- Trade Secrets

Intangible
- Distribution Networks
- Supply Contracts
- Licenses
- Customer Lists
- Manufacturing Practices
- Trained Work Force
- Research Capabilities

EXHIBIT 8.2 Typical Business Enterprise Framework

- Exclusive and non-exclusive licenses
- Co-marketing and promotion agreements
- Food and Drug Administration regulatory approvals

Beyond Commodity Earnings

Working capital, fixed assets, and intangible assets are commodity assets that all businesses can possess and exploit. A company possessing only these limited assets will enjoy only limited amounts of earnings, because of the competitive nature of commodities. A company that generates superior, or excess, earnings must have something special, usually in the form of IP, such as patented technology, trademarks, or copyrights. The contribution of excess earnings to commercial operations generally occurs in three ways:

Price premiums can be obtained from the sale of technology-based products, where the marketplace is willing to pay a higher price than it otherwise would, for products lacking the technologically-based enhancement of utility. When all, or a portion, of the premium survives manufacturing costs and operating expenses, the enhanced, bottom-line profit margins are considered to be directly attributed to the existence of unique technology, or other IP.

- *Cost savings* can enhance the bottom-line profits, though the marketplace may not provide a product price premium. When a technology allows for a product or service to be produced and/or delivered at a reduced cost, the enhanced earnings are attributed to the technology used in the operations.
- *Expanded market share* can also generate incrementally higher profit margins, from economies of scale that come from high volume production. This can occur even when premium product pricing, or manufacturing cost savings, are not possible.

Gravel quarries are generally an excellent example of a commodity business. The products delivered by quarries lack the enhanced utility introduced by technological IP. These companies possess the typical business enterprise asset categories previously discussed, except for IP. They may even possess extensive amounts of intangible assets, in the form of customer lists, corporate procedures, and favorable contracts. Yet the nature of their product places gravel quarries in a very competitive position, where excess earnings beyond those obtainable in a commodity business are not sustainable for the long term. Overall, profit margins in the quarry business are slim. The reason is the absence of IP.

Later in this chapter, we will show that the allocation of earnings, among the asset categories of a business enterprise, is the foundation of deriving royalty rates. The allocation is based on each asset category earning a fair rate of return on the value of the category. When the profits of the company are allocated, among the investment rate of return requirements for working capital, fixed and intangible assets, sometimes little earnings are available for allocation to IP. Such would be the case for a gravel quarry business enterprise. In other industries, like medical therapies, substantial amounts of earnings are still available, after the rate of return requirements of non-IP assets are satisfied. The excess amount of earnings is derived from the existence of IP. In many cases, technology is the driving force.

DRIVING FORCES BEHIND ROYALTY RATES

The primary forces driving the value of IP and royalty rates are listed below.[3] It is important to remember that these forces must be considered within the framework of the business enterprise previously discussed.

Amount of Profits

Duration of Profits

Risk Associated with the Expected Profits

Amount of profits is the economic benefit generated, by the subject IP, after allowing for the economic benefits derived from the investment in complementary assets[4] used in the business enterprise. A technology that requires less investment in fixed assets to achieve its potential is more valuable than a technology requiring large, complementary asset investments. A larger royalty rate is appropriate for a technology that can be commercialized, while using less complementary assets.

Duration of profits refers to the future period during which the economic benefit will continue. This can be determined by patent lives or technology obsolescence.

Risk of receiving the expected economic returns captures the investment rate-of-return requirements to associate with an invention, when calculating its value.

Listed below are some of the complex factors that should be reflected in technology pricing and valuation, even if only on a qualified basis, when negotiating royalty rates. Three economic factors are identified, along with a subset of factors for each of the primary ones.

- Economic Benefits Derived from the Technology
    - Benefits derived from complementary assets
    - Competitor efforts impacting the economic benefits
    - Consumer reactions
    - Management competency
    - Production efficiencies
    - Commercialization expenses
    - Commercialization time-frame requirements

- Duration of the Economic Benefits
  - Rapid technological obsolescence
  - Alternate technologies
  - Validity of patent risks
  - Changing consumer reactions
- Risk of Receiving the Economic Benefits
  - Technology risk
  - Economic risk
  - Regulatory risk
  - Market risk
  - Inflationary risk
  - Unexpected conditions and events

INFRINGEMENT DAMAGES ANALYSIS

The courts have provided some guidance for deriving royalty rates, in the form of a differential profit calculation, often referred to as the "analytical approach."

The Analytical Approach

This method for deriving a reasonable royalty was first expressed in a patent infringement court decision. While a license negotiation may be independent of any legal actions, insight can be gained from considering the royalty rate models that are used in legal proceedings. The analytical approach, according to the courts, determines a reasonable royalty by evaluating the difference between profits expected from infringing sales and a normal industry profit level. The analytical approach can be summarized by the following equation:

$$\text{Expected Profit Margin} - \text{Normal Profit Margin} = \text{Royalty Rate}$$

The analytical approach is a profit differential calculation, where the profits derived from use of the technology are subtracted from the profits that would be expected without access to the technology. The difference is attributed to the technology, and is considered by some as an indication of a royalty.

In *TWM Manufacturing v. Dura Corporation,* a royalty for damages was calculated, based on an analysis of the business plan of the infringer, prepared just prior to the onset of the infringing activity. The court discovered the profit expected from using the infringed technology by reviewing internal memorandums, written by top executives of the company. Internal memorandums showed that company management expected to earn gross profit margins of almost fifty-three percent from the proposed infringing sales. Operating profit margins were then calculated by subtracting overhead costs, to yield an expected profit margin of between thirty-seven and forty-two percent.

To find the portion of this profit level that should be provided as a royalty to the plaintiff, the court considered the standard, *normal,* profits earned in the industry at the time of infringement. These profit levels were determined to be between 6.6 and 12.5 percent, and were considered to represent profit margins that would be acceptable to firms operating in the industry. The remaining thirty percent of profits were found to represent a reasonable royalty from which to calculate infringement damages. On appeal, the federal circuit court affirmed.

The analytical approach can work well when normal industry profits are derived from the analysis of commodity products. The analysis requires that the benchmark commodity's profit margin be derived from products competing in the same, or similar, industry as the infringing product, for which a reasonable royalty is being sought. The benchmark profits should also reflect similar investment requirements in complementary assets; similar to those required to exploit the enhanced product, based on the infringed IP.

Hypothetical Example

Presented in Exhibit 8.3 are profit margin expectations, for the hypothetical Exciting Biotech, associated with commercialization of a new, patented drug therapy. The average expected profit margin is fifty percent. By subtracting this enhanced operating profit margin from an industry *norm,* the portion of profits that can be attributed to proprietary technology are isolated, and can serve as the basis for setting a royalty.

Presented in Exhibit 8.4 are the operating profit margins for a group of generic drug companies, producing commodity products. The products

| EXHIBIT 8.3 | NEW PRODUCT REVENUE FORECAST EXCITING BIOTECH, INC. ($ MILLIONS) |

	2006	2007	2008	2009	2010
Primary Market Revenues	0	25	100	300	400
Operating Profit	−25	9	50	175	225
Profit Margin	deficit	36%	50%	58%	56%
Average Profit Margin					**50%**

are competitively priced, mass produced, widely distributed, and provide their makers with lower profit margins in comparison to proprietary products. The profit margins were derived from information downloaded from the Reuters.com database on public corporations. As a group, the average profit margins of these companies can be looked at as the commodity profit margin for drugs without patent protection.

The analytical approach indicates a royalty rate of approximately 28.4 percent, calculated by subtracting the 21.6 percent generic drug company profit margin from the 50 percent profit margin expected by Exciting Biotech, from commercialization of the new proprietary invention. It is important to note that the 28.4 percent advantage is the starting point for royalty rate negotiations. This is the economic benefit that should be divided, or shared, between the licensor and the licensee. In infringement litigation, it can be argued that the entire 28.4 percent can be awarded as a reasonable royalty.

| EXHIBIT 8.4 | GENERIC DRUG COMPANIES OPERATING PROFIT MARGINS |

Company	Profit Margin
Barr Pharmaceuticals, Inc.	26.75%
Mylan Laboratories Inc.	24.1%
Watson Pharmaceuticals	14.0%
Average Profit Margin	**21.6%**

General Profit Margins

More data showing the profit differential between generic and patented drugs can be found in The Risk Management Association (RMA) Annual Statement Studies. RMA compiles information about the balance sheets and income statements of thousands of companies. The information is classified by Standard Industry Classifications (SIC), a U.S. government system developed by the Office of Management and Budget, for classification of commercial enterprises. A comparison of the operating profit margins for different company classifications can generally provide royalty rate insight. Two SIC classifications are described below.

Pharmaceutical Preparations (SIC #2834) are companies primarily engaged in manufacturing and processing drugs, in pharmaceutical preparations, for human or veterinary use. This broad classification likely includes companies that make and sell both patented and generic products.

Medicinal, Chemicals and Botanical Products (SIC #2833) are companies engaged in the manufacture of bulk organic and inorganic medicinal chemicals, and their derivatives and processing (grading, grinding, and milling), bulk botanical drugs, and herbs. This broad classification likely includes companies that make and sell non-proprietary products.

The RMA Annual Statement Studies (2003/2004) indicated that pharmaceuticals companies with annual sales over $50 million generated operating profit margins of nearly 14.4 percent in 2003. In comparison, companies classified as medical chemical companies earned no more than 6.6 percent of operating profit on sales. A general royalty rate of 7.8 percent is indicated by this broad comparison.[5]

GENERIC PRICING

Considering the price differential between proprietary drugs (under patent protection) and the same product, sold as a generic drug (after patent protection expires), provides additional information that supports a royalty rate. Generic drugs are the chemical equivalent of brand name products, for which patents have expired. The primary difference is the absence of patent protection. The following information indicates the enormous value of patent protection.

Eon Labs states that generic drugs sell for twenty to eighty percent below branded counterparts, depending on the number of generic equivalents in the marketplace.[6]

The Center for Medicare and Medicaid Services recently conducted a study, showing that using generic drugs in place of brand name drugs can save between forty-three and ninety-six percent. Details of the study are presented in Exhibit 8.5.[7]

A 2004 press release, from Leiner Health Products, reports that the company supplies nearly thirty retailers with ten mg Loratadine tablets, retailing for about thirty-seven cents per pill, compared to the branded equivalent, Claritin®, priced at ninety-six cents per pill. This represents a savings of fifty-nine cents per pill, or 61.5 percent.[8]

Business Week reported, in 1994, that the patent protection for the ulcer drug Tagamet® was about to expire, and "Mylan Laboratories is planning a clone of Tagamet® for half the price."[9] In the same story, *Business Week* reported "gross margins for generics are fifty to sixty percent, vs. ninety to ninety-five percent for branded products . . ." A profit differential analysis indicates a royalty rate of between thirty and forty-five percent.

Business Week also discussed a strategy being followed by the proprietary drug companies.[10] Faced with huge market share losses when a proprietary drug loses patent protection, these companies introduced their own versions of generics. *Business Week* said "the majors often price

EXHIBIT 8.5   GENERIC DRUG SAVINGS

Generic versus (*Brand Name*)	Brand Price	Generic Price	Savings %
Warfarin (*Coumadin*)	19.76	11.20	43%
Metformin (*Glucophage*)	76.65	18.24	76%
Furosemide (*Lasix*)	7.44	3.84	48%
Benazepril (*Lotesin*)	31.31	7.96	75%
Glyburide (*Micronase*)	18.88	5.63	70%
Lisinopril (*Prinivil*)	28.04	6.51	77%
Fluoxentine (*Prozac*)	106.26	4.18	96%
Enalapril (*Vasotec*)	46.14	6.10	87%
Verapamil hcl SR (*Verelan SR*)	62.76	20.83	67%
Lisinopril (*Zestril*)	29.01	9.86	66%

Source: U.S. Department of Health and Human Services, Center for Medicare and Medicaid Services. Medical Price Compare 09/27/04.

generics at only ten to twenty-five percent less than the brand-name product, while generics ideally should be half the full price."

Forbes reported in 1994 that patent protection for Naprosyn®, a $500 million (1992 annual sales) arthritis drug made by Syntex, expired in December 1993.[11] Prior to the loss of patent protection, the company introduced, in October 1993, a generic version of the drug, to try to ease the loss of its market share. A few months after the launch of Syntex's generic version, five other generic drug companies entered the market. Forbes said "Soon the generics were selling at one-tenth [ten percent] the price of Naprosyn®, and had over eighty percent of the market." A royalty rate of ninety percent is indicated by this information.

Pharmaceutical Business News, a medical and health industry publication, reported "Generic drugs typically cost thirty to fifty percent less than their brand-name counterparts."[12]

Chemical Marketing Reporter a pharmaceutical industry publication, reported "industry analysts agree that brands will continue to be new drug innovators, and generics will provide off-patent copies at one-fifth to one-half of the price."[13]

Comparison of drug prices between developed and third world countries also demonstrates the generic-versus-patented drug differential. A comparison of prices for HIV/AIDS medicines illustrates the fact, that the pharmaceutical companies sell their patented medicines at much higher prices than those charged by generic producers.

Glaxo prices 3TC® (Lamivudine) in the United States at $3,271 for a year's supply, per patient, but in India, generic manufacturers Cipla and Hetero Drugs charge $190 and $98, respectively, for a year's supply. The savings are 94 and 97 percent, respectively.[14]

Bristol-Myers Squibb sells Zerit® (Stavudine) in the United States for $3,589 for a year's supply, per patient. In India, Cipla and Hetero sell the generic version for $70 and $47, respectively. The savings are 98 percent, and almost 99 percent, respectively.[15]

Boehringer-Ingelheim sells Viramune® (Nevirapine) in the United States for $3,508, per patient, per year, while Cipla and Hetero sell the generic equivalent in India for $340 and $202, respectively. The savings is 90 percent for Cipla's product, and 94 percent for Hertero's version.[16]

Cipla offers a year supply of the generic versions of 3TC®, Zerit® and Viramune® for $350 to $600, compared to the price of the patented medicines, of between $10,000 and $15,000. The savings range between 94 and 97.7 percent.[17]

Another example of the price pressure provided by generic drugs can be illustrated by fluconazole. In Thailand, this generic drug costs twenty-nine cents, and in India, it costs sixty-four cents. The patented version costs $10.50 in Kenya, $27.00 in Guatemala, and $8.25 in South Africa.[18] When the Brazilian government began producing AIDS drugs generically, the price of equivalent patented products dropped by 79 percent.[19]

Profit differentials are just one way to calculate royalty rates.

CHAPTER 9

Investment Rates of Return and Royalty Rates

This section presents an approach for determining a royalty rate based on investment rate of returns. This analysis requires consideration of the profits expected from exploitation of the various assets of a business, including the technology that will be licensed. By allocating a fair rate of return to all of the integrated assets of a business, including the licensed technology, a fair rate of return for use of a specific patent can be derived and expressed as a royalty rate.

BASIC PRINCIPLES

The basic principles in this type of analysis involve looking at the total profits of a business, and allocating the profits among the different classes of assets used in the business. When a business demonstrates an ability to earn profits above that which would be expected from operating a commodity-oriented company, then the presence of IP, such as patented technology, is identified. An allocation of the total profits derived, from using all assets of the company, can attribute a portion of the profits to the technology of a business. When the profits attributed to technology are expressed as a percentage of revenue, royalty rate guidance is obtained.

The investment rate-of-return analysis yields an indication of a royalty rate for a technology license, after a fair return is earned on investment in the other assets of the business. Thus, a royalty rate conclusion, that is supported by an investment rate-of-return analysis, allows for payment of a royalty to a licensor, while still allowing a licensee to earn a fair investment rate-of-return on its own, non-licensed assets used in the business.

INVESTMENT RATE OF RETURN ROYALTY RATES

This section of the report explores the use of financial analysis techniques to derive royalty rates. The method is based on the idea of allocating the total earnings of a technology-based business, among the different asset categories employed by the business. Exhibit 9.1 starts with the concepts introduced earlier, and adds notations that will be used in the following paragraphs to develop the method.

The earnings of a business are derived from exploiting its assets. The number of assets in each category, along with the nature and quality of the assets, determines the level of earnings that the business generates. Working capital, fixed assets, and intangible assets are generally commodity-type assets, that all businesses can possess and exploit. As previously discussed, a company that possesses only these limited assets will enjoy only limited amounts of earnings, because of the competitive nature of commodity-dominated businesses.

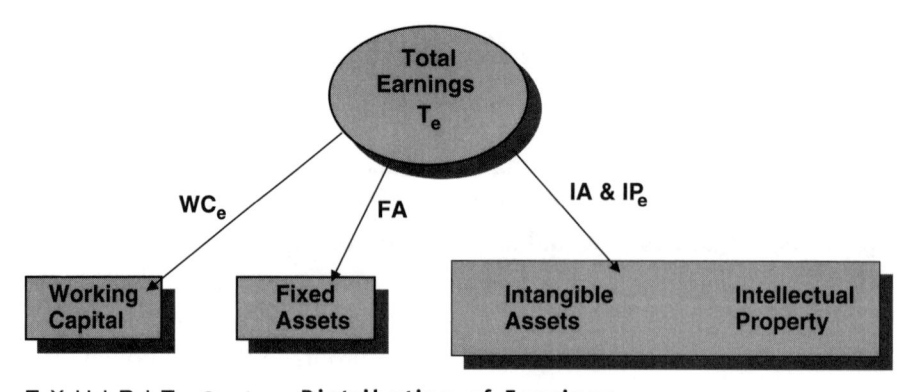

EXHIBIT 9.1   Distribution of Earnings

A company that generates superior earnings must have something special—IP, in the form of patented technology, trademarks, or copyrights. The distribution of earnings among the assets is primarily driven by the value of the assets, and the investment risk of the assets. The total earnings of the company (Te), as expressed below, are comprised of earnings derived from use of working capital (WCe), earnings derived from use of fixed assets (FAe), and earnings derived from use of intangible assets and IP (IA and IPe).

$$T_e = WC_e + FA_e + IA \text{ and } IP_e$$

The earnings associated with use of intangible assets and IP are represented by IA and IPe. This level of earnings can be further subdivided into earnings associated with the use of the intangible assets (IAe), and earnings associated with the use of IP (IPe) as shown below:

$$IA \text{ and } IP_e = IA_e + IP_e$$

ROYALTY RATES

An appropriate royalty rate is equal to the portion of IP_e that can be attributed to the use of the subject technology. The royalty rate to associate with a specific technology equals the earnings derived from the technology, divided by the revenue derived with the technology, as shown in Exhibit 9.2.

Specifically, a company lacking intangible assets and technology would be reduced to operating a commodity-oriented enterprise, where competition and lack of product distinction would severely limit the potential for profits. Conversely, companies possessing proprietary assets can throw-off the limitations of commodity-oriented operations, and earn superior profits.

When a portion of the profit stream of a company is attributed to the proprietary assets of a company, an indication of the profits contributed by the existence of the proprietary assets is provided, and a basis for a royalty is established, when the attributed profits are expressed as a percentage of the corresponding revenues. The total profits can be allocated among the different asset categories, based on the number of assets in each category, and the relative investment risk associated with each asset category.

Shown in Exhibit 9.3 is an allocation of the weighted average cost of

Excess Earnings as a Percent of Revenues

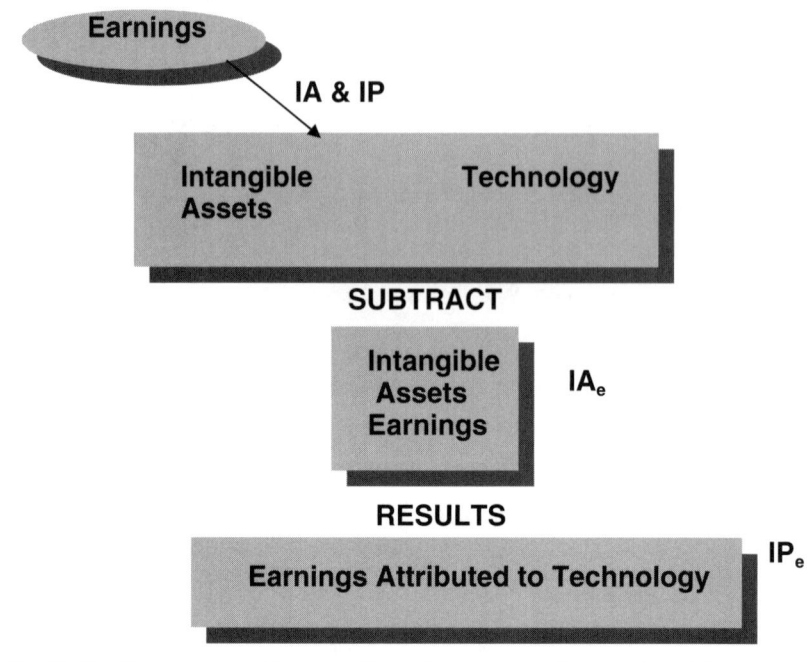

EXHIBIT 9.2 Excess Earnings as a Percent of Revenue

capital[1], for an example business enterprise, allocated among the business assets used in the business enterprise. The various rates of return assigned to each of the assets reflect their relative risk.[2] The relative returns provided by each asset category are also indicated.

Appropriate Return on Monetary Assets

The monetary assets of the business are its net working capital. This is the total of current assets minus current liabilities. Current assets are comprised of accounts receivable, inventories, cash, and short-term security investments. Offsetting this total are the current liabilities of the business, such as accounts payable, accrued salaries, and accrued expenses. The value of this asset category can usually be taken directly from a company's balance sheet.

Working capital is considered to be the most liquid asset of a business. Receivables are usually collected within sixty days and inventories are

EXHIBIT 9.3   EXAMPLE COMPANY, INC. REQUIRED RETURN ON INTANGIBLE ASSETS & INTELLECTUAL PROPERTY (IA & IP)

Asset Category	Amount	Percent	Required Return	Weighted Required Return	Allocated Weighted Return
Net Working Capital	10,000	10%	7.00%	0.70%	7.7%
Fixed Assets	20,000	20%	11.00%	2.20%	2.0%
IA & IP	70,000	70%	13.85%	9.70%	90.3%
Invested Capital	100,000	100%		12.60%	100.0%

usually turned over in ninety days. The cash component is immediately available, and security holdings can be converted to cash with a telephone call to the firm's broker. Further evidence of liquidity is the use of accounts receivable, and/or inventories, as collateral for loans. In addition, accounts receivable can be sold for immediate cash to factoring companies, at a discount on the book value. Given the relative liquidity of working capital, the amount of investment risk is inherently low. An appropriate rate of return to associate with the working capital component of the business enterprise is that which is available from investment in short term securities, of low risk levels. The rate available on ninety-day certificates of deposit, or money market funds, serves as an appropriate benchmark.

Appropriate Return on Tangible Assets

The tangible or fixed assets of the business are comprised of production machinery, warehouse equipment, transportation fleet, office buildings, office equipment, leasehold improvements, office equipment, and manufacturing plants. The value of this asset category may not be accurately reflected on company balance sheets. Aggressive depreciation policies may state the net book value at an amount lower than the fair market value, on which a return should be earned. Correction of this problem can be accomplished by estimating fair market value, somewhere in between original equipment costs and net book value. A midpoint between the two is usually a reasonable compromise.

```
┌─────────────────────────────────┐
│ Investment Rate of Return Associated │
│   with all Intangible Assets    │
│   and Intellectual Property of  │
│ Example Company, Inc. *Including* the │
│   Patented Therapeutic Drug     │
└─────────────────────────────────┘

             **Minus**

┌─────────────────────────────────┐
│ Investment Rate of Return Associated │
│   with all Intangible Assets    │
│   and Intellectual Property of  │
│   Surrogate Pharmaceutical      │
│   Companies *Excluding* the     │
│   Patented Therapeutic Drug     │
└─────────────────────────────────┘

             **Equals**

┌─────────────────────────────────┐
│ Royalty Rate Associated with the │
│      Patented Technology        │
└─────────────────────────────────┘
```

EXHIBIT 9.4   Example Company, Inc. Royalty Rate for Patented Therapeutic Drug

Accuracy in this area is not crucial for the drug business. The amount and value of tangible assets used in the industry is usually minor, relative to the value of revenue, earnings, markets, and the value of the entire business enterprise. An indication of the rate of return that is contributed by these assets can be pegged, at about the interest rate at which commercial banks make loans, using the fixed assets as collateral. While these assets are not as liquid as working capital, they can often be sold to other companies. This marketability allows a partial return on the investment in fixed assets, should the business fail.

Another aspect of relative risk-reduction relates to the strategic redeployment of fixed assets. Assets that can be redirected for use elsewhere in a corporation have a degree of versatility, which can still allow an economic contribution to be derived from their employment, even if it isn't from the originally intended purpose.

While these assets are more risky than working capital investments, they possess favorable characteristics, which must be considered in the weighted, average cost of capital allocation. Fixed assets that are very specialized in nature must reflect higher levels of risk, which of course demands a higher rate of return. Specialized assets are those which are not easily redeployed for other commercial exploitation, or liquidated to other businesses, for other uses.

Appropriate Return on Intangible Assets and Intellectual Property

Intangible assets can be considered the most risky asset components of the overall business enterprise. These assets may have little, if any, liquidity, and poor versatility for redeployment elsewhere in the business.[3] This increases their risk. Customized computer software for tracking the results of clinical studies may have very little liquidation value if the company fails. The investment in trained employees who know how to get government approvals may be altogether lost, along with the value of other elements directly related to the success of the business. A higher rate of return on these assets is therefore required.

An appropriate investment rate of return is then derived, and assigned to the intangible assets and IP of the business, including the infringing technology, by using the weighted average cost of capital for the business, the return on fixed assets deemed appropriate, and the return on working capital deemed appropriate. The earnings associated with the IP, and intangible assets of the company, are then calculated as depicted in Exhibit 9.3. Conversion of these earnings into a royalty rate can be accomplished by dividing earnings by the associated revenue.

Exhibit 9.3 tells us that over ninety percent of the profits of Example Company are derived from intangible assets and IP. If Example Company shows operating profits of twenty percent on sales, then eighteen percent of sales should be attributed to intangible assets and IP. Depending on the characteristics of the subject technology, it may deserve to have the majority of the eighteen percent attributed to its contribution to the business. The final allocation requires considering the amount, types, and importance of other IP used in the business. The royalty just derived may include earnings derived by the business from exploitation of IP, and intangible assets unrelated to specific technology.

ROYALTY RATE FOR THE SPECIFIC PATENTED INVENTION

The next step answers the question "How much of a royalty rate should be subtracted from the derived eighteen percent royalty rate, to isolate the portion that is attributable to only the subject patents?" It must be remembered that the eighteen percent rate is for all of the intangible assets and IP possessed by Example Company, including use of the patented invention.

The answer to the question in the preceding paragraph can be estimated by focusing on a company operating in a similar industry, that possesses most of the intangible assets found in a typical company. However the selected company must be one that does not possess, or use, proprietary and patented inventions.

By duplicating the same analysis presented in Exhibit 8.4 for a surrogate company, we can isolate the amount of income to associate with all intangible assets and IP, *except* for the subject patent. When this analysis was concluded, the royalty rate to associate with everything other than the subject patent was ten percent. The difference is the royalty rate to associate with the subject patent, or eight percent:

When IP_e includes earnings from non-licensed IP, another step is needed to develop a proxy, for earnings that represent the contribution from the non-infringing IP_e. Attribution of earnings for intangible assets can be accomplished by an investment rate-of-return analysis, that derives a royalty for a company that possesses intangible assets, but not technology. These earnings can serve as a proxy for the intangible assets earnings of the subject company. When they are subtracted from the earnings associated with IA and IP_e, then only the earnings for IP_e are left. When these remaining earnings are converted to a royalty, a royalty rate for use of specific technology is indicated.

BENEFITS OF INVESTMENT RATE-OF-RETURN ANALYSIS

An investment rate-of-return analysis enhances royalty rate determination by:

- considering the investment risk associated with the business, and industry environment in which the licensed technology will be used.

- reflecting specific commercialization factors associated with the licensed technology, as embedded in forecasts associated with sales, production costs, and operating expenses.
- allowing for an investment return to be earned on the fixed assets used in the business.
- allowing for an investment return to be earned on the working capital assets used in the business.
- allowing for an investment return to be earned on the other intangible assets and IP used in the business, *other than* the subject patent.

CHAPTER 10

Discounted Cash Flow Analysis and Royalty Rates

A variation of the investment rate-of-return analysis can also be used for royalty rate derivation. This alternate method makes use of a discounted cash flow analysis, which converts a stream of expected cash flow into a present value. The conversion is accomplished by using a discount rate, reflecting the risk of the expected cash flow. In addition to the benefits previously listed, from using an investment rate-of-return analysis, the discounted cash flow analysis also reflects the

- time period during which economic benefits will be obtained.
- timing and amount of capital expenditure investments.
- timing and amount of working capital investments.
- timing and amount of other investments in intellectual property and intangible assets not associated with the subject technology.

The basis of all value is cash. The net amount of cash flow thrown-off by a business is central to corporate value. Net cash flow, also called "free cash flow," is the amount of cash remaining, after reinvestment in the business, to sustain continued viability of the business. Net cash flow can be used for dividends, charity contributions, or diversification investments. Net cash flow is not needed to continue fueling the business. Aggregation of all future net cash flow derived from operating the business, modified with respect to the time value of money, represents the value of a business. A basic, net cash flow calculation is depicted below:

NET SALES minus
MANUFACTURING COSTS equals
GROSS PROFITS

GROSS PROFITS minus
MARKETING EXPENSES and
GENERAL OVERHEAD EXPENSES and
ADMINISTRATION EXPENSES and
SELLING EXPENSES equals
OPERATING PROFITS

OPERATING PROFITS minus
INCOME TAXES equals
NET INCOME

NET INCOME plus
DEPRECIATION equals
GROSS CASH FLOW

GROSS CASH FLOW minus
ADDITIONS TO WORKING CAPITAL and
ADDITIONS TO FIXED PLANT INVESTMENT equals
NET CASH FLOW

Sales represent the revenue dollars collected by the company from providing products or services to customers. Net sales is the amount of revenue that remains after discounts, returns, and refunds.

Manufacturing costs are the primary costs associated with making or providing the product or service. Included in this expense category are expenses associated with labor, raw materials, manufacturing plant costs, and all other expenses directly related to transforming raw materials into finished goods.

Gross profit is the difference between net sales and manufacturing costs. The level of gross profits reflects manufacturing efficiencies and a general level of product profitability. It does not, however, reflect the ultimate commercial success of a product or service. Many other expenses associated with commercial success are not accounted for at the gross profit level. Other expenses contributing to successful commercialization of a product include

- research expenses associated with creating new products, and enhancing old ones.
- marketing expenses required for motivating customers to purchase the products or service.
- general overhead expenses required for providing basic corporate support for commercialization activities.
- selling expenses associated with salaries, commissions, and other activities, that keep product moving into the hands of customers.

Operating profits reflect the amount left over after non-manufacturing expenses are subtracted from gross profits.

Income taxes are expense of doing business, and must be accounted for in valuing any business initiative.

Depreciation expense is calculated based on the remaining useful life of equipment purchased for business purposes. It is a non-cash expense that allocates the original amount invested in fixed assets to annual operations. Depreciation is calculated to account for the deterioration of fixed assets, as they are used to produce, market, sell, deliver, and administer the process of generating sales. Depreciation accounts for the using-up of assets. It is called a "non-cash" expense, because the cash associated with the expense was disbursed long ago, at the time that fixed assets were purchased and installed. The depreciation expense is subtracted before reaching operating profit, so that income taxes will reflect depreciation as an expense of doing business.

Gross cash flow is calculated by adding the depreciation expense, previously subtracted to calculated operating income, back into the after-tax income of the business. Gross cash flow represents the total amount of cash that the business generates each year. Additions to working capital, and additions to fixed plant investment, are investments in the business required to fuel continued production capabilities. Net cash flow is everything that remains of gross cash flow, after accounting for reinvestment in the business for fixed plant and working capital additions.

Value is derived from net cash flow by converting the expected amounts into a present value, using discount rates that reflect investment risk and time value of money, as previously discussed in the investment rate-of-return section of this chapter.

GENERIC AND MATURE COMMODITY CORPORATE VALUE

Consider the discounted cash flow analyses, presented in Exhibits 10.1 through 10.4, as a simple example of using discounted cash flow analysis for royalty rate derivation, where the licensed technology is on the cusp of commercialization.

Exhibit 10.1 represents the future net cash flow for Generic and Mature Commodity Corporation, as it currently operates. The sales, expenses, and earnings for the company reflect the commodity-like nature of the current business and its products. Product prices are under pressure from strong competition, translating into low profitability. Strong competition also severely limits the opportunity for the company to achieve any substantial growth in the future.

The present value calculation, contained in Exhibit 10.1, shows a value for the company at $190 million, using a discount rate of thirteen percent. The calculation of the value of the company includes the present value of the net cash flow expected after year eleven. Constant growth, reflecting inflation and minimal volume growth in perpetuity, is captured in the eleventh year's discount rate factor. The $190 million value equals the aggregate value of all the assets of the company. This amount indicates that the company has earned its required weighted average cost of capital, and an excess present value of $190 million.

Generic and Mature Commodity Corporation is planning to embark on a major business initiative, with the introduction of a patented product using new technology, changing itself into a company that has both commodity and fast-growth products. It will continue to offer its commodity product, but will add a new, proprietary product to its offerings. The underlying technology for the new product will be licensed from another company.

Exhibit 10.2 represents the present value of the company, including the net cash flow from the existing operations, and the net cash flow from

Exhibit 10.1 (DCF #1)
Generic and Mature Commodity Corp.
Business Enterprise Value

Year		1	2	3	4	5	6	7	8	9	10
Sales		$500,000	$515,000	$530,450	$546,364	$562,754	$579,637	$597,026	$614,937	$633,385	$652,387
Cost of Sales		$300,000	$309,000	$318,270	$327,818	$337,653	$347,782	$358,216	$368,962	$380,031	$391,432
Gross Profit		$200,000	$206,000	$212,180	$218,545	$225,102	$231,855	$238,810	$245,975	$253,354	$260,955
Gross Profit Margin		40%	40%	40%	40%	40%	40%	40%	40%	40%	40%
Operating Expenses:											
General and Admin.		$60,000	$61,800	$63,654	$65,564	$67,531	$69,556	$71,643	$73,792	$76,006	$78,286
R&D		$10,000	$10,300	$10,609	$10,927	$11,255	$11,593	$11,941	$12,299	$12,668	$13,048
Marketing		$50,000	$51,500	$53,045	$54,636	$56,275	$57,964	$59,703	$61,494	$63,339	$65,239
Selling		$40,000	$41,200	$42,436	$43,709	$45,020	$46,371	$47,762	$49,195	$50,671	$52,191
Operating Income		$40,000	$41,200	$42,436	$43,709	$45,020	$46,371	$47,762	$49,195	$50,671	$52,191
Operating Profit Margin		8%	8%	8%	8%	8%	8%	8%	8%	8%	8%
Provision for Income Taxes		$16,000	$16,480	$16,974	$17,484	$18,008	$18,548	$19,105	$19,678	$20,268	$20,876
Net Income		$24,000	$24,720	$25,462	$26,225	$27,012	$27,823	$28,657	$29,517	$30,402	$31,315
Net Profit Margin		5%	5%	5%	5%	5%	5%	5%	5%	5%	5%
Cash Flow Calculation											
+ Depreciation		$0	$1,000	$1,386	$1,784	$2,194	$3,194	$2,629	$2,690	$2,753	$2,819
- Working Capital Additions		$0	$1,500	$1,545	$1,591	$1,639	$5,000	$1,739	$1,791	$1,845	$1,900
- Capital Expenditures		$0	$5,000	$1,931	$1,989	$2,049	$5,000	$2,174	$2,239	$2,306	$2,375
Net Cash Flow		$24,000	$19,220	$23,372	$24,429	$25,518	$21,016	$27,373	$28,177	$29,005	$29,858
Discount Factor	13%	0.8849558	0.7831467	0.6930502	0.6133187	0.5427599	0.4803185	0.4250606	0.3761599	0.3328848	2.2360642
Present Value		$21,239	$15,052	$16,198	$14,983	$13,850	$10,095	$11,635	$10,599	$9,655	$66,764
Total Present Value		**$190,070**									

Exhibit 10.2 (DCF #2)
Generic and Mature Commodity Corp.
with New Product Based on Licensed Technology
Business Enterprise Value without Royalty Payment

Year	1	2	3	4	5	6	7	8	9	10
Sales	$500,000	$515,000	$530,450	$546,364	$562,754	$579,637	$597,026	$614,937	$633,385	$652,387
Cost of Sales	$300,000	$309,000	$318,270	$327,818	$337,653	$347,782	$358,216	$368,962	$380,031	$391,432
Gross Profit	$200,000	$206,000	$212,180	$218,545	$225,102	$231,855	$238,810	$245,975	$253,354	$260,955
New Product Sales	$5,000	$25,000	$75,000	$100,000	$110,000	$121,000	$133,100	$137,093	$141,206	$145,442
New Product COS	$2,250	$11,250	$33,750	$45,000	$49,500	$54,450	$59,895	$61,692	$63,543	$65,449
New Product Gross Profit	$2,750	$13,750	$41,250	$55,000	$60,500	$66,550	$73,205	$75,401	$77,663	$79,993
Total Sales	$505,000	$540,000	$605,450	$646,364	$672,754	$700,637	$730,126	$752,030	$774,591	$797,829
Total Cost of Sales	$302,250	$320,250	$352,020	$372,818	$387,153	$402,232	$418,111	$430,654	$443,574	$456,881
Total Gross Profit	$202,750	$219,750	$253,430	$273,545	$285,602	$298,405	$312,015	$321,376	$331,017	$340,948
Total Gross Profit Margin	40%	41%	42%	42%	42%	43%	43%	43%	43%	43%
Operating Expenses:										
General and Admin.	$60,600	$64,800	$72,654	$77,564	$80,731	$84,076	$87,615	$90,244	$92,951	$95,739
R&D	$10,000	$5,000	$12,109	$12,927	$13,455	$14,013	$14,603	$15,041	$15,492	$15,957
Marketing	$50,500	$54,000	$60,545	$64,636	$67,275	$70,064	$73,013	$75,203	$77,459	$79,783
Selling	$40,400	$43,200	$48,436	$51,709	$53,820	$56,051	$58,410	$60,162	$61,967	$63,826
Operating Income	$41,250	$52,750	$59,686	$66,709	$70,320	$74,201	$78,375	$80,726	$83,148	$85,643
Operating Profit Margin	8%	10%	11%	12%	12%	13%	13%	13%	13%	13%
Provision for Income Taxes	$16,500	$21,100	$23,874	$26,684	$28,128	$29,680	$31,350	$32,291	-$238,066	$34,257
Net Income	$24,750	$31,650	$35,812	$40,025	$42,192	$44,521	$47,025	$48,436	$15,491	$51,386
Net Profit Margin	5%	6%	7%	7%	7%	8%	8%	8%	$77,459	8%
									$154,918	
Cash Flow Calculation										
+ Depreciation	$0	$1,000	$2,636	$3,659	$4,319	$5,319	$5,056	$3,967	$3,509	$3,430
- Working Capital Additions	$0	$3,500	$6,545	$4,091	$2,639	$2,788	$2,949	$2,190	$2,256	$2,324
- Capital Expenditures	$20,000	$5,000	$8,181	$5,114	$3,299	$5,000	$3,686	$2,738	$2,820	$2,905
Net Cash Flow	$4,750	$24,150	$23,722	$34,479	$40,573	$42,051	$45,446	$47,475	$75,891	$49,587
Discount Factor 14%	0.877193	0.7694675	0.6749715	0.5920803	0.5193687	0.4555865	0.3996373	0.3505591	0.3075079	1.8967415
Present Value	$4,167	$18,583	$16,011	$20,414	$21,072	$19,158	$18,162	$16,643	$23,337	$94,053
Total Present Value	$251,601									

148

the new product initiative. Additional sales, manufacturing costs, and expenses are reflected in the analysis. Additions to working capital, and fixed assets required for the new product commercialization effort, are also reflected.

Included in the analysis are research and development expenses, needed to prove the technology, and obtain FDA approvals.[1] As a result of the initiative, the present value of the company increases to $251.6 million. The higher value reflects the added revenue and earnings of the new product, at the higher profit margins of the new product. A comparison of Exhibit 10.1 and Exhibit 10.2 shows that research, marketing, working capital additions, and fixed asset additions are all higher—and by more than just a proportional share of the higher sales forecasts. This is especially true for the early years in the discounted cash flow analysis, because the new product initially does not contribute significant sales volume, but definitely has expenses.

NEW PHARMAPROD CORPORATION ROYALTY RATE

What royalty rate should the company pay for use of the new product technology? The highest amount of royalty the company should be willing to pay for the licensed technology is shown in Exhibit 10.3. A royalty expense of 18.3 percent of sales associated with the new product represents a royalty expense, and yields a present value of $190 million for the business—the initial value of the company. At this royalty, the company has earned a return on the additional investment required to commercialize the new product technology, and not a penny more. A royalty rate of less than 18.3 percent would increase the value of the company.

In Exhibit 10.4, the maximum royalty rate that could be paid, without harming company value, is determined assuming a first-year license fee of $10 million associated with the license. In this case, the maximum royalty rate would be seventeen percent of sales.

RISK-ADJUSTED NET PRESENT VALUE

In the previous section, investment risk was reflected in the discount rate. The fourteen percent discount rate, used in Exhibits 1 through 4, indicated

Exhibit 10.3 (DCF #3)
Generic and Mature Commodity Corp.
with New Product Based on Licensed Technology
Business Enterprise Value with Royalty Payment

Year		1	2	3	4	5	6	7	8	9	10
Sales		$500,000	$515,000	$530,450	$546,364	$562,754	$579,637	$597,026	$614,937	$633,385	$652,387
Cost of Sales		$300,000	$309,000	$318,270	$327,818	$337,653	$347,782	$358,216	$368,962	$380,031	$391,432
Gross Profit		$200,000	$206,000	$212,180	$218,545	$225,102	$231,855	$238,810	$245,975	$253,354	$260,955
New Product Sales		**$5,000**	**$25,000**	**$75,000**	**$100,000**	**$110,000**	**$121,000**	**$133,100**	**$137,093**	**$141,206**	**$145,442**
New Product COS		**$2,000**	**$10,000**	**$30,000**	**$40,000**	**$44,000**	**$48,400**	**$53,240**	**$54,837**	**$56,482**	**$58,177**
New Product Gross Profit		**$3,000**	**$15,000**	**$45,000**	**$60,000**	**$66,000**	**$72,600**	**$79,860**	**$82,256**	**$84,723**	**$87,265**
Total Sales		$505,000	$540,000	$605,450	$646,364	$672,754	$700,637	$730,126	$752,030	$774,591	$797,829
Total Cost of Sales		$302,000	$319,000	$348,270	$367,818	$381,653	$396,182	$411,456	$423,799	$436,513	$449,609
Total Gross Profit		$203,000	$221,000	$257,180	$278,545	$291,102	$304,455	$318,670	$328,231	$338,077	$348,220
Total Gross Profit Margin		40%	41%	42%	43%	43%	43%	44%	44%	44%	44%
Operating Expenses:											
General and Admin.		$60,600	$64,800	$72,654	$77,564	$80,731	$84,076	$87,615	$90,244	$92,951	$95,739
R&D		**$10,000**	**$5,000**	**$12,109**	**$12,927**	**$13,455**	**$14,013**	**$14,603**	**$15,041**	**$15,492**	**$15,957**
Royalty Payments	18.3%	**$914**	**$4,568**	**$13,704**	**$18,272**	**$20,099**	**$22,109**	**$24,319**	**$25,049**	**$25,800**	**$26,574**
Marketing		$50,500	$54,000	$60,545	$64,636	$67,275	$70,064	$73,013	$75,203	$77,459	$79,783
Selling		$40,400	$43,200	$48,436	$51,709	$53,820	$56,051	$58,410	$60,162	$61,967	$63,826
Operating Income		$40,586	$49,432	$49,732	$53,438	$55,722	$58,142	$60,711	$62,532	$64,408	$66,340
Operating Profit Margin		8%	10%	9%	10%	10%	10%	10%	10%	10%	10%
Provision for Income Taxes		$16,235	$19,773	$19,893	$21,375	$22,289	$23,257	$24,284	$25,013	$25,763	$26,536
Net Income		$24,352	$29,659	$29,839	$32,063	$33,433	$34,885	$36,426	$37,519	$38,645	$39,804
Net Profit Margin		5%	6%	6%	6%	6%	6%	6%	6%	6%	6%
Cash Flow Calculation											
+ Depreciation		$0	$1,000	$2,636	$3,659	$4,319	$5,319	$5,056	$3,967	$3,509	$3,430
- Working Capital Additions		$0	$3,500	$6,545	$4,091	$2,639	$2,788	$2,949	$2,190	$2,256	$2,324
- Capital Expenditures		**$20,000**	$5,000	$8,181	$5,114	$3,299	$5,000	$3,686	$2,738	$2,820	$2,905
Net Cash Flow		$4,352	$22,159	$17,749	$26,516	$31,814	$32,416	$34,847	$36,558	$37,077	$38,005
Discount Factor	14%	0.877193	0.7694675	0.6749715	0.5920803	0.5193687	0.4555865	0.3996373	0.3505591	0.3075079	0.2696561
Present Value		$3,817	$17,051	$11,980	$15,700	$16,523	$14,768	$13,926	$12,816	$11,402	$72,087
Total Present Value		**$190,070**									

Exhibit 10.4 (DCF #4)
Generic and Mature Commodity Corp.
with New Product Based on Licensed Technology
Business Enterprise Value with License Fee & Royalty Payment

Year		1	2	3	4	5	6	7	8	9	10
Sales		$500,000	$515,000	$530,450	$546,364	$562,754	$579,637	$597,026	$614,937	$633,385	$652,387
Cost of Sales		$300,000	$309,000	$318,270	$327,818	$337,653	$347,782	$358,216	$368,962	$380,031	$391,432
Gross Profit		$200,000	$206,000	$212,180	$218,545	$225,102	$231,855	$238,810	$245,975	$253,354	$260,955
New Product Sales		$5,000	$25,000	$75,000	$100,000	$110,000	$121,000	$133,100	$137,093	$141,206	$145,442
New Product COS		$2,000	$10,000	$30,000	$40,000	$44,000	$48,400	$53,240	$54,837	$56,482	$58,177
New Product Gross Profit		$3,000	$15,000	$45,000	$60,000	$66,000	$72,600	$79,860	$82,256	$84,723	$87,265
Total Sales		$505,000	$540,000	$605,450	$646,364	$672,754	$700,637	$730,126	$752,030	$774,591	$797,829
Total Cost of Sales		$302,000	$319,000	$348,270	$367,818	$381,653	$396,182	$411,456	$423,799	$436,513	$449,609
Total Gross Profit		$203,000	$221,000	$257,180	$278,545	$291,102	$304,455	$318,670	$328,231	$338,077	$348,220
Total Gross Profit Margin		40%	41%	42%	43%	43%	43%	44%	44%	44%	44%
Operating Expenses:											
General and Admin.		$60,600	$64,800	$72,654	$77,564	$80,731	$84,076	$87,615	$90,244	$92,951	$95,739
R&D		$10,000	$5,000	$12,109	$12,927	$13,455	$14,013	$14,603	$15,041	$15,492	$15,957
Royalty Payments	17%	$10,000	$4,266	$12,799	$17,065	$18,772	$20,649	$22,714	$23,395	$24,097	$24,820
Marketing		$50,500	$54,000	$60,545	$64,636	$67,275	$70,064	$73,013	$75,203	$77,459	$79,783
Selling		$40,400	$43,200	$48,436	$51,709	$53,820	$56,051	$58,410	$60,162	$61,967	$63,826
Operating Income		$31,500	$49,734	$50,637	$54,644	$57,049	$59,602	$62,317	$64,186	$66,112	$68,095
Operating Profit Margin		6%	10%	10%	10%	10%	10%	10%	10%	10%	10%
Provision for Income Taxes		$12,600	$19,894	$20,255	$21,858	$22,820	$23,841	$24,927	$25,674	$26,445	$27,238
Net Income		$18,900	$29,840	$30,382	$32,786	$34,229	$35,761	$37,390	$38,512	$39,667	$40,857
Net Profit Margin		4%	6%	6%	6%	6%	6%	6%	6%	6%	6%
Cash Flow Calculation											
+ Depreciation		$0	$1,000	$2,636	$3,659	$4,319	$5,319	$5,056	$3,967	$3,509	$3,430
- Working Capital Additions		$0	$3,500	$6,545	$4,091	$2,639	$2,788	$2,949	$2,190	$2,256	$2,324
- Capital Expenditures		$20,000	$5,000	$8,181	$5,114	$3,299	$5,000	$3,686	$2,738	$2,820	$2,905
Net Cash Flow		-$1,100	$22,340	$18,292	$27,240	$32,610	$33,292	$35,811	$37,551	$38,099	$39,058
Discount Factor	14%	0.877193	0.7694675	0.6749715	0.5920803	0.5193687	0.4555865	0.3996373	0.3505591	0.3075079	1.8967415
Present Value		-$965	$17,190	$12,347	$16,128	$16,937	$15,167	$14,311	$13,164	$11,716	$74,084
Total Present Value		$190,079									

that the new proprietary product didn't add much additional risk to the value of the company. When new initiatives involve unproven technologies, risk of market rejection, or regulatory hurdles, a substantial discount rate is appropriate. Business initiatives at early stages might easily require discount rates of fifty percent, venture capital rates.

Instead of reflecting investment risk in the discount rate, there is another way. Use a standard industry discount rate, reflecting typical industry risk and rewards, then introduce a probability-of-success factor into the calculations.

Some industries have established success rates for new inventions. Some companies have historic data, allowing for creation of their own unique success rates. These success rates can be converted into factors, reflecting the unique risk associated with a unique project. The pharmaceutical industry is a classic example.

This next section shows how to implement a risk adjusted net present value analysis, using a standard industry discount rate and probability factors. While this section focuses on the pharmaceutical industry, the exact same method can be used for any business initiative, where success rate data can be estimated.

Incorporation of clinical trial success rates is a means for applying risk-adjusted, net present value to pharmaceuticals and biotechnology initiatives.

Drug development is expensive, time-consuming, complex and risky. The drug research process is categorized by the following development stages: Preclinical Testing, Phase I, II and III clinical trials, and Regulatory Review by the Food and Drug Administration (FDA). Sometimes the FDA asks for Phase IV clinical trials, to gain more information about side effects, or how the new compound interacts with other medicines. Before any new medical product can hit the market, the FDA must approve it. New products start out as new molecular (biological-based) entities (NME), or new chemical entities (NCEs). To gain FDA approval for commercialization, clinical trials are typically performed on humans and animals in three phases.

> *Phase I*—Healthy volunteers are given a new compound, to determine toxicity and proper dosage. Information about absorption, distribution, metabolism, and excretion is obtained. A small number of volunteers are used for this first phase, between twenty and eighty people. This phase typically takes a year. Costs are between $8,000 and $15,000 per test subject, plus $500,000 for supplemental animal studies.[2]

Phase II—If the Phase I trial shows promising results, then one hundred to three hundred patients are given the new compound. More information is obtained about efficacy, optimal dosage, side effects, and regimen. This phase typically takes two years. Costs are again between $8,000 and $15,000 per test subject, plus $1 million for supplemental animal studies.[3]

Phase III—If the new compound passes Phase II, it is then given to thousands of patients, to confirm efficacy, monitor long-term side effects, and confirm safety. Costs per test subject are between $4,000 and $7,500. Supplemental animal studies are approximately $1.5 million,[4] and this phase takes three years.[5]

FDA Approval—Once all the clinical trials are completed, approval for commercialization must be obtained from the FDA. This final hurdle can take between one and two years. Costs are between $800,000 and $1.8 million, plus a $300,000 fee for the Prescription Drug User Fee Act II.

SUCCESS RATES

A large amount of data exists about clinical trial success rates. The Tufts University Center for the Study of Drug Delivery periodically publishes summaries of this data. Success rates for NCEs vary by therapeutic class. On average, for NCEs entering into Phase I clinical trials, the success rate for ultimately becoming a commercialized product is 22.6 percent. For NCEs in Phase II the success rate is 32.7 percent, and for NCEs in Phase III trials the success rate is 78.5 percent. After Phase III is completed, there is still a chance the FDA might not approve the NCE. The data show the FDA approves eighty percent of all NCEs submitted. The FDA typically takes years to review data and process an approval (see Exhibit 10.5).

The chances of success for a preclinical NCE are more difficult to estimate. Obviously, these NCEs are less likely to be successful than Phase I NCEs, but the data on preclinicals is not exact. Drug companies investigating an NCE, never reaching Phase I, might never publicize the failure. As such, preclinical data is difficult to accurately find. Nonetheless, the Pharmaceutical Research and Manufacturers of America (PhRMA) cites the success rate of preclinical NCEs at ten percent.

Exhibit 10.6 shows data available regarding success rates for specific categories of therapeutic classes.

154 CHAPTER 10 DISCOUNTED CASH FLOW ANALYSIS

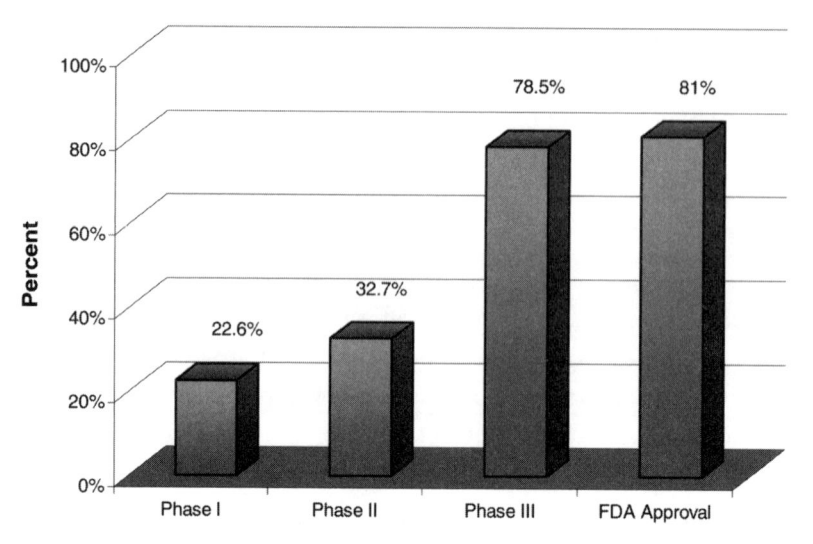

[Bar chart showing: Phase I: 22.6%, Phase II: 32.7%, Phase III: 78.5%, FDA Approval: 81%]

Source: DiMasi, J. A. Risk in new drug development: Approval success rates for investigational drugs. *Clinical Pharmacology & Therapeutics,* Fig. 8, May 2001, 69:5. ©Elsevier. Used with permission.

EXHIBIT 10.5   **Approval Success Rates for Different Clinical Phases**

EXHIBIT 10.6   CURRENT AND MAXIMUM POSSIBLE SUCCESS RATES BY THERAPEUTIC CLASS FOR SELF-ORIGINATED NCEs WITH INDS FIRST FILED FROM 1981 TO 1992

Therapeutic Class	NCEs	Approved NCEs	Open NCEs	Current Success Rate	Maximum Success Rate
Analgesic/anesthetic	49	10	4	20.4%	28.6%
Anti-infective	57	16	3	28.1%	33.3%
Antineoplastic	38	6	6	15.8%	31.6%
Cardiovascular	120	21	6	17.5%	22.5%
Central Nervous System	110	16	14	14.5%	27.3%
Endocrine	33	6	4	18.2%	30.3%
Gastrointestinal	15	3	2	20.0%	33.3%
Immunologic	13	2	0	15.4%	15.4%
Respiratory	25	3	0	12.0%	12.0%
Miscellaneous	43	3	4	7.0%	16.3%

Source: DiMasi, J. A. Risk in new drug development: Approval success rates for investigational drugs, *Clinical Pharmacology & Therapeutics,* Table 1, May 2001, 69:5. ©Elsevier. Used with permission.

SUCCESS RATE ADJUSTED DCF EXAMPLE

Incorporating success rates into a discounted cash flow can be accomplished, as illustrated in the following example. At different stages of development, there is strong interest in knowing the value of the project. The first step is to start at the end.

A discounted cash flow calculation, as previously demonstrated in this book, might be used to find the fair market value of a new compound, at the date of commercialization. Assume, for example, that at the start of commercialization—the end of the development process—a highly profitable therapy is expected in the marketplace. Commercialization is expected to run for twelve years, before expiration of the underlying patents. All research, clinical trials, and regulatory hurdles have been successfully completed. Consequently, no technical or regulatory risk exists at the commercialization date. Market acceptance is strongly anticipated and the DCF analysis indicates a huge amount of value ($1 billion) for the new therapy, at the future date when commercialization begins. This is the starting point for determining the value at different developmental stages. Finding the value at the different stages of development can be graphically displayed, as shown in Exhibit 10.7. Success rates for this example are based on data developed and published by DiMasi.[6]

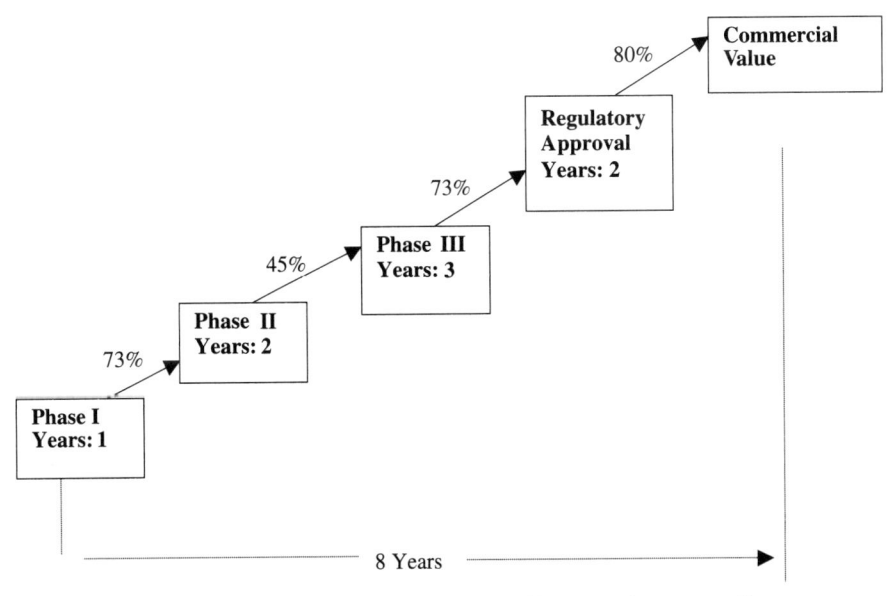

EXHIBIT 10.7 **Value at the Different Stages of Development**

EXHIBIT 10.8 VALUATION OF NEW COMPOUND USING SUCCESS RATE ADJUSTED PRESENT VALUE CALCULATIONS (DOLLARS IN MILLIONS)

Stage	Success Rate	Discount Years	Discounted Factor	Success Rate & Research Value	Cost	FMV
Commercial Value	100%	0	1.000	$1,000	$0	$1,000
FDA Approval	80%	1	0.893	$714	$2	$712
Phase III	73%	2	0.797	$415	$25	$390
Phase II	45%	3	0.712	$125	$6	$119
Phase I	23%	2	0.797	$22	$2	$20
Discount rate	12%					

Exhibit 10.8 shows a calculation incorporating success rates into a value determination. Also reflected in the calculation is a discount rate, for the years of clinical trials and regulatory approvals, as well as the cost to fund the different developmental stages. As this illustrative new venture enters Phase I, its end-stage $1 billion value is worth $67 million. The discount rate of twelve percent is estimated as a typical industry rate of return, and does not need to account for technical risks because the success probabilities incorporate those specific risk elements, directly into the calculation.

VALUATION USING THE RELIEF-FROM-ROYALTY METHOD

A popular method for valuing patented technology is called the relief-from-royalty method. This method is popular because it is relatively easy to implement, and can provide a very credible indication of value. The ease of implementation derives from the limited number of inputs needed to fuel the model. However, each of the inputs must be appropriate and precise if the model is to yield a worthwhile result.[7]

The relief-from-royalty method can be used to value a patented invention. Alternately, it can be used to determine the combined value of a patented invention, and the underlying technological know-how used to commercialize the technology. The valuation of a patent is more accurately characterized as valuing the rights associated with ownership of a patent, or patent portfolio. Remember, a patent provides its owner with rights to exclude others from making, using, offering for sale, or selling an invention in the United States, or importing the invention into the United States. What is granted is not the right to make, use, offer for sale, sell, or import, but the right to exclude others from doing so.

The underlying theory of this method is based on the present value of forecasted income. The forecasted income takes the form of savings, and the savings come from owning a patent. Ownership of a patent relieves the owner from having to license it from another party, which typically requires payment for use of patent rights. Most often, payment is made in the form of running royalties. The royalty a licensee must pay is calculated, based on a percentage of company revenue. Sometimes the royalty is based on a fixed amount per unit, but typically the royalty is expressed as a percentage of future sales. Examples of the royalty rates associated with licensed pharmaceutical biotechnology patents can be found throughout the remainder of this book.

INPUTS FOR THE RELIEF-FROM-ROYALTY METHOD

This method calculates the present value of the money saved by owning a patent, and not having to pay royalties to a third party for a license to the patent. It can also be looked at as the present value of future savings.

Five inputs must be determined to implement this method. The key inputs of this method include the following:

- Remaining life of the patent protection
- Forecast revenue
- Royalty rate
- Tax rate
- Discount rate

REMAINING LIFE OF THE PATENT PROTECTION

This input determines the period over which the forecasted savings will be enjoyed from owning the patent. Make sure the remaining life reflects not only the remaining life of the patent protection, but also the remaining life of the underlying invention. Forecasting beyond the remaining life of the invention captures value that does not exist. A patent lasts for twenty years, but in some industries a new technology may become obsolete far sooner than the expiration of the patent. So, the forecast period must reflect not only the remaining life of the patent, but may be subordinate to the time remaining in a technology's life cycle.

A key question becomes "Will the patented invention provide utility for as long as the patent lasts?" One way to answer this question is to look into the history of the subject technology. By studying the historic changes in technology for the relevant industry, insight can be gained for answering this key question. Investigation of current research and development efforts can also indicate when a new technology will replace a current one.

FORECAST REVENUE

This input is a powerful component of the future savings enjoyed by owning a patent. It must be based on forecast revenue expected, from the products or services that commercialize the patented invention. Revenue forecasts must be limited to only those products or services benefiting from the patent protection. They do not have to be based solely on the revenue of the owner, and can include other applications that are reasonable to anticipate.

Licensing trends continue to develop. In many industries corporations are licensing their inventions to others, including direct competitors, as a new source of income. Texas Instruments earns billions of dollars licensing its patent portfolio. Sometimes they earn more from licensing than they do from operations. Alternately, Procter and Gamble rarely licenses its patents, preferring to internalize them, exclusively.

Usually, the value of the patent to the owner is dominated by the protection enjoyed from its exclusive exploitation. An assumption may be required that the exclusive use of the patent rights is the best, or possibly the only, use. Otherwise, in order to capture the full economic value of a patent, applications beyond those of the owner's must be considered.

ROYALTY RATE

This input is the third component required to calculate the future savings enjoyed by owning the patent. It is estimated as the rate the owner would have had to pay to license the patent rights, had it not owned them. Most often a royalty for the specific patented invention being valued is not available, because the patent at issue has not been licensed. As a result, a proxy royalty rate must be developed. A proxy is often obtained from market data, reporting the royalty rate at which similar patent rights have been licensed, between independent third parties. Alternately, a proxy royalty rate for use in the relief-from-royalty method can be estimated using the profit split rule of thumb, profit differential calculation, or a discounted cash flow analysis. All of these royalty estimation methods have already been discussed in this book.

TAX RATE

This input converts the royalty savings into an after tax cash flow, which is converted into a patent value. Use an effective tax rate, but not one that is impacted by unique events, not associated with normal business operations. A business, for example, may enjoy unusually low tax rates from loss carry-forwards. Use of such tax rates distort the benefits associated with the patents, by capturing value associated with tax strategies, and not the technology.

DISCOUNT RATE

This input reflects the risk associated with obtaining the forecast income. This rate should reflect more than the weighted average cost of capital (WACOC) for the business using the patented invention. When considering the WACOC of a business, you must remember that it is comprised of a portfolio of assets, including net working capital, fixed assets, intangible assets, and intellectual property. Each of these asset classes carries different levels of risk. Some have very definite liquidation values, such as cash, accounts receivable, and fixed assets. Others have no liquidation value, such as the intangible asset of a trained and assembled workforce.

All together, the collection of assets that comprise a business contribute to the WACOC. When valuing a distinct element of the overall business, such as a patent, be aware that the appropriate discount rate is not always the overall WACOC of the business. That said, if forecasts are subject to discounts, for success probabilities, then a typical WACOC is appropriate.

EXHIBIT 10.9 RELIEF-FROM-ROYALTY METHOD OF VALUATION

Year	Revenues	Saved Royalties	After-tax Savings	Discount Factor	Present Value
1	20,000,000	600,000	360,000	0.8696	313,043
2	21,000,000	630,000	378,000	0.7561	285,822
3	22,050,000	661,500	396,900	0.6575	260,968
4	23,152,500	694,575	416,745	0.5718	238,275
5	24,310,125	729,304	437,582	0.4972	217,556
6	25,525,631	765,769	459,461	0.4323	198,638
7	26,801,913	804,057	482,434	0.3759	181,365
8	28,142,008	844,260	506,556	0.3269	165,594
9	29,549,109	886,473	531,884	0.2843	151,195
10	31,026,564	930,797	558,478	0.2472	138,047
				Total	2,150,504

5%	Revenue growth rate
3%	Royalty rate
40%	Tax Rate
15%	Discount rate

PRESENT VALUE CALCULATION

Exhibit 10.9 is an example of the relief-from-royalty method. In this example, the inputs are as follows:

- Revenue is expected to grow at an annual rate of five percent.
- Royalties saved on future sales of the product or service protected by the underlying patent rights are calculated, using a proxy royalty rate of three percent of net revenue.
- Income taxes have been calculated at forty percent of income.
- The remaining life of the patented invention is ten years from the date of the valuation.
- The after-tax income saved has been discounted to present value, using a required investment rate of return of fifteen percent.

The value indicated for the patented protection is $2.1 million. It is important to note the difference between patent rights and technological know-how. The royalty rate of three percent was determined, based on third-party licenses, at which similar, "naked" patent rights have been exchanged, on an exclusive basis. Consequently, this value does not capture any proprietary technological know-how that the company using the patent rights created, for commercializing the protected invention. The value expressed in this example is solely for the patent rights.

CHAPTER 11

Court-Awarded Royalty Rates

By Michele M. Riley, CPA, CFE[1]

This chapter provides a review of court-awarded royalty rates in patent infringement cases, from 1990 through 2006. Patent licensing agreements are time-consuming to negotiate and difficult to administer. What happens when parties just can't come to an agreement, and the patent holder decides to take the other party to court? How much time and effort should patent holders spend trying to enforce their patent rights? This chapter will address the royalty rates awarded at the district court level, by examining statistics relating to these rates, the considerations given by the courts to varying factors when determining those rates, and comments made by the Court of Appeals when reviewing lower court decisions.

TOP TEN

A glance at the top ten royalty rate awards, shown in Exhibit 11.1, would convince even the faintest of heart that it is worth it to go to court. As the exhibit shows, the highest rate awarded at the district court level, in any

EXHIBIT 11.1 TOP TEN REASONABLE ROYALTY RATE AWARDS: 1990–2006 (DISTRICT COURT)

Year	Plaintiff	Defendant	Technology	Rate
2001	Mikohn Gaming Corporation	Acres Gaming, Inc.	System of networked gaming devices designed to provide promotional bonuses	42%
1999	Biacore, AB and Biacore, Inc.	Thermo Bioanalysis Corporation	Biosensors used in the study of interactions between biologically active molecules	40%
1994	Lonnie Williams	Skid Recycling, Inc. et al.	Machine for disassembling wooden pallets	35%
1994	Dr. Sakharam D. Mahurkar	C.R. Bard, Inc., Davol, Inc. and Bard Access Systems, Inc.	Double-lumen catheter designed to simultaneously remove and restore fluids to the body during a transfusion	34.88%
1991	TP Orthodontics, Inc.	Professional Positioners, Inc. and Bristol-Myers Co.	Tooth positioner with clasps	30%
2006	Mitutoyo Corporation, et al.	Central Purchasing, LLC	Digital calipers	29.2%
1990	Modine Manufacturing Company	The Allen Group, Inc.	Vehicle radiator with welded tube-to-header joints	28%
2006	Honeywell International, Inc. and Honeywell Intellectual Properties, Inc.	Universal Avionics Systems Corporation and Sandel Avionics, Inc.	Ground proximity warning system for aircraft to use on final approach to an airport	26%
1999	C.R. Bard	Boston Scientific Corporation	Esophageal dilation catheter	25%
1993	Additive Control and Measurement Systems, Inc.	Flowdata, Inc. and Titan Industries, Inc.	Flowmeter	25%
1994	Zygo Corporation	Wyko Corporation	Interferometer system	25%
1991	Smithkline Diagnostics, Inc.	Helena Laboratories Corporation	Method for detecting invisible blood in fecal matter	25%
2004	GE-Harris Railway Electronics, LLC et al.	Westinghouse Air Brake Company	Radio-based distributed power systems for railroad locomotives	25%

patent case, was in 2001, when a Nevada court awarded Acres Gaming a royalty on Mikohn's sales of progressive jackpot gaming machines (*Mikohn Gaming v. Acres Gaming, Inc.* (D. Nev. 2001)). In its order pertaining to an additional accounting of damages, the district court noted that evidence of damages presented to the jury was based on a royalty rate of forty-two percent for products without slot machines, and twenty-eight percent for products with slot machines. Since the jury awarded more than Acres' damages expert calculated as a reasonable royalty, the court noted that "the jury exceeded the rates proposed by Acres' expert."

Two of the rates in our top ten were awarded in 2006: Mitutoyo Corporation was awarded a 29.2 percent royalty, on a patent covering digital calipers (*Mitutoyo Corporation et al. v. Central Purchasing, LLC* (N.D. Ill. 2006)), while Honeywell International received twenty-six percent on a patent relating to a ground proximity warning system, used by aircraft on final approach (*Honeywell International et al. v. Universal Avionics, Inc.* (D. Del. 2006)).

In the Mitutoyo case, the plaintiff was seeking damages based on lost profits, but failed to show that the infringing calipers and its own calipers competed in the same market. Accordingly, the court found that any claim from the plaintiff for lost profits would be entirely speculative, and instead awarded a reasonable royalty.

In the Honeywell case, the court entered the jury's award of a twenty-six percent royalty, after finding that the award was supported by the weight of the evidence presented. It was deemed that the parties to the suit were direct competitors, and the jury's award was within the range of royalties typically agreed to by participants in that field.

The lowest rate awarded in our survey was 0.75 percent, which went to Slimfold Manufacturing Company (*Slimfold Manufacturing Company v. Kinkead Industries, Inc.* (N.D. Ga. 1990)). The patent in suit covered folding doors, used for closets and cabinets.

FREQUENCY OF RATES AWARDED

As Exhibit 11.2 shows, most rates awarded were in the six to ten percent range, with forty-nine awards made during the period covered by our survey. The most commonly awarded rate was ten percent, awarded twenty times during the relevant time period. As for the rest of the distribution,

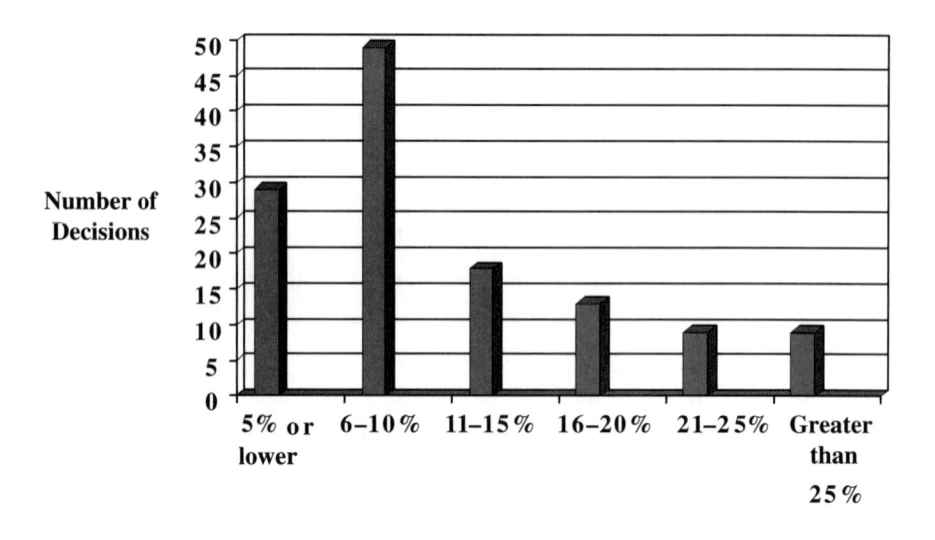

[Bar chart: Number of Decisions vs Rate, with bars approximately at 29 (5% or lower), 49 (6-10%), 18 (11-15%), 13 (16-20%), 9 (21-25%), 9 (Greater than 25%)]

EXHIBIT 11.2 Royalty Rates Awarded by District Courts (1990–2006)

there are twenty-nine awards of five percent or less, thirteen awards of rates between sixteen and twenty percent, and only nine awards with rates higher than twenty-five percent.

INDUSTRY CATEGORIZATIONS

The royalty rates in this study have been categorized according to the U.S. Census Bureau's North American Industry Classification System (NAICS). As Exhibit 11.3 shows, the industry with the most rates awarded was computer and electronic products manufacturing, which had thirty-eight rates awarded during the relevant period, with an average rate awarded equal to 11.01 percent.

The industry with the highest average rate was furniture and related products manufacturing, with an average rate of 15.54 percent for the three cases included in that category. The industry with the lowest average rate was paper manufacturing, which had an average rate of 3.83 percent, based on three cases. Chart 3 also shows statistics for the other industry categories in our survey.

EXHIBIT 11.3 ROYALTY RATE AWARDS BY INDUSTRY: 1990-2006 (DISTRICT COURT)

NAICS Description	No. of Awards	Mean	Median	Maximum
Computer and Electronic Product Manufacturing	38	11.01	6.50	42.00
Medical Equipment and Supplies Manufacturing	20	14.63	11.00	34.88
Miscellaneous Manufacturing	14	10.20	9.00	24.00
Transportation Equipment Manufacturing	8	12.31	10.00	28.00
Machinery Manufacturing	8	13.35	10.55	35.00
Chemical Manufacturing	7	8.36	6.50	28.00
Plastics and Rubber Product Manufacturing	6	11.67	11.75	15.00
Fabricated Metal Product Manufacturing	3	11.00	10.00	21.00
Electrical Equipment, Appliance and Component Manufacturing	3	12.50	10.00	17.50
Furniture and Related Product Manufacturing	3	15.54	18.00	20.00
Paper Manufacturing	3	3.83	3.50	6.00
Building, Developing and General Contracting	3	8.58	12.50	12.50
Publishing Industries	2	11.32	11.32	12.64
Apparel Manufacturing	2	10.00	10.00	10.00
Printing and Related Support Activities	2	6.75	6.75	7.50

CONSIDERATIONS CITED BY THE COURTS IN DETERMINING A REASONABLE ROYALTY

Existing Licenses

The Court of Appeals found that a royalty may be awarded based on an established royalty, if there is one, or if none exists, upon the result of a hypothetical negotiation between plaintiff and defendant (*Rite-Hite Corporation et al. v. Kelley Corporation* (Fed. Cir. 1995)). Because of this finding, existing licenses are often introduced as evidence at trial. In *Mickowski v. Visi-Trak Corporation et al.* (S.D.N.Y. 1999), the court awarded plaintiff a royalty rate of twenty percent of sales, because the plaintiff introduced evidence of other license agreements, for which he had received royalties of fifteen to twenty percent of sales, on products covered by his patent on computer software for monitoring die casting or injection molding manufacturing processes. The court chose the high end of this range, because the parties to the suit were direct competitors in the manufacturing and sale of die casting monitoring systems in the United States.

Similarly, in *Glenayre Electronics v. Philip Jackson et al.* (N.D. Ill. 2003), the court found there was somewhat of an established licensing policy on the part of the counter-plaintiff. However, the licenses introduced as evidence at trial, for the patent in suit, applied to the patent as a whole. In this case, the jury found that only two claims of the patent were infringed. Therefore, the hypothetical negotiation would necessarily be for a limited portion of the patent. In order to comply with this limitation on the award, the court ordered a remittitur (a judge's order reducing a judgment awarded by a jury when the award exceeds the amount asked for by the plaintiff) on the jury's $12 million award, to $2.65 million. The jury's award amounted to a thirty percent royalty rate, while the remitted award, which was accepted by the counter-plaintiff, equaled a six percent royalty.

In *Promega v. LifeCodes Corporation et al.* (D. Utah 1999), the court awarded a 22 percent royalty rate on a patent relating to DNA probes for use in human genetic identification. During trial, there was evidence introduced regarding a license agreement for the patent in suit that carried a rate equaling thirty percent of sales. The court gave great weight to this existing license agreement, but lowered the rate it awarded to 22 percent because the hypothetically negotiated royalty would be based on a co-exclusive license (rather than an exclusive license), the parties to the lawsuit were direct competitors, and the plaintiff generally did not grant licenses for patents it held.

The jury awarded a 6.5 percent royalty rate in *Tristrata Technology, Inc. v. Mary Kay, Inc.* (D. Del 2006) for Mary Kay's infringement of a patent covering skin care products containing alpha hydroxy acids. This award was apparently based on evidence of a license agreement between Tristrata and another party, and there was no evidence in the record, other than this license agreement, for awarding a royalty rate greater than six percent.

During post-trial motions, Mary Kay said the court erred in admitting this license into evidence, arguing that Federal Rule of Evidence 408 prohibits the introduction into evidence of a license made in settlement of litigation. However, the court upheld the jury's finding of a 6.5 percent royalty rate as reasonable, stating that the licensee was not a party to relevant litigation at the time the license was entered into.

Importance of Expert Testimony

The opinions of experts are often considered by the courts in making a determination as to a reasonable royalty rate. For example, in *Segan Limited Partnership v. Trendmasters,* which involved a patent on combat vehicle toys, the judge recommended (and the court awarded) a ten percent royalty, apparently based solely on the testimony of a witness who had twenty-five years of experience in designing and licensing toys.

Another case that demonstrates the importance of credible expert testimony on damages is *Medical Instrumentation and Diagnostics v. Elekta AB*. In this case, involving a patented system for planning surgical treatment using a presentation of images from multiple scanning sources, the defendant did not produce evidence of its infringing sales data for several of the years during the period of infringement. Therefore, plaintiff's estimates of infringing revenue for those periods of time, as opined by its damages expert, were apparently accepted by the jury as the actual royalty base, when it determined its damage award. The district court found that the jury could have reasonably relied on the estimates in determining its damages award, because the defendant did not disclose its actual infringing sales figures.

In addition, the court found that the plaintiff's expert relied on sound economic theory, in basing his projection of the infringing sales data on previous sales growth rates. Although the defendant did subsequently introduce some testimony regarding actual infringing sales, the court discredited the testimony because it appeared to be based on estimates, and did not cite any document disclosed in discovery. The court found that if the jury had relied on the defendant's actual infringing sales numbers, instead of the plaintiff's expert's estimates, the damages award would have been $9 million instead of $15.6 million. Therefore, credible expert testimony almost doubled the damages award received by the plaintiff.

The courts, however, are not compelled to rely on expert testimony at all. In *Smithkline Diagnostics v. Helena Laboratories,* the lower court awarded the plaintiff a twenty-five percent royalty, to compensate for defendant's infringement of a patent describing a method of detecting invisible blood in fecal matter. However, the district court judge did refer to the royalty rates set forth by both parties during trial, stating that if he were forced to choose, the defendant's case for a three percent royalty was more credible than the plaintiff's case for forty-eight percent.

On appeal, the defendant argued that their asserted rate was more credible than the plaintiff's, so the district court judge was necessarily compelled to enter the three percent royalty rate. The federal circuit did not see it that way, stating that "a district court is not limited to selecting one or the other of the specific royalty figures urged by counsel as reasonable," also noting that the district court appropriately relied on the factors enumerated in *Georgia-Pacific v. U.S. Plywood,* in finding what it considered to be a reasonable royalty of twenty-five percent. The federal circuit, therefore, affirmed the lower court's decision, in its entirety.

Use of Projections

Because the hypothetical negotiation is a legal fiction, that necessarily occurs at the date of first infringement, certain estimates and assumptions relating to the future must be considered. Courts have accepted revenue projections available to the parties at the time of the hypothetical negotiation, even though actual sales figures differed from the projections. For example, in *Frank A. Calabrese v. Square D,* the court accepted the jury's recommendation of a seventeen percent royalty, even though actual sales figures turned out much lower than projections available at the time of the hypothetical negotiation.

Likewise, the federal circuit affirmed the lower court's decision in *Interactive Pictures v. Infinite Pictures,* where the lower court used projected sales from the plaintiff's business plan as the royalty base. The Federal Circuit found that the projections would have been available to the parties at the time of the hypothetical negotiation, and it was irrelevant whether or not the sales projections were met.

Entire Market Value Rule

The entire market value rule allows for recovery of damages based on the value of an entire apparatus, containing numerous features, when the patented feature constitutes the basis for customer demand. In *Immersion v. Sony,* the jury awarded Immersion a royalty rate of 1.37 percent, to be applied to Sony's sales of PlayStation gaming systems. The patented technology described a mechanism for providing tactile feedback to users of game controllers, thereby allowing the user to feel vibrations through the controller that correspond to activity on the screen. Although the patented technology was, by definition, only contained in the game controllers, the jury used Sony's sales of PlayStation monitors, games, and controllers as a royalty base.

It was Sony's contention that each of the components of a PlayStation has non-infringing uses, noting that the infringing vibration function can be turned off, and also noting that there are games which do not utilize the vibration function. However, the judge noted in her opinion that it was reasonable for the jury to use the entire PlayStation system as a royalty base, because the jury may have taken these non-infringing uses into account when awarding its relatively low royalty rate of 1.37 percent. The jury could also have calculated damages using a higher rate, but a smaller royalty base.

Another fairly recent application of the entire market value rule is found in *Bose v. JBL.* The district court found that the patented feature, described as a port inside a loudspeaker enclosure used to radiate acoustic energy, "shared a substantial nexus with the demand for the products incorporating it." The district court also found that the defendants sold almost all of their infringing products as part of complete speaker systems, and therefore determined that the royalty base should equate to the sales of the speaker systems, rather than the sales of the infringing products alone. This ruling was subsequently affirmed by the federal circuit, in its entirety.

FEDERAL CIRCUIT DECISIONS ON ROYALTY RATES

Because there are many issues that must be addressed in a patent case, before making a determination relating to a royalty rate in particular, the Federal Court of Appeals rarely opines on royalty rates awarded by the district courts. For example, in *C.R. Bard v. Boston Scientific,* which was affirmed in its entirety by the appeals court, the award of a reasonable royalty rate of twenty-five percent was not even appealed; the plaintiff appealed only the lower court's award of lost profits, and its construction of two patent claim terms.

In *Biacore v. Thermo Bioanalysis,* the plaintiff sought lost profits, but could not prove it would have made the defendant's sales, absent the infringement. The district court ultimately awarded a forty percent royalty rate on the defendant's sales of infringing biosensors, used in the study of interactions between biologically active molecules. This rate was awarded despite the fact that the district court did not find that the invention described in the patent formed the basis for customer demand for the entire product. This favorable royalty rate was affirmed by the federal circuit, in its entirety. This royalty award, the second-highest in our survey, may have helped make the plaintiff feel better about not receiving an award of lost profits.

The most well-known federal circuit decision addressing reasonable royalty rate determinations is *Sakharam D. Mahurkar v. C. R. Bard*. After conducting a hypothetical negotiation, the lower court awarded the plaintiff a 34.88 percent royalty on the defendant's sales of double-lumen catheters. The lower court expressly stated that the plaintiff was entitled to a 25.88 percent royalty, which it calculated by adding the defendant's savings in research and development costs, to the defendant's profit margin on the infringing products. The federal circuit agreed with the calculation up to this point, but did not agree with the lower court's addition of nine percent to the royalty rate, which it referred to as a "Panduit kicker," designed to compensate the plaintiff for having to bring the matter to court. The federal circuit remanded the case for recalculation of a reasonable royalty.

Two more instances of the federal circuit addressing a lower court's award of a royalty rate are found in *Total Containment v. Environ Products* and *Unisplay v. American Electronic Sign*. In the Total Containment case, the district court determined that the plaintiff was entitled to a royalty rate of 10.75 percent, based on both its profit margin on products incorporating the patent, as well as its lost sales of ancillary products. The district court then added an additional ten percent, to account for the plaintiff's policy of not licensing its patents, and the fact that the parties were direct competitors.

The Federal Circuit found that the addition of ten percent lacked evidentiary support, stating that there may have been non-infringing alternatives the defendant might have chosen, rather than pay the plaintiff such a high royalty. In the Unisplay case, the district court awarded a royalty rate of fourteen percent. However, the federal circuit ordered a new trial on damages, because it found that evidence did not support a royalty rate higher than ten percent. The federal circuit found that the fourteen percent rate was based on a discredited, "poison the market" theory, whereby the plaintiff argued that its sales of the product at issue did not reach original expectations, because the defendants' infringing products were of inferior quality.

CONCLUSION

There are numerous considerations that must factor in to any court-awarded reasonable royalty rate. In order to prevail, parties to patent infringement litigation must present royalty rates supported by evidence generated in the normal course of business, as well as the testimony of experts.

CHAPTER 12

Litigation Rates are Higher

Exhibit 12.1 shows royalty awards (in cases with percentage royalties) distributed by industry. The information in this chapter is taken from the book *Patent Infringement Damages Statistics and Trends,* 1990–2004, by Navigant Consulting, and published by Intellectual Property Research Associates (IPRA, Inc.).

The industry with the highest mean rate award, as well as the highest median award, is fabricated metal product manufacturing. Unlike the royalty rate guidance presented throughout this book, enormous royalty rates—forty percent for computers; thirty-five percent for machinery; and twenty-five percent for electrical—are not unheard of as infringement damages awards.

COMPARISON OF LITIGATED AND NON-LITIGATED LICENSES

Exhibit 12.2 compares the data on non-litigated royalty rates, with data on reasonable royalty rates awarded by the courts, presented earlier. For both litigated and non-litigated rates, an overwhelming majority are concentrated

EXHIBIT 12.1 REASONABLE ROYALTY RATES AWARDED BY INDUSTRY: 1990-2004 (U.S. DISTRICT COURTS)

Industry	# of Awards	Mean	Rates (%) Median	Low	High
Apparel Manufacturing	2	10.0	10.0	10.0	10.0
Chemical Manufacturing	7	9.9	8.0	3.0	24.0
Computer and Electronic Product Mfg.	29	10.2	6.0	1.0	40.0
Electrical Equipment/Component Mfg.	4	12.9	12.0	2.5	25.0
Fabricated Metal Product Manufacturing	7	12.4	13.0	3.0	21.0
Furniture and Related Product Mfg.	3	9.8	8.6	0.8	20.0
Machinery Manufacturing	9	12.3	8.0	1.0	35.0
Miscellaneous Manufacturing	28	12.0	9.0	0.5	34.9
Paper Manufacturing	2	4.0	4.0	2.0	6.0
Plastics and Rubber Products Mfg.	2	12.5	12.5	10.0	15.0
Printing and Related Support Activities	2	6.8	6.8	6.0	7.5
Transportation Equipment Mfg.	7	11.7	10.0	7.5	16.3
All Industries	107	11.0	10.0	0.5	40.0

Source: Navigant Consulting Patent Damages Database.

in the zero to ten percent range. However, the rates from litigation appear, on average, to be higher than those negotiated outside of litigation.

Among those in the zero to ten percent range, the litigated rates tend to be in the six to ten percent range, while a greater proportion of the non-litigated rates are between zero and five percent. Licenses in excess of ten percent are much more prevalent among the litigated rates. Thirty-five percent of the litigated rates are over ten percent, while only fifteen percent of the non-litigated rates are that high. In fact, the concentration of litigated rates is much higher in each range above ten percent. Rates between eleven and twenty percent, and over twenty percent, are more than twice as common among litigated rates.

In Exhibit 12.3, the data is broken down further. Royalties negotiated outside of litigation are compared to royalties awarded by the courts in two industries: medical equipment and supplies, and computer and electronic products. These two industries have the highest number of published rates, for both litigated cases and licenses negotiated outside litigation.

It is clear that the pattern of litigated and non-litigated rates in these two industries is similar to the overall trend. The distribution of the litigated

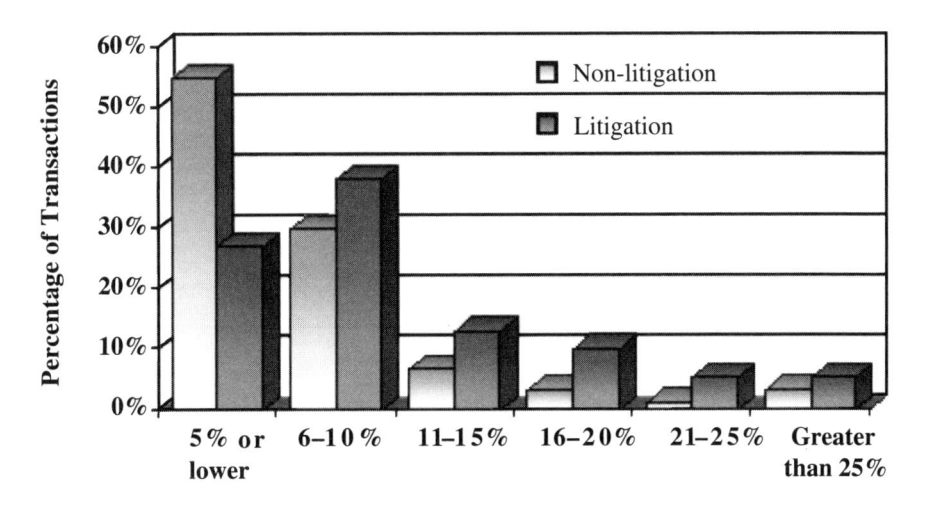

Exhibit 12.2 Royalty Rates: Litigation v. Non-Litigation

Source: Navigant Consulting Patent Damages Database.

rates differs from the distribution of the non-litigated rates in both cases, with the litigated rates more prevalent in the six to ten percent range, while the non-litigated rates are clustered in the zero to five percent range.

Both the overall data, and the data from the two industries, provide an indication that royalty rates allowed by the courts as reasonable royalties in damage awards may, on average, be higher than the typical award arrived at by parties negotiating outside of litigation.

In discussions with counsel, licensing experts, and other experts in the intellectual property field, we found a consensus on several factors that might explain the higher litigated rates.

One key factor driving this difference is probably the assumption made in litigation that the parties to the hypothetical negotiation—on which a reasonable royalty determination is usually based—are directed by case law to assume that the patents in question are valid, and that the prospective licensee's planned actions will infringe the licensor's rights.

This assumption is almost never made by parties in an arms-length licensing negotiation. In fact, a standard bargaining chip used by a prospective licensee, in real world licensing negotiations, may be to argue that the patents are not valid and, even if the patents are valid, the licensee's actions will not infringe them. Similarly, the prospective licensor in an actual negotiation will generally argue strongly, about the strength

Medical Equipment and Supplies Manufacturing

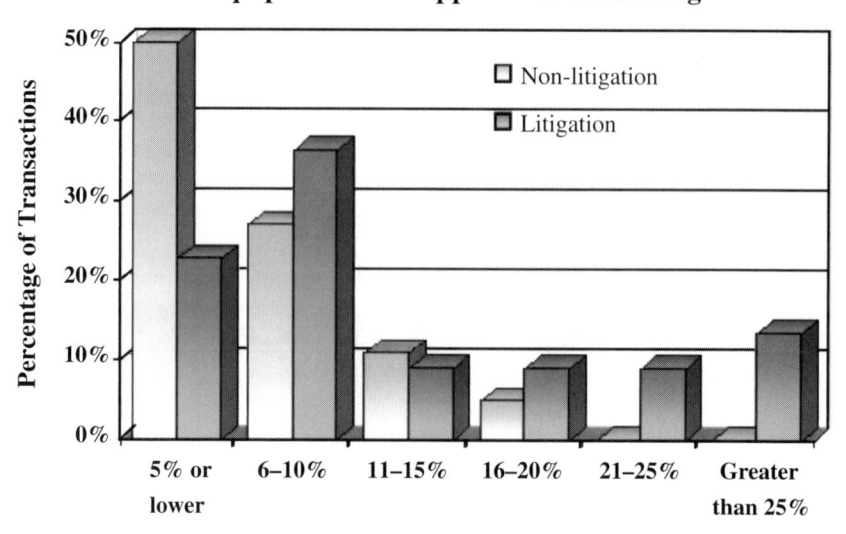

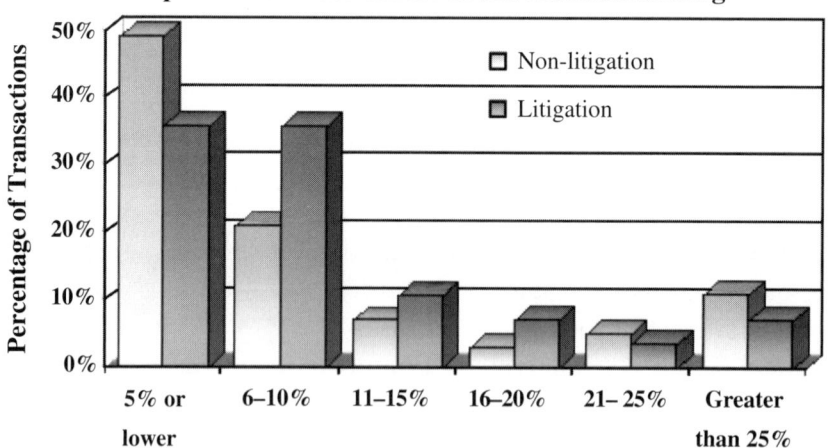

Computer and Electronics Product Manufacturing

Source: Navigant Consulting Patent Damages Database.

EXHIBIT 12.3 **Royalty Rates: Litigation v. Non-Litigation**

of the patents, and of the clear evidence that the licensee's activity will infringe.

In an actual negotiation, each party can maintain his or her position without contradiction, the reason being that until the judge and/or the jury complete their rule (and increasingly, until the federal circuit approves the trial result), neither party can be certain as to either validity or infringement.

Another factor that may have a positive impact on the amount of litigated royalties is that there is a natural selection process that tends to lead to more litigation involving commercially successful patents, than on patents that fail to achieve such success. With licenses derived from negotiations apart from litigation, there is general uncertainty about the prospective success of ventures attempting to use the patented technology after the license agreement is completed.

The discovery process in litigation allows both parties to see what the other's profitability expectations were at the time of the hypothetical negotiation for the product. Parties also typically find out what the actual profitability of the infringing product has been since. In real-world deals, these things are generally unknown, because the licensee may have not begun production of the licensed product as of the date of the negotiation, or if

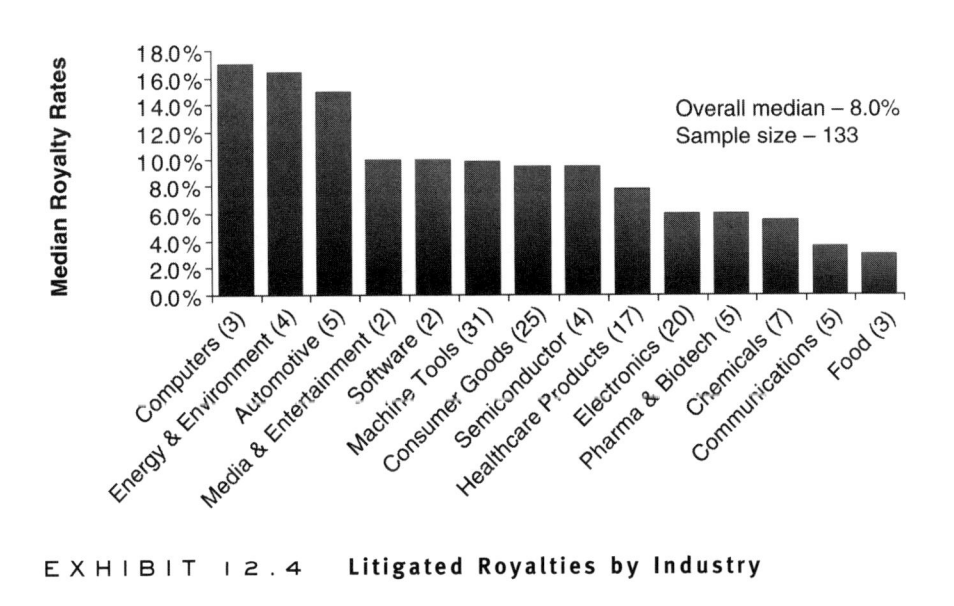

EXHIBIT 12.4 Litigated Royalties by Industry

Overall median – 8.0%
Sample size – 133

the licensee has begun production, he would not necessarily share his records, or projections of profitability, with the licensor.

In most actual license negotiations, the parties may not know whether the marketplace will accept the commercial version of the technology. In litigation, the parties know exactly how well the product or service performed, giving a better basis for establishing the commercial success of the product manufactured under the patent.

In Exhibit 12.4, Analysis Group Economics considered one hundred and thirty-three deals, in fifteen industries, from the AG Database. The data was taken from published legal decisions.

CHAPTER 13

Royalty Rate Services

This chapter provides information about sources of royalty rate information, derived from researching license agreements.

ROYALTYSOURCE®™

Through the RoyaltySource® website, you can access helpful tools, and expert advice, on various aspects of IP valuation, and reasonable royalty rates for transactions. Their continuous investigation has yielded a searchable database of technology and trademark sale and licensing transactions, that can minimize the time spent researching the marketplace for this information.

RoyaltySource® continues to research all forms of media for reported transactions. Their IP transaction database includes

- licensee and licensor, including industry description, or code;
- description of the property licensed or sold;
- royalty rate details;
- other compensation, such as up-front payments, or equity positions;

- transaction terms, such as exclusivity, geographical restrictions, or grant-backs; and
- the source of the information.

A table of the many industries represented is shown below

Agriculture	Chemicals	Financial	Manufacturing	Semiconductors
Apparel	Communications	Food	Medical	Software
Automotive	Computer	Franchises	Services	Sports
Beverages	Hardware	Household	Pharmaceutical	Universities
Biotechnology	Electronics	Goods	Publishing	Waste
	Entertainment	Lodging	Retailing	Management

The RoyaltySource® service is designed as an economic tool, for users looking to maximize their search efforts at a minimum cost. The research begins after you define the technology, industry and SIC codes, industry players, and any key words that might assist in the search. You can also detail your search request on a contact form, found on their website.

If RoyaltySource® finds up to ten transactions of interest, the charge is $250. If they find up to twenty transactions, the charge is $300. In other words, the charge increases $50 for every additional ten transactions. If no relevant transactions are found, the charge is $100. Major credit cards are accepted.

To receive a sample copy of their reports, or to discuss further details visit their website at www.royaltysource.com.

ROYALTYSTAT®

RoyaltyStat® is a subscription database of royalty rates and license agreements, compiled from the U.S. Securities and Exchange Commission (SEC) EDGAR archives. With RoyaltyStat® you can find comparable royalty rates for valuing, or licensing, intangible assets. Every license agreement in the database contains at least one numerical (non-redacted) royalty rate or license fee, and the database is updated every business day.

RoyaltyStat® is useful for the following purposes:

- Finding royalty rates for licensing intangible property
- Complying with tax laws requiring arm's length, intercompany transactions

- Finding industry, or comparable, royalty rates
- Determining buy-in payments, for cost-sharing arrangements under transfer pricing regulations
- Determining purchase price allocation (class IV assets acquisition, under IRS section 1060—see Form 8594, Asset Acquisition Statement)
- Establishing damages in IP disputes
- Valuing intangible property for mergers, acquisitions, divestitures, bankruptcy, or other transactions.

The database may be searched by Standard Industrial Classification (SIC) code, or by full-text queries. The time-saving Royalty Tableau™ contains the name of the licensor, licensee, property description, royalty rate, exclusivity, duration, and territory covered by the selected license agreements. The search results, including the full text of each license agreement, can be viewed online or archived for future analysis. You can view statistics, including count, average, standard deviation, and quartiles, of selected royalty rates.

INTELLECTUAL PROPERTY RESEARCH ASSOCIATES (IPRA)

Three books are published by IPRA, Inc., a company owned by the author of this book. They are dedicated to reporting royalty rates on technology, trademarks, and copyrights. The three books are described below, and can be purchased at www.ipresearch.com.

Royalty Rates for Pharmaceuticals and Biotechnology, Sixth Edition, reports royalty rates for an incredible range of compounds, manufacturing techniques, therapies, and other patented pharmaceutical and biotechnology inventions. Just some of the technology categories covered include attention deficit disorder, Alzheimer's detection, anti-inflammatory, antifungal, antiviral, arthritis, bone marrow production, cancer, cardiovascular, cartilage regeneration, chromosome analysis, cold remedies, contraception, cystic fibrosis, dermatology, diabetes, drug delivery, gene alteration, hepatitis, HIV, humanized antibodies, monoclonal antibodies, neurological, pain therapy, personal care, psychotherapy, research processes, sleep therapy, stem cells, transdermal drug delivery, and vaccines.

The book presents detailed financial information about third-party transactions, that center on the transfer of biotechnology and pharmaceutical technology. The parties are identified, the technology is described, and all of the financial terms available are reported, including royalty rates, license fees, and milestone payments. This edition also presents seven financially-based models, for pricing and valuing biotech and pharmaceutical technology. Comprehensive illustrations are provided.

Royalty Rates for Technology, Third Edition, reports royalty rates, license fees, and milestone payments, for twenty-five different industries, including technologies from aeronautics, agriculture, automotive, chemistry, communications, computer hardware, computer software, construction equipment, electrical equipment, electronics, entertainment, food, franchises, glass, household products, Internet, mechanical devices, medical devices, natural resources, photography, semiconductors, sports, steel, toys, and waste.

Royalty Rates for Trademarks and Copyrights, Third Edition, reports royalty rates and transaction values for trademarks and copyrights, for the period 1990 through 2004. Industries covered include airline, apparel, architecture, art, autos, boats, celebrities, communications, corporate names, electronics, food and beverage, franchises, furniture, general merchandise, domain names, medical, movies, music, party goods, restaurants and hotels, sports toys, and university names. Also included is a new section describing financial methods for royalty rate development.

SECURITIES AND EXCHANGE COMMISSION EDGAR ARCHIVES

The mission of the SEC is to protect investors, maintain fair, orderly, and efficient markets, and facilitate capital formation. The laws and rules that govern the securities industry in the United States derive from a simple and straightforward concept: all investors, whether large institutions or private individuals, should have access to certain basic facts about an investment prior to buying it, and so long as they hold it. To achieve this, the SEC requires public companies to disclose meaningful financial, and other, information to the public. This provides a common pool of knowledge, for all investors to use, to judge for themselves whether to buy, sell, or hold a particular security. Only through the steady flow of timely, comprehensive, and accurate information can people make sound investment decisions.

The SEC offers the public a wealth of educational information on its website, which also includes the EDGAR database of disclosure documents, that public companies are required to file with the Commission. EDGAR, the Electronic Data Gathering, Analysis, and Retrieval system, performs automated collection, validation, indexing, acceptance, and forwarding of submissions by companies, and others, who are required by law to file forms with the SEC. Its primary purpose is to increase the efficiency and fairness of the securities market, for the benefit of investors, corporations, and the economy, by accelerating the receipt, acceptance, dissemination, and analysis of time-sensitive corporate information filed with the agency.

Companies file their annual reports, called "10Ks," with the SEC. These reports provided a wealth of information about the financial and operating results of the filing company. Often, when a company has entered into license agreements, details about the agreements, including royalty rate information, are provided. For the do-it-yourself researcher, the EDGAR database can be an important source for significant amounts of royalty rate information.

The EDGAR database can be accessed at www.sec.gov/edgar.

CHAPTER 14

Monitoring License Agreements and Financial Compliance

BY DEBORA ROSE STEWART, CPA,
AND JUDY A. BYRD, CPA, CIRA

INTRODUCTION

Licensors and licensees alike spend enormous amounts of time negotiating license agreements for intellectual property. Such negotiations generally include not only the royalty rate, but also how that rate is applied, and if and when it might vary. It is hoped this investment of time will result in a license agreement that is not only acceptable to both parties, but also clearly stated.

After the agreement is signed, however, the license is often put in a file drawer, never to be looked at again, except when problems arise. Why don't licensors spend the same amount of time and effort in license monitoring as they do in securing the license agreement? After all, in a typical business transaction, parties do not rely on trust alone to document the exchange of goods and services; payment amounts are compared against invoices, shipping logs, or other documents from an accounting system.

It is the licensor's fiduciary duty to insure that optimal royalties, at the negotiated royalty rate, are realized under each license agreement. This is true for both non-profit foundations and for-profit companies. Licensing provisions must be monitored, and prompt action taken if a licensee fails to comply with the agreement's reporting, and royalty payment, requirements. This is not to suggest that licensors should become skeptical of business partners, or assume they are not trustworthy. Rather, it is just the best business practice to keep abreast of the situation so discrepancies can be identified early, before money is lost and the business relationship jeopardized.

Underpayment of royalties is common (see Exhibit 14.1). Even reputable and trustworthy licensees, who intend to pay the correct amount of royalties, often pay less than what is owed, due to misunderstandings and errors. As such, unmonitored license agreements leave valuable assets unprotected.

Why is it that licensors rarely monitor the process under which royalties are calculated and paid? Sometimes the lack of monitoring is due purely to a shortage of resources. In addition, for licensees, staff responsible for royalty calculations and license compliance are typically not the same people who negotiated the agreement. There may be interpretation differences, or simply a lack of understanding concerning what data are to be gathered and reported, or where to obtain required elements for calculations and reports. There also may be a disconnect because information systems are not available, or programmed, to accumulate the required items. For licensors, staff tasked with responsibility for monitoring compliance may be

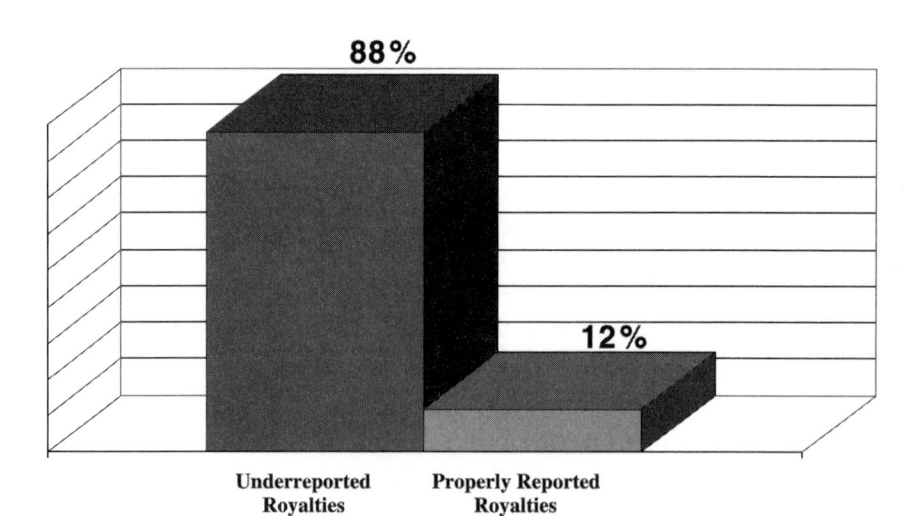

EXHIBIT 14.1 **Percentage of Licenses with Underreported Royalties**[1]

unfamiliar with the license terms, or mistakenly concerned that a monitoring program will send the wrong message.

Breaking Through Old Perceptions

License agreements can be complex, with the actual royalty calculation based on variable data, from multiple sources. Royalty audits are a common means of monitoring license compliance. Historically, companies have avoided royalty audits because they do not want to insinuate mistrust, and jeopardize the relationship. To respond to these concerns, licensors should be reminded of the similarities between license transactions and sales transactions. Just as sales customers are not insulted by verifying payments against invoices, licensees will not be upset by a similar examination of royalty streams.

Licenses create a symbiotic relationship; licensees need the license to develop, manufacture, or sell a product or service; licensors may become dependent on royalty income, or the research channel. It must be understood that the use of a royalty audit is not an accusation of fraud, but rather an acceptance of the potential for human error. In fact, license agreements generally include a clause permitting royalty audits; often the right is negotiated, and agreed to, as a condition of the license. Often, the licensee has agreed to retain documents specifically for this purpose. Licensors should guarantee accurate royalty streams, by invoking the system of checks and balances offered by a royalty audit.

Still concerned? There are several ways to minimize the likelihood that the licensee will be offended by an audit. Give them early notice, make audits routine, rather than in response to a suspected problem, and make it clear that all licenses of a certain size, or type, are always audited.

The give-and-take of the negotiating process often forces the licensor to agree to a lower royalty rate, or less favorable terms, than originally desired. If the licensor's monitoring procedures are lax, then the gap between desired royalties, and royalties actually realized, is going to widen.

Many people think monetary license monitoring is limited to royalty audits. However, there is a great deal more to a compliance program. Below we discuss these topics, which include the agreement language, royalty audits, desk audits, and, most importantly, proactive communication between licensor and licensee.

WHAT IS A ROYALTY AUDIT?

The term "audit" is a term of art in the accounting profession that refers to an examination performed under generally accepted accounting principles (GAAP), resulting in an "opinion" on a company's financial statement, taken as a whole. In contrast, when the term "royalty audit" is used, it refers to an analysis of information, to determine whether a licensee is performing in accordance with a license agreement.

A royalty audit is used to determine whether a licensor is receiving the proper amount of contractual information, and payments, due under a license. If the royalty audit uncovers non-compliance, the auditors then generate a quantification of the unreported sales, and/or units, and outline understated royalties owed to the licensor.

A royalty audit is the primary tool used to determine if a licensee is in compliance, with all the terms and conditions of the licensing agreement. By performing a royalty audit, licensors are not only assured that licensees are paying all royalties due, but also that the licensees are adhering to all other provisions of the agreement. Licensors are also able to verify that sales are within the licensed territory, only authorized products are sold, and any other requirements are followed.

When is it appropriate to audit? If performed early in the licensing relationship, licensors gain assurance that royalties are being calculated, reported, and paid as required, from the onset of the agreement period. It also sets expectations and standards. By performing just one royalty audit, licensors set a precedent, applicable to all of their licensees, demonstrating that royalty streams will be monitored on a regular basis, under-reporting will not be tolerated, and that the licensor values and protects its assets. Regularly scheduled audits, throughout the agreement term, maintain these expectations, lessening the likelihood of lost revenue, not only as it is earned, but also the cumulative effect of an error (potentially with interest) that may need to be negotiated just to get it paid.

Red Flags

No matter how thorough both parties are in negotiating and selecting the final language of the agreement, individuals who were not on the original negotiation team are generally charged with enforcing agreement compliance. Therefore, misreporting can be expected as a part of doing business.

Although all licensees should be part of a royalty audit program, certain "red flags" are indicators of potential under-reporting or misreporting of royalties, and highlight licenses that require immediate attention. Red flags can appear in the royalty report, or can be found by scrutinizing the licensee's performance in the marketplace. Licensors should pay close attention to reports that include unsupported calculations, or an insufficient level of detail. Similarly, licensors should become cautious if the licensee is unable to answer questions about its royalty calculation.

Other indications of potential problems surface when a royalty payment is made. The licensor should be aware of late royalty reports, minimum payments not in complete contractual compliance, or royalty payment amounts that are neither as high as anticipated, or are not within current market expectations. Likewise, a licensor should be alerted to potential problems if the royalty report shows poor performance of a licensed product, compared to other licensee products, or sales inconsistent with market performance, or a poor, or failing, financial condition of the licensee.

Some additional red flags include

- recurring miscalculations of royalties due,
- licensee's poor internal controls,
- evidence of product combinations,
- complex distribution channels for licensed product, and
- inconsistent, or nonexistent, contact person at licensee's business, with detailed knowledge of the agreement.

AUDITOR SELECTION

Once a licensor has decided to implement a royalty audit program, the licensor must determine who will perform the audit. Agreements commonly specify that an independent CPA is to perform the audit. Not only is an independent CPA unbiased, but licensees favor the unrelated third-party, to help protect competitive information.

Royalty auditing requires specialized skills and a unique approach. A royalty auditor should have extensive experience, and knowledge, of both intellectual asset management, and intellectual property licensing. The audit is best handled by someone capable of interpreting the accounting provisions of a contract, and trained to dig beneath the surface.

The chosen auditor should also be one who represents the licensor in an appropriate manner. The licensor-licensee relationship is a partnership, which must be preserved and strengthened. The selection of an appropriate, non-adversarial, professional, third-party auditor will help a licensor maintain a positive relationship with the licensee.

HOW IS THE ROYALTY AUDIT DONE?

The royalty audit is generally performed in three phases, as follows:

Pre-site research

Site investigation

Post-site analysis and report generation

In general, phase one will include research and analysis of all relevant information, prior to the site visit. Phase two will include an onsite investigation, and phase three will consist of continued analysis, and completion of the audit report.

At the completion of site work, the audit team will draft conclusions, or prepare a report. Depending on the situation, this report will be discussed with the licensor and, sometimes, the licensee. Changes will be made, and a final report will be issued. This report may be verbal, or it may take the form of a detailed, written report that includes supporting schedules and data.

The underpayment of royalties is usually not intentional. Rather, underpayment is likely due to a flaw in the royalty tracking system. Therefore, the auditor should work with the licensee to explain how the mistake occurred, and address possible actions that should be taken to insure that the problem is resolved.

To maintain the maximum value of a licensing agreement, an audit should be performed within two years of commencement of sales of covered products. Although the audit may identify under-reported royalties, the under-reported amounts at this time may not be material. If errors are caught early, licensee collections are optimized. It is unfortunate, but when an audit is put off and large errors are found, the licensor generally is forced to negotiate for less than what they are due contractually. More importantly, since lack of communication often contributes to misreporting, an early audit will keep lines of communication between the licensor and licensee open.

After the first audit is complete, the licensor should perform future audits, on a regular basis, to make sure new misunderstandings have not developed. To the uninitiated, these audits may seem like an unnecessary expense. But for those with experience, it is clear that the minimal expense of regular audits pays dividends that far exceed the costs.

DESK AUDITS

In general, a license agreement that is monitored is less likely to have significant royalty reporting mistakes. A well-thought-out compliance program to monitor license agreements should include several types of checks and balances, in addition to the full royalty audit. The desk audit is one such example.

The licensor should analyze payments, as they are received, for trends. A review of sales by country of origin, if applicable, should be performed, as well as a more customized review, based on the license. This could include the reconciliation of product catalogs to reported sales, review of public information, including press releases for indications of sales growth, matched with royalty payments. Finally, a non-exclusive license can lend itself to the comparison of the performance among different licensees.

DRAFTING A LICENSE AGREEMENT TO LOWER THE LIKELIHOOD OF MISTAKES

The best way to receive full royalty payments is to draft an agreement that does not contain vague terms, subject to misinterpretation. Definitions should be precise. Terms such as "gross sales," "net sales," "other consideration," and "discounts" should be reviewed for clarity.

The agreement should specify all information required to be included in the royalty report. It should also include a sample report, showing the exact format in which the information should be provided to the licensor. This report should be provided in hard, and electronic, format. At a minimum, the following should be included:

- Period included on the report
- Product name, number, and SKU
- Units sold (and sublicense information identified, if applicable)
- Sales dollars (and sublicense information identified, if applicable)
- Itemized deductions from gross to net sales (if applicable)

- Country in which product was sold (if applicable)
- Foreign currency (if applicable)
- Conversion rate to U.S. dollars (if applicable)
- Converted U.S. dollars (if applicable)
- Applicable royalty rate
- Extended royalty dollar amount
- Contact person, knowledgeable about the report contents

In addition, the license agreement should

determine how combination products should be handled.

define and determine how to consider "free" items.

allow the licensor to receive interest on any late or understated royalties (including specification of a rate, and compounding frequency).

contain language that provides for an unlimited right to audit, with the cost to be paid by the licensee if an understatement is found that exceeds a threshold (frequently five percent of royalties). Further, record retention requirements should be detailed.

if sublicensing is granted, include at a minimum the right to receive copies of agreements, reports, and pass-through audit rights.

contain a clause that allows a royalty auditor to set up a royalty reporting system for the licensee, as a preemptive strategy. This service is usually not a significant investment in time or money in the short term, but pays valuable dividends of more accurate royalty reports in the long run.

COMMON ERRORS

The following is a list of common errors that lead to reporting mistakes:

- Neglecting to report royalties on a new product
- Incorrectly processed credit memos
- Misapplication of "free" items
- Incorrect royalty base
- Unreported sales
- Under-reported sales

- Excessive price discounts, or use of estimates rather than actual prices
- Inappropriate deduction for chargebacks and/or allowances
- Sales to unauthorized territories, markets and/or customers
- Non-escalation of royalty rates
- Unaccounted production
- Inappropriate exchange rates
- Clerical errors
- Transfer prices to affiliates used as royalty base
- Failure to account for all distribution channels
- Failure to account for sales of other products that contain the licensed product
- Failure to pay interest on late payments
- Failure to report sublicenses
- General misinterpretation of the agreement

COMMUNICATIONS BETWEEN LICENSOR AND LICENSEE

The common thread, woven into all components of a license-monitoring program, is communication between licensor and licensee. This communication should take place throughout the life of the license, whether or not problems arise. Upon initiation of the monitoring program, a letter of introduction should be sent to each licensee, so that each is aware of the program, and no one feels singled out for scrutiny. Likewise, the licensee should be called if a desk audit procedure uncovers a problem with the calculation method.

The licensee should also be called after receiving a royalty report, to acknowledge receipt, as well as to thank them for sending it in a timely fashion. Such time is also propitious to discuss any new developments with the licensee, as such communication can only improve the relationship.

CONCLUSION: BENEFITS OF A SOUND MONITORING PROGRAM

The establishment of a monitoring program is a necessary part of licensing. Audits should be performed early in the licensing relationship, so both parties can eliminate potential ambiguities within the contract, without having a financial dispute. When there appears to be a problem with contract interpretation, communication with the licensee or auditor will help take care of it immediately. The irony is that delaying, while often intended to save money, or spare the licensee's feelings, will almost always cost a considerable amount more than an audit performed earlier, thus impacting the effective royalty rate.

Most misreporting errors are not fraudulent. As prudent business people, it is important to remember that royalty reports are prepared by humans, and humans make mistakes. To overcome these mistakes, businesses implement systems of checks and balances. License agreements should not be excluded from scrutiny; licensors deserve to receive the revenue that was agreed upon. The use of a royalty audit as an agreement-monitoring tool is imperative. Its use makes sound business sense.

Notes

Chapter 1

1. www.oceantomo.com.
2. Keith Cardoza, Justin Basara, Liddy Cooper, and Rick Conroy, "The Power of Intangible Assets: An Analysis of the S&P 500," *Les Nouvelles—The Journal of the Licensing Executives Society,* March 2006: Page 4.
3. Ibid., 5.
4. http://www.loc.gov/about.
5. R. Mark Halligan, Esq., "What Is A Trade Secret? Trade Secret Audits: Part One" http://my.execpc.com/~mhallign/tradesec.html.
6. James Bone, "Three Charged With Stealing Coca-Cola Trade Secrets," *Times Online,* July 6, 2006, http://www.timesonline.co.uk/article/0,11069-2259092,00.html
7. Associated Press, "Pepsi Alerted Coca-Cola to Stolen-Coke-Secrets Offer" Thursday, July 06, 2006, http://www.foxnews.com/story/0,2933,202439,00.html.

Chapter 2

1. "Returns of Active Corporations, Form 1120", www.irs.gov.
2. In 1994, Computer and Electronics, and Miscellaneous, were not separate categories.
3. M. Yamasaki, "Determining Pharmaceuticals Royalties," *Les Nouvelles* (September 1996): 112.
4. Thomas Ginsberg, "Big Pharma faces tough competition in biotech industry," *Philadelphia Inquirer* (posted on the Internet June 20, 2005).
5. Ibid.
6. Linda Lloyd, "Wyeth signs three biotech product deals, *The Philadelphia Inquirer* (January 9, 2006): C1.
7. Richard Razgaitis, "US/Canadian Licensing In 2004: Survey Results", *Les Nouvelles,* (December 2005): 145.
8. Stephen A. Degnan and Corwin Horton, "A Survey of Licensed Royalties," *Les Nouvelles* (June 1997): 91.

Chapter 3

1. D.J. Neil, "Realistic Valuation of Your IP," *Les Nouvelles 32* (December 1997): 182; Stephen A. Degnan, "Using Financial Models to Get Royalty Rates," *Les Nouvelles 33* (June 1998): 59; Daniel Burns, "DCF Analyses in Determining Royalty", *Les Nouvelles 30* (September 1995): 165; Russell L. Parr and Patrick H. Sullivan, *Technology Licensing:*

Corporate Strategies for Maximizing Value," (1996): 233–46; Richard Razgaitis, *Early Stage Technologies: Valuation and Pricing,* (1999): 121–58.
2. Robert Reilly and Robert Schweihs, *Valuing Intangible Assets,* (1999): 159–66.
3. Parr and Sullivan, *Technology Licensing: Corporate Strategies for Maximizing Value,* 223–33.
4. V. Walt Bratic, et al., "Monte Carlo Analyses Aid Negotiation," *Les Nouvelles 33* (June 1998): 47; Razgaitis, *Early Stage Technologies: Valuation and Pricing,* 160–77.
5. Dr. Nir Kossovsky and Dr. Alex Arrow, "*TRRU*™ *Metrics: Measuring The Value and Risk of Intangible Assets,*" *Les Nouvelles 35* (September 2000): 139; F. Peter Boer, *The Valuation of Technology: Business and Financial Issues in R&D,* (1999): 302–06.
6. Razgaitis, *Early Stage Technologies: Valuation and Pricing,* 96.
7. Richard S. Toikka, "In Patent Infringement Cases, the 25 Percent Rule Offers a Simpler Way to Calculate Reasonable Royalties. After Kumho Tire, Chances are the Rule Faces Challenges to its Daubert Reliability," *Legal Times* (August 1999): 34.
8. Robert Goldscheider, "Litigation Backgrounder for Licensing" *Les Nouvelles 29* (1994): 25; Robert Goldscheider, "Royalties as Measure of Damages" *Les Nouvelles 31* (1996): 115–19.
9. Robert Goldscheider, *Technology Management: Law/Tactics/Forms §10.04* (1991). cite page numbers used from this book.
10. Robert Goldscheider and James T. Marshall, "The Art of Licensing—From the Consultant's Point of View," *The Law and Business of Licensing 2* (1980): 645.
11. Robert Goldscheider, *Technology Management: Law/Tactics/Forms §10.04.*
12. Albert S. Davis, Jr., *Basic Factors to be Considered in Fixing Royalties,* Patent Licensing, Practicing Law Institute, 1958.
13. *Horvath v. McCord Radiator and Mfg. Co. et al.,* 100 F.2d 326, 335 (6th Cir. 1938).
14. In the reasonable royalty determination in *Standard Manufacturing Co., Inc. and DBP, Ltd. v. United States,* both sides' experts focused on the patent holder's profit rate. The Court took exception noting that defendant's profits were a "more realistic and reliable estimation of profits which were to [the plaintiff] by the infringement since they are derived from the actual sale of [the infringing product]." *Standard Manufacturing Co., Inc. and DBP, Ltd. v. United States,* 42 Fed. C1. 748, 767 (1999). The Court noted that a variety of federal courts held the same, citing *Mahurkar v. C.R. Bard, Inc., Davol Inc. and Bard Access System, Inc.* 79 F.3 d 1572, 1580 (Fed. Cir. 1996) (district court did not err in calculating portion of award when it initially used infringer's profit rate); *TWM Manufacturing Co., Inc. v. Dura Corp. and Kidde, Inc.* 789 F.2 d 895, 899 (Fed. Cir. 1986) (affirming district court's computation of damages based on infringer's profits); *Trans-World Manufacturing Corp. v. Al Nyman & Sons, Inc. and Al-Site Corporation,* 750 F.2d 1552, 1568 (among factors considered in determining reasonable royalty was the infringer's anticipated profit from invention's use, and evidence of infringer's actual profits probative of anticipated profit).
15. Baruch Lev, "Rethinking Accounting," *Financial Executive Online Edition,* (March/April 2002) http://www.fei.org/maggable/articles/3-4-2002.coverstory.cfm.
16. In some circumstances, the *licensor's* profits may provide some guidance. That is, those profits may, in part, reflect his/her appetite for a license and those profits may serve as a surrogate for missing or unknown licensee profits.
17. Razgaitis, *Early Stage Technologies: Valuation and Pricing,* 108. *Fonar Corporation and Dr. Raymone V. Damadian v. General Electric Company and Drucker & Genuth, MDS, P.C. d/b/a South Shore Imaging Associates,* 107 F.3d 1543 (Fed. Cir. 1997). *Hanson v. Alpine Valley Ski Area, Inc.,* 718 F.2d 1075 (Fed. Cir. 1983).
18. Richard Brealey and Stewart C. Myers, *Principles of Corporate Finance* (2000): 123.
19. Razgaitis, *Early Stage Technologies: Valuation and Pricing,* 108.
20. Gordon V. Smith and Russell L. Parr, Valuation of Intellectual Property and Intangible Assets (1994): 362.
21. Russell Parr, *Intellectual Property Infringement Damages, A Litigation Support Handbook,* 1993, pp. 170–71.

22. Robert Goldscheider, *Technology Management: Law/Tactics/Forms* § *10.04* (1991), Razgaitis, *Early Stage Technologies: Valuation and Pricing,* 103.
23. Brealey and Myers, *Principles of Corporate Finance,* Chapters 2 & 6.
24. Shannon P. Pratt, et al., *Valuing Business: The Analysis and Appraisal of Closely Held Companies,* (1996): 149–285; Shannon P. Pratt et al., *Valuing Small Businesses and Professional Practices,* (1993): 507–524; Gordon V. Smith and Russell L. Parr, *Valuation of Intellectual Property and Intangible Assets,* (1994): 127–136; Reilly and Schweihs, Valuing Intangible Assets, 118–203.
25. Paul E. Schaafsma, "An Economic Overview of Patients," *Journal of the Patent Trademark Office Society* (April 1997): 251–53.
26. Jon Paulsen, "Determining Damages for Infringements," *Les Nouvelles 32* (June 1997): 67.
27. Paul A. Samuelson and William D. Nordhaus, *Economics* (2001): 47. *Crystal Semiconductor v. Tritech Microelectronics International, Inc.,* 246 F. 3d 1336 (Fed. Cir. 2001).
28. *Standard Manufacturing Co., Inc. and DBP, Ltd. v. United States,* 42 Fed. C1 748, 764–765 (1999). *Ajinomoto Inc. v. Archer-Daniels-Midland Co.,* No. 95-218-SLR, 1998 U.S. Dist. LEXIS 3833, (D. Del. March 13, 1998). *Tights, Inc. v. Kayser-Roth Corp.* 442 F. Supp. 159 (M.D.N.C. 1977). *Dow Chemical Co. v. United States,* 226 F. 3d 1334 (Fed. Cir. 2000) Razgaitis, *Early Stage Technologies: Valuation and Pricing,* 117–18.
29. Stephen A. Degnan and Corwin Horton, "A Survey of Licensed Royalties," *Les Nouvelles 32* (June 1997): 91, 95.
30. *Ajinomoto Inc. v. Archer-Daniels-Midland Co.,* No. 95-218-SLR, 1998 U.S. Dist. LEXIS 3833, at 44 n.46 (D. Del. March 13, 1998).
31. *Odetics, Inc. v. Storage Technology Corp.* 185 F. 3d 1259, 1261 (Fed. Cir. 1999).
32. *Grain Processing Corp. v. American Maize-Products Co.,* 185 F. 3d 1341, 1345 (Fed. Cir. 1999).
33. Robert E. Bayes, "Pricing the Technology," *Current Trends in Domestic and International Licensing* (1977): 369, 381. Marcus B. Finnegan and Herbert H. Mintz, "Determination of a Reasonable Royalty in Negotiating a License Agreement: Practical pricing for Successful Technology Transfer", *Licensing Law and Business Report 1* 1 (June–July 1978): 19. Lawrence Gilbert, "Establishing a University Program", *The Law and Business of Licensing 1,* (1980): 506.267. Robert Goldscheider and James T. Marshall, "The Art of Licensing—From the Consultants Point of View", *The Law and Business of Licensing 2* (1980): 645. H.A. Hashbarger, "Maximizing Profits as a Licensee", *The Law and Business of Licensing 2* (1980): 637. Alan C. Rose, "Licensing a 'Package' Lawfully in the Antitrust Climate of 1972," *The Law And Business of Licensing 1* (1980): 637. Yoshio Matsunaga, "Determining Reasonable Royalty Rates," *Les Nouvelles* (December 1983): 216–18. *The Basics of Licensing: Including International License Negotiating Thesaurus,* LES 13 (1988) Edward P. White, *Licensing: A Strategy for Profits* (1990): 104. Martin S. Landis, "Pricing and Presenting Licensed Technology," *The Journal of Proprietary Rights 3* (August 1991): 18–21. William Marshall Lee, "Determining Reasonable Royalty," *Les Nouvelles* (September 1992): 124. David C. Munson, *Licensing Technology: A Financial Look at the Negotiational Process* what is all this? (January 1996): 78; Schaafsma, "An Economic Overview of Patients", 251. David C.? Munson, "Figuring the Dollars in Negotiations", *Les Nouvelles 33* (June 1998): 88; Reilly and Schweihs, *Valuing Intangible Assets,* 193–94, 503.
34. Degnan and Horton, "A Survey of Licensed Royalties", 92.
35. Ibid.
36. *Standard Manufacturing Co., Inc. and DBP, Ltd. v. United States,* 42 Fed. C1. 748 (1999 U.S. Claims LEXIS 11).
37. *Georgia-Pacific Corp. v. U.S. Plywood Corporation,* 318 F. Supp. 1116 (S.D.N.Y. 1970) modified and aff'd, 446 F.2d 295 (2d Cir. 1971).
38. *Standard Manufacturing Co., Inc. and DBP, Ltd. v. United States,* 42 Fed. C1. 748, 763–64 (1999 U.S. claims LEXIS 11).
39. *Ajinomoto Co., Inc. v. Archer-Daniels-Midland Co.,* No. 95-218-SLR, 1998 U.S. Dist. LEXIS 3833, at 052 n.46 (D. Del. March 13, 1998); *W.L. Gore & Associates, Inc. v. International Medical Prosthetics Research Associates, Inc.,* 16 USPQ 2d. 1241 (D. Ariz. 1990); *Fonar Corporation and*

Dr. Raymond V. Damadian v. General Electric Company and Drucker & Genuth MDS, P.C. d/b/a/ South Shore Imaging Associates, 107 F.3d 1543 (Fed. Cir. 1997). See also Donald S. Chisum, *Chisum on Patents,* 7 § 20-03[3] [iv], 20-188, 20-189 (1993 and Supp. 1997) *Fromson v. Western Litho Plate & Supply Co.,* 853 F. 2d 1568 (Fed. Cir. 1988).

40. Robert Goldscheider, "Litigation Backgrounder for Licensing", *Les Nouvelles 29* (March 1994): 20, 25.
41. *Georgia Pacific v. United States Plywood Corp.,* 318 F. Supp. 1116 (S.D.N.Y. 1970) modified and aff'd, 446 F.2d (2d Cir. 1971), the court set forth 15 factors that should be considered in determining a reasonable royalty. See also, Stephen A. Degnan, "Using Financial Models to Get Royalty Rates", Les Nouvelles 33 (June 1998): 59–60.
42. Razgaitis, *Early Stage Technologies: Valuation and Pricing,* 99–102.
43. Schaafsma, "An Economic Overview of Patients", 251–52.
44. Mark Berkman, "Valuing Intellectual Property Assets for Licensing Transactions," *The Licensing Journal 22* (April 2002): 16.
45. 509 U.S. 579 (1993).
46. 526 U.S. 137 (1999).
47. Schaafsma, "An Economic Overview of Patients," 252.
48. Parr, *Intellectual Property Infringement Damages: A Litigation Support Handbook* (1993): 171.
49. Robert Goldscheider, "Litigation Backgrounder for Licensing," *Les Nouvelles 29* (March 1994): 20, 25.
50. Parr, *Intellectual Property Infringement Damages: A Litigation Support Handbook,* 169. Mark Berkman, "Valuing Intellectual Property Assets for Licensing Transactions", 16; Gregory J. Battersby and Charles W. Grimes, *Licensing Royalty Rates* (2002), 4–5.
51. Parr, *Intellectual Property Infringement Damages: A Litigation Support Handbook,* 169.
52. Ibid., 169–171.
53. Degnan and Horton, "A Survey of Licensed Royalties", 95.
54. *The Procter & Gamble Company v. Paragon Trade Brands,* 989 F. Supp. 547 (D. Del. 1997).
55. Ibid. 547, 595.
56. Ibid.
57. Ibid. 547, 596. The expert's "Rule-of-Thumb" analysis obtained a range of 1.975 percent to 2.6 percent.
58. Lee, 2073.
59. We were unable to gather (or evaluate) information from proposed transactions that were never consummated. Presumably, in those instances, IP sellers were asking for more than IP buyers were willing to pay. We have no *a priori* reason to think, however, that exclusion of such "data" biases our results.
60. The RoyaltySource™ database tracks licensing transactions for other industries as well. The industry categories used here were developed by the authors and are somewhat different than the internal classification system used by RoyaltySource™.
61. Data available to us from RoyaltySource.com did not allow us to easily convert lump-sum or the per unit royalties into royalties per dollar, which terms were needed for testing our hypothesis. As a result, we excluded those observations from our analysis. We have no *a priori* reason to think, however, that exclusion of such data biases our results.
62. Razgaitis, *Early Stage Technologies: Valuation and Pricing,* 118.

Chapter 4

1. Dr. Michael Gross, *Actual Royalty Rates in Patent, Know-How and Computer Program License Agreements* (1998).

Chapter 6

1. Russell L. Parr, *Royalty Rates for Technology, Third Edition* (2005): p. 76.
2. Ibid. p. 80.

3. Ibid. p. 81.
4. Royalty Rates for Technology, Third Edition, IPRA, Inc., 2005 p. 91.
5. Ibid. p. 92.
6. Junko Yoshida, "3G Intellectual Property Licensing Strategy Comes Under Fire," *EE Times* (posted November 27, 1999): http://www.us.design-reuse.com/news/news1965.html.
7. Royalty Rates for Technology, Third Edition, IPRA, Inc., 2005 pgs. 101–2.
8. Ibid. p. 111.
9. http://www.internetnews.com/wireless/article.php/1496321.
10. David Guenther and John Wills, "A Survey of PC Royalty Rates," *Les Nouvelles,* (December 1995): 198.
11. Ibid. p. 198.
12. Royalty Rates for Technology, 3rd Edition, IPRA, Inc., 2005 p. 123.
13. Ibid. p. 126.
14. Ibid. p. 125–6.
15. Royalty Rates for Technology, 3rd Edition, IPRA, Inc. 2005 p 148.
16. Id p. 147.
17. http://www.internetnews.com/ent-news/article.php/2243671.
18. Royalty Rates for Technology, 3rd Edition, IPRA, Inc. 2005 p. 156.
19. Id p. 156.
20. M. Yamasaki, "Determining Pharmaceuticals Royalties," *Les Nouvelles* (September 1996): 112.
21. IMS Health, 2005.
22. www.royaltysource.com.
23. Stephen A. Degnan and Corwin Horton, "A Survey of Licensing Royalties," *Les Nouvelles* (June 1997): 91.
24. www.medius-associates.com.
25. http://www.cptech.org/ip/health/royalties/.
26. Ibid.
27. Bob H. Sotiriadis, Sophie Coret and Jacques Lemoine, "Patents And Technology Transfers in a Biotechnology Context."
28. http://www.cptech.org/ip/health/royalties/.

Chapter 7

1. Richard Stim, *Licensing Artwork: Negotiating and Monitoring Royalty Payments* (May 5, 2006) http://www.keepmedia.com/pubs/Nolo/2005/02/15/676882?extID=10038&data=royalty_rate.
2. http://www.restaurant.org/research/economy/commentary_20060720.cfm.

Chapter 8

1. Current assets are defined by generally accepted accounting principles as assets, which are to be converted into cash, within twelve months of the date of the balance sheet on which they appear. Current liabilities are financial obligations that are expected to be satisfied within twelve months of the same date.
2. Earnings are the basis of value. The valuation of corporate stock is most often based on the present value of the expected future earnings of a company. The amount, growth rate, and risk associated with expected earnings are typically converted into a value, or price, of a company's stock.
3. An underlying assumption in this discussion is that rights associated with the intellectual property in question are valid and enforceable.
4. Complementary assets are all the other business enterprise assets—working capital, fixed assets, and intangible assets.
5. It should be stressed that the operating profit margin of 14.4 percent is most likely weighted

downward, by the lower profit margins associated with generic drugs, that are part of the pharmaceutical preparations classification.
6. Eon Labs, 12/31/2003 SEC 10K Report.
7. http://www.cms.hhs.gov/medicarereform/drugcard/drugcardreports.asp.
8. Leiner Health Products press release, June 22, 2004, www.leiner.com.
9. "A Big Dose of Uncertainty—An industry plagued by high costs faces health-care reform," *Business Week*, (January 10, 1994): 85.
10. "*The Drugmakers vs. The Trustbusters,*" *Business Week*, (September 5, 1994): 67.
11. "*Drug Wars,*" *Forbes* (August 29, 1994): 81.
12. "Market forces usher in a golden age of generic drug," *Pharmaceutical Business News* (November 29, 1993).
13. "Into the mainstream: greater cooperation between generic drug and name-brand drug makers," *Chemical Marketing Reporter* (March 9, 1992).
14. "Patents vs patients: AIDS, TNCs and Drug Price Wars" report from Kavaljit, Public Interest Research Centre (2001).
15. Ibid.
16. Ibid.
17. Ibid.
18. "Patent Injustice: How World Trade Rules Threaten the Health of Poor People," Oxfam Briefing paper (2001).
19. *Prescriptions for Action,* MSF Briefing for the European Parliament of Accelerated Action targeted at Major Communicable Diseases with the Context of Poverty Reduction, Medicines Sans Frontiers, 2001.

Chapter 9

1. The weighted, average cost of capital is an investment rate of return, required from business investments that is a weighting of the rate of return required by debt and equity investors. More information about the appropriate rate of return for this type of analysis can be found in: *Valuation, Exploitation and Infringement Damages,* by Gordon V. Smith and Russell L. Parr, published by John Wiley and Sons.
2. The rates used in this example are for demonstration purposes only. Changing economic conditions must be considered each time this method is used.
3. The liquidity of IP is starting to change. Recently, music copyrights served as the basis for investment securities, when musician David Bowie pledged a large collection of music copyrights, and the royalties they generate, as the foundation for bonds.

Chapter 10

1. The time span for pharmaceutical projects is greater than depicted in this example. For illustrative purposes, a short time span has been used.
2. Office of Technology Assessment, "Pharmaceutical R&D: Costs, Risks and Rewards," (1998) GPO stock #052-003-01315-1.
3. Ibid.
4. Ibid.
5. Dale E. Wierenga, PhD and Robert Eaton, "Phases of Product Development," Office of Research and Development, Pharmaceutical Manufacturers Association.
6. J.A. DiMasi, "Risk in new drug development: Approval success rates for investigational drugs," *Clinical Pharmacology and Therapeutics Volume 69, Number 5,* (May 2001).
7. Please note that the examples presented in this section, as with the other examples already presented, are for illustrative purposes only. Inputs used for the examples may not be appropriate for every application of the relief-from-royalty method. Each case is specific, and will require development of appropriate inputs.

Chapter 11

1. ©2006 Invotex Group. This study is based on information contained in a proprietary, licensing database, developed and maintained by Invotex Group.

Chapter 14

1. Findings based on License Agreements actually audited by an independent party.

Index

A

AccuMed International (AI), 89
Acer Laboratories, 101
Additive Control and Measurement Systems, Inc. (court-awarded royalty rate), 164
Advanced Oxygen Technologies (AOT), 87
After-tax income saved, discounting, 160
Ajinomoto ruling, district court writings, 38
Alfimeprase, rights (sale), 21
Allied Energy, 71
Altria Group, advertising spending, 11e
Alza, Johnson & Johnson purchase, 21–22
Alzheimer's diagnostic test, license deals, 95e
American Express, megabrand ranking, 12e
American Innovations (AI), 86
American Water Star (AWS), 113
Ampersand Medical, 89
Analysis Group, study, 54–55
Andretti™, royalty statistics, 111
AOT. *See* Advanced Oxygen Technologies

Apparel, royalty statistics, 107–109
Apple operating system (Apple OS), technology royalty statistics, 80–81
Applied Nanotech (AN), 85
Arm's length intercompany transactions, requirement, 182
Arm's length negotiation, 62
Artwork, royalty statistics, 109–112
Asphalt roofing debris recycling, technology royalty statistics, 103
AT&T, patent number, 5e
AT&T Wireless, megabrand ranking, 12e
Auditor selection, 191–192
Audits. *See* Desk audits; Royalty audits
Automotive industry, technology royalty statistics, 67–70
Automotive manufacturing industry, technology royalty statistics, 69–70
AWG, license agreement, 111

B

Bard, C.R. (court-awarded royalty rate), 164e
Battery terminals, technology royalty statistics, 68

Bayer AG, patent number, 6e
Benazepril, generic drug savings, 129e
Benihana Japanese restaurants, royalty statistics, 118
Berkman, Mark, 42
Best Buy, megabrand ranking, 12e
Biacore AB, court-awarded royalty rate, 164e
Biacore v. Thermo Bioanalysis, 172
Big League Chew, royalty statistics, 111
Biotechnology
  license deals, fees, 95e
  patent transfers, royalty rates, 97
  royalty rates, 58–60
  technology
    royalty statistics, 92–97
    transfers, royalty rates, 97
Bloomberg database, 46
BMS. *See* Bristol-Myers Squibb
Book publishers, conglomerate ownership, 114–115
Bose v. JBL, 171
Breast cancer detection, technology royalty statistics, 88–89
Bristol-Myers Squibb (BMS) acquisition, 22
Business enterprise
  equation, 119
  framework, 119–128
    illustration, 122e
  value
    equation, 120
    example, 147e
Business groups, identification, 22–23
Business Week, reports, 129–130
Buy-in payments, determination, 183

C

Cancer screening, technology royalty statistics, 89

Canon Kabushiki Kaisha, patent number, 5e
Capital expenditure investments, timing/amount, 143
Capital Grille Steakhouse, royalty statistics, 117–118
CAS. *See* Computer Automation Systems
Catheter, technology royalty statistics, 89–90
CDMA. *See* Code Division Multiple Access
Cell Robotics International (CRI), 90
Centocor, biotech acquisition, 21
Chemical companies, royalty rate guidelines, 54e
Chemical industry, technology royalty statistics, 70–72
Chemical manufacturers, focus, 70
Chemical Marketing Reporter, 130
Chevrolet, megabrand ranking, 12e
Chrysler. *See* DaimlerChrysler
  megabrand ranking, 12e
Cingular, megabrand ranking, 12e
Citibank, megabrand ranking, 12e
Clark, Marcia (royalty statistics), 115
Clearly Canadian Beverage Corporation, 86–87
Clinical phases, approval success rates, 154e
Clinical trial data/information, 121
Clinton, Bill (royalty statistics), 115
Clinton, Hillary Rodham (royalty statistics), 115–116
Coca-Cola Company, trade secrets, 14–15
Cochran, Johnnie (royalty statistics), 116
Code Division Multiple Access (CDMA) technology, royalty statistics, 75

Co-marketing agreements, 122
3Com Corporation, 78–79
Commercialization
　expenses, 124
　FDA approval, phases, 152–153
　time-frame requirements, 124
Commercial relationship, 28
Commodity
　corporate value. *See* Generic
　　commodity corporate value;
　　Mature commodity corporate
　　value
　earnings, 122–123
Communications equipment/services,
　　technology royalty statistics,
　　72–76
Company patents, number, 5e–6e
Comparative analysis, summary, 65–66
Competitive advantage, creation, 23
Complementary assets, benefits, 124
Computer
　architecture, technology royalty
　　statistics, 77
　hardware, technology royalty statistics,
　　76–80
　manufacturing, royalty rates
　　(litigation/non-litigation
　　comparison), 178e
　software, technology royalty statistics,
　　80–82
　technology royalty statistics. *See* PS/2
　　computers
Computer Automation Systems (CAS),
　　77–78
Condiment names, royalty statistics, 112
Construction industry, technology
　　royalty statistics, 82–83
Consumer reactions, 124
　change, 125
Contraceptive regime alternative, license
　　deals, 95e

Convoyed sales, 28
Copyright Act (1976), 10–11
Copyrights, 10–13
　royalty rates, 57–58
　royalty statistics, 107
Corporate royalty rate, 149
Corporate value, 1. *See also* Generic
　　commodity corporate value
Cost savings, impact, 123
Cost-sharing arrangements, usage,
　　183
Cough medicine, license deals, 95e
Court-awarded royalty rates, 163
　ranking, 163–165
Cox, Richard, 97
C.R. Bard v. Boston Scientific, 171
Cypress stem cells research, license deals,
　　95e

D

Dabek, Rose Ann, 97
DaimlerChrysler
　advertising spending, 11e
　profit share, 67
Dannon, royalty statistics, 111–112
Data mining, technology royalty
　　statistics, 81–82
Daubert v. Merrill Dow Pharmaceuticals, 42
Davis, Albert S., 33
DCF. *See* Discounted cash flow
DeCecco, Dave, 15
Decision technology, royalty statistics,
　　81–82
Dell Computers, 77
　megabrand ranking, 12e
Dermatology products, license deals, 95e
Design patents, 3
Desk audits, 193
Detection monitoring, technology
　　royalty statistics, 85

208   INDEX

Diabetes treatment, license deals, 95e
Digital Information Communications and Electronics (DICE)
  companies, IP development reasons, 23
  licensing
    income, generation, 24
    insights, 23
    payments, minimization, 24
  out-licensing, 24
  patents, importance, 23
Digital scanner, technology royalty statistics, 90
Discounted cash flow (DCF), 31
  analysis, 155
    performing, 40
    royalty rates, relationship, 143
  example. See Success rates
Discount rate, determination, 157, 159
Disney, royalty statistics, 108
DNA binding invention, license deals, 95e
Dodge, megabrand ranking, 12e
Drug. See Patented drugs
  development stages, value, 155e
  discovery, difficulty, 19, 92
  introduction, cost, 19
  inventions, dominance, 6
  market share, worth, 96
DSL modems, demand, 72
DVD/video players, technology royalty statistics, 84

E

Early-stage technology, 29, 59
Earnings
  capitalization, 31
  distribution, 121e, 134e
  revenue percentage. See Excess earnings

Eastman Kodak, patent number, 5e
Eating-and-drinking establishments
  characteristic, 117
  small business, frequency, 117
Economic benefits
  competitor efforts, impact, 124
  derivation. See Technology
  duration, 125
  receiving, risk, 125
  time period, 143
Economic factors, identification, 124–125
Economic life, remainder. See Property
Economic returns, receiving (risk), 124
Economic risk, 125
Eggs, technology royalty statistics, 87–88
E.I. DuPont De Nemours, patent number, 6e
Electronic Billboard Technology (EBT), 85
Electronic Data Gathering Analysis and Retrieval (EDGAR), 185
  archives. See Securities and Exchange Commission
Electronics
  product manufacturing, royalty rates (litigation/non-litigation comparison), 178e
  royalty rate guidelines, 54r
  technology royalty statistics, 84–86
Eli Lilly, 114
Enalapril, generic drug savings, 129e
Entire market value rule, 170–171
Environmental Solution Agency (ESA), 104–105
Equity positions, 181
Ericsson, 76
Ernst and Young, report, 20
Established trademarks, 121
Everlast™, royalty statistics, 108
Excess earnings, revenue percentage, 136e

Exclusive licenses, 122
Exclusivity, 64–65. *See also* Licensing
  aspects, comparison, 66
Expected profits
  focus, 34
  margin, equation, 125
Expert testimony, importance, 169–170

F

Fabrics, royalty statistics, 109
Fair market royalty
  establishment, 65–66
  negotiation, 65
Fiberchem, 85
Financial compliance
  monitoring, 187–189
  perceptions, 189
Fixed assets, 137–139
  inclusion, 120
  investment return, earning, 131
  return, 137–139
Fixed capital, illustration, 122e
Flame-retardant products, technology
  royalty statistics, 71
Flat panel display technology, royalty
  statistics, 85
Fluoxentine, generic drug savings, 129e
Food, household expenditures, 117
Food and Drug Administration (FDA)
  approval, 149, 153
    phases. *See* Commercialization
  regulatory approvals, 122
Food/beverage industry
  packaging, technology royalty
    statistics, 87
  technology royalty statistics, 86–88
Forbes, Naprosyn patent protection
  report, 130
Ford Motor Co.
  advertising spending, 11e

  megabrand ranking, 12e
  profit share, 67
Forecast revenue, 157, 158
Frank A. Calabrese v. Square D., 170
Fuel reactor technology, technology
  royalty statistics, 71–72
Fuel technology, technology royalty
  statistics, 72
Fuji Photo Film, patent number, 6e
Fujitsu, patent number, 6e
Fully-loaded profits, 34–35
Furosemide, generic drug savings, 129e

G

GAAP. *See* Generally accepted
  accounting principles
GE-Harris Railway Electronics, LLC
  (court-awarded royalty rate),
    164e
GEM Edwards, 90–91
General Electric Co.
  advertising spending, 11e
  patent number, 5e
Generally accepted accounting
  principles (GAAP), 190
General Motors Corp.
  advertising spending, 10, 11e
  megabrand ranking, 12e
  profit share, 67
General profit margins, 128
Generic commodity corporate value,
  146–149
Generic drugs
  companies, operating profit margins,
    127e
  savings, 129e
Generic pricing, 128–131
Genetic research, license deals, 95e
Georgia-Pacific v. U.S. Plywood, 40, 170
Gift wrap, royalty statistics, 109

Gingrich, Newt (royalty statistics), 116
GlaxoSmithKline, advertising spending, 11e
Glenayre Electronics v. Philip Jackson et al., 168
Glyburide, generic drug savings, 129e
GNB Battery Technologies, 68
Goldscheider, Robert, 31–33
Greeting cards, royalty statistics, 109
Gross cash flow, calculation, 145

H

Hawaiian Tropic®, royalty statistics, 113
Hayes Microcomputer Products, 79–80
Healthcare, licensing insights, 23
Health Technologies International (HTI), 88–89
Hepatitis A vaccine, license deals, 95e
Hewlett-Packard, megabrand ranking, 12e
High-bandwidth chip connection technology, royalty statistics, 98–99
Hitachi, patent number, 5e
HIV/AIDS medicines, price comparisons, 130–131
Home Depot
  advertising spending, 11e
  megabrand ranking, 12e
Honda, megabrand ranking, 12e
Honeywell International, Inc. (court-awarded royalty rate), 164e
Honeywell International et al. v. Universal Avionics, Inc., 165
Household items, royalty statistics, 109
Hughes Danbury Optical Systems (HDOS), 99
Hydro Environmental Resources (HER), ECHFR system, 71
Hypoix tumor cell radiosensitizer, license deals, 95e

I

IBM, patent number, 5e
Illinois Trade Secrets Act, 13
Income taxes, 145
  calculation, 160
Incremental savings, 38
Independent publishers/bookstores, competition, 115
INDS, first filing, 154e
Industrial companies, licensing insights, 23
Industriy categorization, 56
Industry litigated royalties, 179e
Industry profits, 46
  rates, 47e
Industry transactions, relevance, 63–64
Inflationary risk, 125
Influenza drug, license deals, 95e
Information
  knowledge, 14
  secrecy, guarding, 14
  source, 182
  value, 14
Infringement damages analysis, 125–128
  analytical approach, 125–126
  example, 126–127
Intangible assets
  growth (1975–2005), 2e
  illustration, 122e
  required return, example, 137e
  return, 139
Intangible property
  licensing, royalty rates (finding), 182
  valuation, 183
Integrated Paving Concepts, 83
Integrated Process Equipment Corporation (IPEC), 99

Intellectual Property Association (IPA), 73
Intellectual property (IP), 1
  contribution, operating profit level (accuracy), 35
  disputes, damages (establishment), 183
  dominance, 2
  illustration, 122e
  investment, timing/amount, 143
  involvement, 65, 66
  licensing, 17, 24
  out-licensing, 24
  required return, example, 137e
  return, 139
  valuation, Twenty-Five Percent Rule (usage), 31
  value, primary forces, 124–125
Intellectual Property Research Associates (IPRA), 183
Interactive Pictures v. Infinite Pictures, 170
Inter-company licenses, 62
Interline Resources, 103
Internal licenses
  identification, 65
  self-serving behavior, 62
Internal research and development pipelines, insufficiency, 19, 92
International transactions, 64
Internet publishers, competition, 115
Investment rate of return
  analysis, benefits, 140–141
  principles, 133–134
  royalty rates, 134–135
    relationship, 133
Investment return, earning. *See* Fixed assets
  allowance, 141
Investment risk, consideration, 140
IP. *See* Intellectual property
IPA. *See* Intellectual Property Association

IPassets, development reasons, 23–24
IPRA. *See* Intellectual Property Research Associates
Issued patent, worth, 96
IXYS, 101

J

J.C. Penney, megabrand ranking, 12e
Johnson & Johnson
  biotech acquisition, 21
Johnson & Johnson, advertising spending, 11e
Jones Medical Industries, 114

K

Kaisha, patent number, 5e
Kumho Tire Co. v. Carmichael, 42

L

Laser finger-perforator technology, royalty statistics, 90–91
Laser hair removal, technology royalty statistics, 91–92
Later-stage technology, risk, 28–29
Law Relating to Inventions Made by Employees (Germany), 54
Lee, William, 43, 44
Leon B. Rosenblatt Textiles v. Griseto, 110
Library of Congress, 12–13
License agreements
  drafting, 193–194
  monitoring, 187–189
  perceptions, 189
Licensed product, distribution channels, 191
Licensed royalty rates, 47e

INDEX

Licensee profits, 46–48
   1999–2000, 48e
   relationship. *See* Royalty rates
   splits, distribution. *See* Profit
   success. *See* Successful licensees
Licensees
   business, contact person, 191
   internal controls, 191
Licenses. *See* Package licenses
   comparison, 61
   fees, distribution, 59e
   rights, transfer, 65
   royalties, court determination, 167–169
   self-serving behavior. *See* Internal licenses
   underreported royalties, percentage, 188e
Licensing. *See* Intellectual property
   agreement royalty rate frequency, 59e
   company engagement, reasons, 25–29
   exclusivity, 25
   forces, 19–22
   motivation, 22–24
   parties, financial condition, 63
   protection, 25
   utility, 25
Licensor/licensee communications, 195
Lightning resistance, technology royalty statistics, 99
Lisinopril, generic drug savings, 129e
Litigated licenses, non-litigated licenses (comparison), 175–180
Litigation rates, increase, 175
Long-run product profits, expectation, 45
L'Oreal, advertising spending, 11e
Lotto™, royalty statistics, 108
Lucky-Goldstar Group, 83

M

Machinery, royalty rate guidelines, 54r
Macintosh enhancement, technology royalty statistics, 77
Macy's, megabrand ranking, 12e
Mahurkar, Sakharam D. (court-awarded royalty rate), 164
Management competency, 124
Manufacturing, technology royalty statistics, 99–100
Manufacturing industries
   royalty income, 18
   technology royalty statistics. *See* Automotive manufacturing industry
Market acceptance, 155
Marketing expenses, 145
Market risk, 125
Market share, expansion (impact), 123
Marks. *See* Trademarks
Massachusetts General Hospital (MGH), 92
Matsushita Electric Industrial, patent number, 5e
Mature commodity corporate value, 146–149
McDonald's Corp.
   advertising spending, 11e
   megabrand ranking, 12e
Medical equipment
   royalty rates, litigation/non-litigation comparison, 178e
   technology royalty statistics, 88–92
Medical supplies, royalty rates (litigation/non-litigation comparison), 178e
Medicinal, Chemicals and Botanical Products (SIC #2833), 128
Medius Associates, 94
Merck & Co., advertising spending, 11e

Metformin, generic drug savings, 129e
Meyer III, Harold A. (royalty rate guideline suggestions), 96
MichellamineB/tropical vine leaves, license deals, 95e
Mickowski v. Visi-Trak Corporation et al., 168
Mikohn Gaming Corporation, court-awarded royalty rate, 164e
Mikohn Gaming v. Acres Gaming, Inc., 165
Mineral water, technology royalty statistics, 86–87
Mitsubishi Denki Kabushiki, patent number, 5e
Mitutoyo Corporation, court-awarded royalty rate, 164e
Mitutoyo Corporation et al. v. Central Purchasing, LLC, 165
Modems
    standards, technology royalty statistics, 78–79
    technology royalty statistics, 79–80
Modified Black-Scholes option valuation methods, 31
Modine Manufacturing Company, court-awarded royalty rate, 164
Monetary assets, return, 136–137
Monte Carlo simulation, 31
Motorola, patent number, 5e
MPEG LA, 74–75

N

NAICS. *See* North American Industry Classification System
NCEs. *See* New chemical entities
NEC, patent number, 5e
Nestor Traffic Systems (NTS), 81
    PRISM® fraud detection solutions, 82
Net cash flow calculation, 144
Net present value. *See* Risk adjusted net present value
Neupogen, license deals, 95e
New chemical entities (NCEs), 152. *See also* Self-originated NCEs
    submission, 153
New compound, valuation, 156e
New molecular entities (NMEs), 152
New product, licensed technology basis (example), 148e, 150e, 151e
New product revenue forecast, example, 127e
New Restatement of the Law Third, Unfair Competition, 13
Nissan Motor Co.
    advertising spending, 11e
    megabrand ranking, 12e
    Samsung Group sale, 69
NMEs. *See* New molecular entities
Nokia, 76
Non-cash expense, 145
Non-exclusive licenses, 122
Non-licensed IP, earnings, 140
Non-litigated licenses, comparison. *See* Litigated licenses
Non-monetary compensation, 64
Normal profit margin, equation, 125
North American Industry Classification System (NAICS), 166
Northeast American Enterprises, 77
Notes, 197–203
Novartis, advertising spending, 11e
NTS. *See* Nestor Traffic Systems
NTT DoCoMo, 76
Nucleic acid probe technology, license deals, 95e
Nuvelo, commercialization rights, 21

O

Odetics, federal circuit court writings, 38
Operating profits, 35, 145
   level, accuracy. *See* Information Processing
   margins. *See* Generic drugs
   rate, expectation, 40
Out-licensing. *See* Digital Information Communications and Electronics; Intellectual property
Overhead expenses, 145
   omission, 35

P

Package licenses, 65
Packaging, technology royalty statistics. *See* Food/beverage industry
Palomar Medical Technologies, 91
Patented drugs, 121
Patented invention
   remaining life, 160
   royalty rate, 140
Patented technology valuation, relief-from-royalty method, 156–157
Patented therapeutic drugs, royalty rate (example), 138e
Patents, 3–8. *See also* Design patents; Plant patents; Utility patents
   applications, 121
   history. *See* United States patents
   importance. *See* Digital Information Communications and Electronics
   number. *See* Company patents
   owner distribution, 5e
   ownership, identification, 4–6
   pending, worth, 96
   protection, remaining life (determination), 157–158
   prototype, presence (worth), 96
   risks, validity, 125
   technology classifications, 6. *See also* United States patents
   transfers, royalty rates. *See* Biotechnology
   trends, 4
   types, 3
   worth. *See* Issued patent
Patent to Profit, guidance, 53–54
Paving, technology royalty statistics, 83
Pentium II processor, technology royalty statistics, 100–101
PepsiCo, advertising spending, 11e
Pepsi-Cola, trade secrets, 14–15
Personal care, royalty statistics, 112–114
Personal digital assistant (PDA), patent example, 4
Pfizer, advertising spending, 11e
Pharmaceutical Business News, 130
Pharmaceutical companies (pharmaceuticals)
   competition, 19, 93
   compound (discovery), pressure (increase), 19, 92
   development stage, royalty rate, 94
   intangible assets, 121–122
   intellectual property, 121–122
   invention, category, 94
   license deals, fees, 95e
   research and development
      deficiencies, licensing activity supplement, 93
      stage, average royalty, 96
   royalty rates, 58–60
      distribution, 94e
      guidelines, 54e
      information, 26–27
   technology royalty statistics, 92–97
Pharmaceutical drug, clinical trials (worth), 96

INDEX 215

Pharmaceutical industry
   development stage, royalty rate, 96
   royalty rates, increase, 19, 92–93
Pharmaceutical preparations (SIC #2834), 128
Pharmaceutical Research and Manufacturers of America (PhRMA), 153
Plant patents, 3
Polo, royalty statistics, 108–109
Polyvinyl chloride pipe products, technology royalty statistics, 83
Posters, royalty statistics, 109
Post-site analysis/report generation, 192
Power conversion, technology royalty statistics, 101
Precision Materials Operation (PMO), 99
Present value calculation, 160–161
Pre-site research, 192
Pretax profits, 35
Price premiums, obtaining, 122–123
Prints, royalty statistics, 109
Probability-of-success factor, 152
Procter and Gamble v. Paragon Trade Brands, 44
Procter & Gamble Co.
   advertising spending, 10, 11e
   licensing restrictions, 158
Product commercialization, expenses, 145
Production efficiencies, 124
Product revenue
   forecast, example. *See* New product revenue forecast
   patent enhancement, 37
Profit. *See* Industry profits; Licensee profits; Operating profits
   amount, 124
   differentials, royalty rates (relationship), 119
   duration, 124
   expectation, risk (association), 124
   margins. *See* General profit margins
   equation. *See* Expected profits; Normal profit margin
   rates. *See* Industry profits
   splits, licensee profits (distribution), 49e, 51e
   twenty-five profit, rule of thumb, 42
Projections, usage, 170
Promega v. LifeCodes Corporation et al., 168
Promotion agreements, 122
Property, economic life (remainder), 40
Protection, duration, 27–28
PS/2 computers, technology royalty statistics, 77–78
Publishing
   houses, complaints, 114
   royalty statistics, 114–116
Purchase price allocation, determination, 182

Q

Qualcomm, 74, 75

R

Ralph Lauren, royalty statistics, 108–109
Ramtron International, 101
Rare Hospitality, 117–118
Raw idea, worth, 96
Razgaitis, Richard, 41
ReClaim, 103
Recycling, 102
Red flags, 190–191
Regulatory risk, 125

Relief-from-royalty method
  inputs, 157
  usage. See Patented technology valuation
Remote metering, technology royalty statistics, 86
Research expenses, 145
Research Frontiers, 70
Restatement of Torts, 13
Restaurants
  consumer spending, 117
  industry, impact (expectation), 116
  royalty statistics, 116–118
  sales, job generation, 117
Return. See Investment rate of return
Return on investment, 31
Revenue, growth expectation, 160
Risk adjusted net present value, 149–153
Risk Management Association (RMA) Annual Statement Studies, 128
Risk reduction, consideration, 138
Rite-Hite Corporation et al. v. Kelley Corporation, 167–168
Royalties
  determination, Sixth Circuit Court of Appeals (impact), 33
  factors, 25e
  income. See Manufacturing industries
  IRS report, 17–18
  miscalculations, recurrence, 191
  reasonableness, court considerations, 167–171
  recipients, ranking, 97
  saving, 160
  statistics. See Technology
  terms
    inclusion, 66
    specification, 66
Royalty audits
  defining, 190–191
  errors, 194–195
  mistakes, likelihood (decrease), 193–194
  monitoring program, benefits, 195–196
  process, 192–193
Royalty rates, 45–46. See also Biotechnology; Copyrights; Corporate royalty rate; Court-awarded royalty rates; Licensed royalty rates; Technology; Trademarks
  appropriateness, 135–137
  awards
    frequency, 165–166
    industry categorization, 167e
    ranking, 164e
    reasonableness, 176e
  details, 181
  district court awards, 166e
  equation, 125
  federal circuit decisions, 171–173
  finding. See Intangible property
  frequency, 57e. See also Licensing; Trademarks
  guidelines, 53. See also Pharmaceutical companies
  ranking, 54e
  industry categorizations, 166–167
  input, determination, 157, 158–159
  licensee profits, relationship, 48–51
  ranking, 49e
  litigation, non-litigation (comparison), 177e
  percentage, 56
  primary factors, 124–125
  relationship. See Discounted cash flow analysis; Profit
  services, 181
  successful licensee profits, relationship, 50–51
  ranking, 50e

Royalty Rates for Pharmaceuticals and Biotechnology, 26–27, 58, 183–184
Royalty Rates for Technology, 55, 184
Royalty Rates for Trademarks and Copyrights, 57, 184
RoyaltySource®, 93, 181–182
　data, Analysis Group study, 56
　information, 45–46
　royalty rates, 55e
RoyaltyStat®, 182–183
　usefulness, 182–183
Ruth's Chris Steakhouse, royalty statistics, 117

S

Sakharam D. Mahurkar v. C.R. Bard, 172
Samsung Group, sale, 69
SBC Communications, advertising spending, 11e
Scantek Medical, 88–89
Schaafsma, Paul, 42
Scientific databases, 121
SciMed Life Systems, 89
Sears, megabrand ranking, 12e
Sears Holdings Corp., advertising spending, 11e
Securities and Exchange Commission (SEC) EDGAR Archives, 182, 184–185
Segan Limited Partnership v. Trendmasters, 169
Self-dimmable rearview mirrors, technology royalty statistics, 70
Self-interests, argument, 62
Self-originated NCEs, 154e
Selling expenses, 145
Semiconductors, technology royalty statistics, 97–102
Sharer, Kevin, 20

SI Diamond Technology, 85
Siemens AG, patent number, 5e
Sign Builders of America (SBOA), 85
Silicon Integrated Systems (SIS), 100
Single inline memory modules (SIMMs), technology royalty statistics, 102
Site investigation, 192
Skoda Klatovy, 104
Slimfold Manufacturing Company v. Kinkead Industries, Inc., 165
Smithkline Diagnostics, Inc. (court-awarded royalty rate), 164e
Sony Corp.
　advertising spending, 11e
　patent number, 5e
Spirulina, license deals, 95e
Spring, megabrand ranking, 12e
Standard Manufacturing and DBP v. United States, 40
Standard & Poor's 500 (S&P500) company assets (1975–2005), 2e
Subject analysis, 65
Successful licensees
　profitability data, 50
　profits, 50
　relationship. *See* Royalty rates
Success rates, 153–154
　adjusted DCF example, 155–156
　adjusted present value calculations, usage, 156e
　therapeutic class, identification, 154e
Sugar Foods, 112
Sunk costs, 34

T

Tangible assets, return, 137–139
Tanning Research Laboratories, 113
Tapazole®, royalty statistics, 114
Target stores, megabrand ranking, 12e

Tax law compliance, 182
Tax rate, determination, 157, 159
Technology
  alternatives, 125
  classifications. *See* Patents; United States patents
  economic benefits, derivation, 124
  obsolescence, 125
  risk, 125
  royalty
    rates, 55–57
    statistics, 67
  transfers, royalty rates. *See* Biotechnology
Territory restriction, 27
Textile patterns, royalty statistics, 110
Thin film ferroelectric technology, royalty statistics, 101–102
Third-generation wireless technology, technology royalty statistics, 73–74
Time period, relevance, 62–63
Time Warner, advertising spending, 11e
Tire recycling, technology royalty statistics, 104–105
Titan Technologies, 104
T-Mobile, megabrand ranking, 12e
Toikka, Richard, 42
Toshiba, patent number, 5e
Total Containment v. Environ Products, 172
Total earnings, 135
Total market, intangible value (percentage), 2e
Toyota Motor Corp.
  advertising spending, 11e
  megabrand ranking, 12e
Toys/dolls, royalty statistics, 109
TP Orthodontics, Inc. (court-awarded royalty rate), 164
Trademarks (marks), 8–10. *See also* Established trademarks
  applications, 9
    foreign nation filers, 10e
  applications (2005), 9
  royalty rates, 57–58
    frequency, 58e
  royalty statistics, 107
Trade secrets, 13–15
  evaluation, 14–15
Transaction terms, 182
Transaxles, technology royalty statistics, 68–69
Transfer pricing regulations, 183
Tristrada Technology, Inc. v. Mary Kay, Inc., 168
Twenty-Five Percent Rule
  application, 39–41
  criticisms, 42–44
  empirical test, 44–45
  employment, 40
  explanation, 33–36
  history, 32–33
  illustration, 36–39
    cost side, 38e
    revenue side, 37e
  indeterminateness, 43
  justification, 41–42
  rule of thumb, 42, 44
  usage. *See* Intellectual property
  introduction, 31–32
TWM Manufacturing v. Dura Corporation, 126

U

UMTS. *See* Universal Mobile Telecommunications System
Unilever, advertising spending, 11e
Unisplay v. American Electronic Sign, 172

United Fire Technology (UFT), 71
United States advertisers, ranking, 11e
United States government, advertising spending, 11e
United States megabrands, ranking, 12e
United States Navy, patent number, 6e
United States Patent and Trademark Office (USPTO), 3
  registration, 8
United States patents
  applications
    1850–2004, 8e
    history, 6–8
  technology classification, 7e
Universal Mobile Telecommunications System (UMTS), 73–74
University/government licensing insights, 23
Unocal Corporation, lawsuit, 72
Up-front payments, 181
Used oil recovery, technology royalty statistics, 103–104
US Philips, patent number, 5e
Utility patents, 3

V

Valero Energy, lawsuit, 72
Valuation. *See* Patented technology valuation
  relief-from-royalty method, 160e
Verapamil hcl SR, generic drug savings, 129e
Verizon Communications
  advertising spending, 11e
  megabrand ranking, 12
Vidal Sassoon, royalty statistics, 114
Video patent pool, technology royalty statistics, 74–75

W

WACOC. *See* Weighted average cost of capital
Wal-Mart, megabrand ranking, 12e
Walt Disney Co., advertising spending, 11e
Warfarin, generic drug savings, 129e
Wart removal products, license deals, 95e
Waste management, technology royalty statistics, 102–105
Water-jel burn dressings, license deals, 95e
Weighted average cost of capital (WACOC), 159
Weiler, David, 93
Wideband code division multiple access (W-CDMA) technology, royalty statistics, 76
Williams, Lonnie (court-awarded royalty rate), 164
Windows operating system (Windows OS) code, technology royalty statistics, 82
Working capital (WC), 135
  illustration, 122e
  investments, timing/amount, 143

X

Xerox, patent number, 6e

Y

YoCream, royalty statistics, 111–112

Z

Zygo Corporation, court-awarded royalty rate, 164